Game Development for iOS with Unity3D

Game Development for iOS with Unity3D

Jeff W. Murray

CRC Press
Taylor & Francis Group
Boca Raton London New York

CRC Press is an imprint of the
Taylor & Francis Group, an **informa** business

AN A K PETERS BOOK

Cover image courtesy of Unity Technologies.

CRC Press
Taylor & Francis Group
6000 Broken Sound Parkway NW, Suite 300
Boca Raton, FL 33487-2742

Printed in the United States of America on acid-free paper
Version Date: 20120703

International Standard Book Number: 978-1-4398-9219-0 (Paperback)

Library of Congress Cataloging-in-Publication Data

Murray, Jeff.
  Game development for iOS with Unity3D / Jeff Murray.
    p. cm.
  Includes index.
  ISBN 978-1-4398-9219-0 (pbk. : alk. paper) 1. Computer games--Programming. 2. iOS (Electronic resource) 3. Unity (Electronic resource) 4. Three-dimensional display systems. I. Title.

  QA76.76.C672M887 2012
  794.8'1526--dc23

2012019335

Visit the Taylor & Francis Web site at
http://www.taylorandfrancis.com

and the CRC Press Web site at
http://www.crcpress.com

This book is dedicated to my Nan. She never doubted me for a second, and without her love and encouragement, I would probably be someone very different, doing something very different, and perhaps enjoying life a lot less.

Table of Contents

Introduction

In my darkest hours, when the going gets tough and the bugs get tougher, one question keeps coming back to me: *Why do I do this?* I could have found a career in anything—I studied theatre and media—but in the end, I chose to make games. Making games ticks all of the boxes for me. I can make music, create graphics, make sounds, and write stories. I can create worlds and play god. Programming gives me the power to change the rules of physics, space, and time, and at the end of all that hard work, I can share my creations and *entertain*. Put simply, my code is my paint and my games are my canvas. I'm not a famous actor or a big movie director and my reward isn't fame or fortune. It is the knowledge that I've confused, puzzled, frustrated, and entertained literally millions of people through my love of what I do. And they don't even know who I am.

When I made my first game, it was on a computer that could only render ASCII characters—numbers, letters, and basic symbols. Being a game designer in 1983 required a lot of imagination and a whole host of optimization tricks to get around the limitations of that technology. To put it plainly, if you wanted to make enough money to buy that helicopter sports car, you really needed to be good at making the most of very little, immersing users in games that looked like the result of a drunken monkey secretary using a broken and probably drunken typewriter.

At the time, this didn't present much of a problem as it was accepted by my fellow 80s gamers that all game graphics would be complete rubbish. We'd all gotten used to that fact and, over time, conventions began to take shape, such as the letter A representing a user's character or an asterisk as a projectile or dangerous object. Simple rules, formed through a collective acceptance of "this is the way that makes the most sense," began to provide game designers of the time with a small amount of grammar to tell their stories.

The very foundation of the language of the games we see today was beginning to take shape thanks to the explosion of the home computer market and the fact that, although our parents said we should use the computers only for homework, all kids wanted to do when they got in front of a monitor was to play games.

Conventions in the mechanisms that make up games have come about to help us tell our stories more effectively; yet, time and time again developers fail to share knowledge. Young game designers repeatedly run into the same walls as their predecessors, techniques held back like a valuable secret recipe for egg on toast. Each person solving the problem fails to share solutions because we believe the solutions themselves to be more valuable than they actually are. The real value is in the quality of their implementation and, most importantly, how they are used to provide an entertainment experience for the end user.

Perhaps the part I find most frustrating is that all the time developers spend solving old problems could be spent developing new mechanics or concentrating on great game play, if only the information had been shared sooner. Building rendering systems, orbiting cameras, inventory systems, or even file handling code has, quite literally, been done by hundreds of thousands of game developers for decades—yet, right now there is still someone out there scratching his or her head and trying to figure out how to do it again. Thanks to the work of *Unity* and the developers sharing their code on wikis and asset stores, this is slowly beginning to change.

If you don't have the resources to make games, Unity also makes it easier than ever for you to buy graphics, 3D models, starter kits, and scripts to bring your dream to life. Need 3D models? Not sure if your programming skills are up to it? You can even buy a drag-and-drop programming system. This empowers smaller development teams to do more than ever. It also helps to spread the knowledge of how games are made, alleviating some of the burden of discovery and allowing game developers to concentrate more on the games themselves.

One of the things I would like to achieve with this book is to lift another little veil of secrecy from game development: you don't need a million dollars, a huge studio, or a brontosaurus with a gold-encrusted sports bike. You just need a little knowledge and a whole lot of commitment. I want you to succeed, and so do my friends, and their friends, too. We all want you to make a game, but if something technical is holding you back, then the best I can do is hope that this book will help you to get over it. If this book saves you three weeks that you would have otherwise had to spend learning how to use the engine, tools, or systems, then it means that you're able to spend three extra weeks making a good game. I like good games. Just remember to drop me a message when you're done, because I want to play it.

Prerequisites

I would love to be able to give you everything you need right here in the text of this book, but for iOS development, there are a few things you will need to buy and download.

- *A paid Apple developer account subscription.* More detail on this may be found later in Chapter 2.

- *An Intel-powered Apple Mac.* At the time of writing this book, iOS development is limited to Mac only. It is not impossible to program an iOS game on the PC, then convert it over to a Mac in the final stages of development, but I don't recommend it. Testing touchscreen controls, accelerometer input, or any other iOS-specific features will only be possible on an Apple Mac system.

- *An iOS device (e.g., an iPod, iPhone, or iPad) and USB connecting cables.* Testing touchscreen controls, accelerometer input, or any other iOS-specific features will only be possible with an iOS powered device. A USB cable will be required to transfer builds from your Mac to your device.

- *Unity Free or Unity Pro.* Available from the Unity store,[1] Unity Free is completely free—no charge at all—which, in my opinion, is a really sweet deal! We are talking about a fully functional game engine here, ready to make 3D games to be sold commercially or otherwise. No royalties at all! Unity Pro adds a whole host of professional functionality to the engine, such as render culling and profiling.

- *A Unity iOS basic or advanced license.* Available from the Unity store, the basic Unity iOS license allows you to do everything you need to make iOS games. There is, however, a caveat in that your games have a Unity *splash screen* and there is no legal way to remove it. A few other features differ from the Pro version, too, in that you don't have the profiler and you can't strip libraries and offer smaller downloads. Don't let this stand in your way, though, as there are already some great games on the *iTunes Store* that were created with a Unity iOS basic license. Unity iOS Pro gives you more of the professional features. You also get access to the culling system, which can be huge for performance-driven game development.

- *Some basic JavaScript programming knowledge.* This book is *not* a programming guide. You will need to know some programming (even if I have tried to make the examples as simple as possible).

What This Book Covers

Chapter 1: Designing Your Game

Having read the rousing introduction to this book, I imagine that you will be raring to go and get started on your first game. That's one option, but, let's face it, the right thing to do is to think a little bit about what it is you are going to be building and how you are going to build it.

The first chapter of this book will try to steer you in the right direction with some helpful advice for planning out your project. We will take a look at project management on a low budget and you will learn about the kinds of things that should be included in a game design document. Also in the chapter, we will highlight some common problems that may arise during planning phases and try to establish methods to avoid them early on.

---

[1] http://www.unity3d.com

We will take a brief look at strategies for testing your game and how you can keep tabs on all of the bugs, along with some helpful tips for staying healthy and keeping your team on track and motivated.

Chapter 2: Getting Set Up for iOS Development

To bring your game to life and take it to iOS, you are going to need the hardware and software to do it. Getting set up can be an intimidating process, so we will cover everything from buying the right Apple Developer subscription, purchasing the correct Unity licenses and, briefly, what hardware you will need. In this chapter, you will find out what you need to buy, borrow, or beg for and how you can keep costs down. Once you know what you will need, we will also look into getting it all set up, downloaded, and ready for action.

Chapter 3: Setting Up Unity and Your Mac for iOS Development

In the third chapter, you will learn how to get set up for development. We will look at the Unity Remote, an iOS app that allows you to send input via a USB cable from your iOS device to the editor. This chapter will cover building the Unity Remote application and any related certificates or profiles that you will need to install. We will look at the various methods for dealing with user input and some of the out-of-the-box solutions Unity provides to make control of your iOS game easy.

Chapter 4: Basics of the Unity Editor

Opening up Unity for the first time could leave you wondering where to click next. This chapter demonstrates the basics of what makes up a Unity project, navigating the game scenes, and other editor functionality.

Chapter 5: Building a Game in Unity iOS: The Roll-a-Ball Game

By now, you should be all set up for your first Unity iOS game project. This chapter will get you started on the path to becoming a full-fledged iOS developer by taking you through the creation of a simple rolling ball maze game. We'll cover basic UI, scripting, physics, collisions, and publishing. You will learn about controlling physics objects with input provided by the accelerometer and some of the core principles of Unity that you will need to effectively script, build, and test the game on your iOS device.

Chapter 6: Making a Kart-Racing Game

In Chapter 6, we take things to the next level to produce a fully featured 3D kart-racing game. You will learn more advanced techniques than those from the previous chapter, delving deeper into the physics engine, collision systems, scripts, UI, and sound effects.

Chapter 7: Debugging and Script Optimization

By now, you have already made two games for iOS. Those last two chapters were hard work, but you made it through. Now we look at effective strategies for debugging, both within the editor and on the device itself, for when things go wrong. It's nothing to fear—all games have bugs until those bugs are squashed!

Chapter 8: Optimizing for File Size and Performance

Now that you are a full-fledged game developer, having made two games already, you may want to learn how to make things work better. There are some secrets that may not be obvious when you are starting out. Here we will look at texture compression settings, sound compression, and occlusion culling (for Unity Pro users only) and how they impact performance. This chapter is all about squeezing extra performance from your Unity iOS games.

Chapter 9: Publishing to the iTunes Store

In this chapter, we will be looking at the process of publishing your game to the Apple iTunes Store: what you will need to submit, how to bring everything together, how to design your iTunes Store page, and even how to promote your game. These are the final steps to your becoming a published game developer, so we're going to cover it all and make sure that you are 100% ready to go.

Chapter 10: Thinking Outside the Box

Where to now? There are several things that you can do outside of the Unity iOS environment to improve upon existing features or bring new functionality to your Unity projects. In this chapter, we look at some tweaks and optimizations that you can make to the Xcode project to make your games work better, followed by a look into some of the third-party plug-ins out there to expand the scope of your iOS games.

What This Book Doesn't Cover

This is not a book about programming and it is not a book about the right or wrong way to do things. I assume that the reader has some experience with the JavaScript programming language, although the first complete game example, intended for nonprogrammers, uses very simple concepts to introduce Unity. I am a self-taught programmer and I understand that there may well be better ways to do things. I've met coders who can write the most beautiful, technically incredible code on the planet but have never been able to finish a game project on their own. Our goal is always to reach the finish line. If you can do it with nice code, please do. The rest of us can just concentrate on making games and stop worrying about the nitty gritty—at the end of the day, Unity takes care of a lot of that for us anyway.

This is a book about concepts, and it is inevitable that there will be better methods for achieving some of the same goals. Techniques and concepts offered in this book are meant to provide solid foundation, not to be the final word on any subject. Instead, I hope that as you gain your own experiences in game development you will make your own rules and draw your own conclusions.

For nonprogrammers, perhaps the biggest reason to own this book might be the free source code. Let's face it, where else will you find full source code to two 3D games ready to publish to mobile devices, all for only the price of a textbook? You never know—perhaps with some hacking around, a nonprogrammer might catch the programming bug. (Pun intended.) This could be the start of something! We're not going to fully explain all of the source code in this book, but we will try to cover the point of each script, at the very least. It is not just about the code, but the problems that the scripts solve and the concepts that surround them.

Hopefully, this book will serve as a good place to start your journey in making games with Unity iOS and in publishing them to the iTunes Store.

Acknowledgments

I am honestly and truly grateful for my life to have been blessed with the light that my friends and family shine on it.

Sincere thanks to my awesome editor Kara Ebrahim, Sarah Chow, and all at A K Peters and CRC Press for being so patient, understanding, and supportive during the production of this book. This book is also for my treasures Ethan and William and for my wonderful wife, Tori. They are the source of motivation for everything I do. Boys, be nice to the cat.

Thank you to my mum and dad, who did a great job in not getting too crazy about all those hours I spent at the computer when I was younger. Thanks to my brother Steve for not hogging the computer too much.

Brian Robbins, thank you for giving me some massive breaks and believing in my work. Thanks to the awesome Si (Psionic[2])—a fantastic artist and a true inspiration to 3D modelers. A sincere thank you to my good friends Tim Bacon, Paul Green, and the White family. Thank you to The Daily Grind café in Ottawa for all the coffee and support when I was writing this book.

Finally, thank *you* for buying this book and for wanting to do something as cool as making games. I hope you can find the same passion for making games as I have and that this book inspires you in some way to get out there and just do it. (Don't forget to let me know when you're done.)

---

[2] http://www.psionic3d.co.uk

CHAPTER 1

Designing Your Game

Let's start on a positive note: projects fail. Okay, that's not very positive, is it? Sadly, project failure rate in independent game development is ridiculously high and there are countless numbers of great programmers who start games and never finish them. Why do so many fail? Here are some of the most common reasons:

- They underestimate how much work it takes to make a game.

- They choose a genre that requires more work than they initially thought.

- A team has too many commitments outside of the project.

- A new or inexperienced team becomes overwhelmed by the sheer amount of work it takes to put a game together.

- They don't have enough time scheduled for the project.

- They have unclear design goals, leading to a loss of focus.

Like any profession or skill, making games is something that takes practice to be truly understood. Just like you can't pick up a book on surgery and go out and do it, you can't pick up a book and suddenly make great games. But you can pick up a book to obtain the tools to make great games and go out and practice until you become awesome!

Up until the point when a game "finds its groove," the development process is relatively mechanical and needs to be focused on day-to-day tasks. It is a project like any other and, just like a building or a renovation project, keeping it on track demands that you do your best to aim to keep a schedule and keep a clear direction. Sure, that may sound like it is taking all the fun out of game development, but believe me, there is still a lot of fun to be had—just make it organized fun!

I'm going to say this once and only once, so pay attention right now and feel free to reread this if you need to. When you are choosing a project to work on, *choose an idea that has the most potential for reaching completion.*

It is a common saying in the games industry that the last 20% of game development takes 80% of the time. That final 20% is the part of the project where everything gets covered in the layers of polish, when the game elements get tuned to perfection, and when all of the bugs and game play problems are supposed to be ironed out. There are hundreds of small details that make a game "feel right" that may not stand out immediately. They may only surface when you are knee-deep in development. These are the details that both the users and the developers sometimes take for granted.

1.1 It's Not as Easy as It Looks!

Making games is an art that looks easy on the surface. As a game developer, I have dedicated a lot of my time to explaining to people that I don't actually just sit around playing games all day and that there are many parts of my job that are mind-numbingly dull. Inexperienced producers or game designers will at some point make a wildly unrealistic request, expecting the amount of work involved to be minimal. Unfortunately, lurking underneath a statement like "we just use a simple orbit camera" could be quite literally months of work.

To the uninitiated, that "simple request" of an orbit camera is just a camera that moves around a character. Simple! Attach the camera to the character and match its rotation, right? Not really. First of all, you are going to want the camera to rotate around with a little lag, otherwise the user doesn't really get a good sense of movement when turning the character in the game world. Okay, now you have smooth rotation. We're done, right? Not quite.

What about when the character stands close to a wall and our camera goes through walls? You need a collision system for it. What about when the camera doesn't go through the wall but gets pushed forward into the back of an avatar's head, clipping the model? You need to check for a minimum distance that the camera can be positioned from the character. What if, when the camera is at its minimum distance from the character, we end up staring at the hair on the back of the character's head and can't see much else? We need an adjustment to the rotation to have its x rotation move up so that we can see over the character's head. Within minutes of looking at our camera, we've already made a whole lot of work. Now take this and apply it to every single mechanism and component of a video game, then bug fix and polish it all. I think you get the idea. Making games can be really hard work!

1.2 Play Testing

Someone, at some point, will say something about your game that will annoy you. It will sound like the most ridiculous comment or bug report that you have ever heard and it may well make you very angry. Your users know nothing about your pain and sometimes, sadly, they will tell you … the truth.

My first game was called *Splodge*, and it was a top-down scroller. This was 1983, so things were pretty limited. Little letter Os moved up the screen as you controlled a letter V at the top of the screen, moving left and right to avoid them. I gave the user an automatic score for each time the screen updated. Users only got one life—hit an O, and it was game over. The proud moment arrived when I demonstrated it to my friends. After the initial "Wow, you made a computer game!" they got bored. Within minutes, we were back to escaping from a maze before a Minotaur made lunch out of us. My friends needed more. They wanted extra lives, jumps, and space aliens. I gave them one life and lots of letter Os. They were bored and I was sad. (At least, I was sad until it was time to watch the A-Team on TV.)

Splodge version 2 worked out some of the kinks. We now had bonus score *pickups* and the automatic scoring was gone. There needed to be a reason for people to grab those pickups. Along with it came three lives, and just to be really fancy about it all, I added sound. Play testing for *Splodge* version 2 ran on for hours and the game was a huge success as we all tried to beat each other's scores.

My first version had been way off. Just because I was having fun didn't mean my users would. But to realize that, I needed to step back and look at the elements that the game was made up of. I needed to think a little more about my users and how I could provide the kind of experience I wanted them to have. Playtesting will tell you about your players, but it is your job as a game designer to try and anticipate what it is that will give the players of your games an immersive and satisfying experience. From scoring systems to the soundtrack, everything in a game should be there for a reason and to support the key themes of the game or goals of the experience. If you design a *powerup* system, try to design one that has relevance in the overall experience. For example, if flying is a powerup how will this improve gameplay or support the themes of the story? If the character is afraid of heights, does it make sense to have it fly? How does flying affect the pace of the level and does that change in pace affect the overall flow of the experience?

When you start putting together ideas, document as many as possible. Ideas that don't necessarily fit the project early on may be of use later, or even with other projects. Using a pen and paper is a great way to get ideas out of your head and onto something that you can refer back to later. Keep all of your game ideas, but do not feel as though you have to use them all at once. A good game designer will make sure that everything has a good reason to be there.

1.3 iOS Platform-Specific Considerations

Before sitting down to write your *game design document* (*GDD*), it makes sense to think a little bit about the concept behind your game and how you can choose a game idea that you can see through to completion and that will complement the iOS platform and maximize the effectiveness of the extra features that the iOS operating system brings to the table.

Think about the environment that your games will be played in. The nature of mobile gaming means that there may be interruptions. Unity iOS helps you with these situations by allowing users to pick up where they left off after switching tasks, but it is still important for you to keep this in mind. Try to either automatically save user data regularly or provide a method for users to save data (such as game-play progression) in case of power loss. Designing smaller levels to be played in quick chunks may suit the mobile play experience. Whether your users are travelling on a bus, riding a train, or killing time in a waiting room, short play sessions are the norm with iOS games. This is why many of the biggest hits in the iTunes Store have been based around two- to five-minute bursts of game play.

The file size of your game will be important to users (some more so than others). This will determine how quickly the game downloads, how much bandwidth it takes out of your potential customer's cellphone plan (if they're downloaded over cell rather than Wi-Fi), and how much space the game takes on their device. At the end of the day, their iOS device is multifunctional; they most likely also use it for listening to music, storing pictures, and watching movies, as well as playing games. An empty Unity iOS file will weigh in somewhere between 10 and 15 megabytes (MB), but this adds up quickly once you get all of your assets (music, sound, graphics, textures) into a project. If the user's allowed storage space is used up, some things are going to have to be deleted, and it is unreasonable to expect users to keep games that use up unnecessary amounts of space, so be sure to make an effort to reduce file size.

Another consideration for iOS development is the amount of memory your game will be allowed to take up in RAM. The Unity engine and all of its libraries uses around 60 MB of RAM. If you're playing on an iPhone 3G or a third generation iPod Touch, that's nearly half of your 128-MB memory allowance gone before you have even started. The iPad 1 has substantially more space, weighing in at 256 MB, both the iPad 2 and iPhones 4 and 4S have 512 MB, and the iPad 3 has a full gigabyte (GB) of RAM. There is a massive difference between the graphics and sounds you can get into 1 GB of RAM versus 128 MB. Memory limitations affect the number of elements that can make up your game (sound effects, music tracks, 3D models, textures, etc.) and the quality of them. If you were hoping for $2,048 \times 2,048$-sized textures with vast environments, many animations, and music, you may want to rethink things to bring down its scope. If you are looking to reach the widest market possible with a single universal build (one that will work on iPods, iPhones, and iPads) you may also have to consider reducing memory usage to cater to older devices.

1.3.1 iTunes Store Guidelines

Apple has strict requirements as to what you can and can't include in an iOS application or game, as well as the ways in which the application can interact with other services if you want your game in the iTunes Store. The iTunes Store Review guidelines are available through the developer portal and contain points to help you understand what will get rejected during the review process and why. Apple refers to this as a "living document," meaning that it is a document that changes according to developments. Be sure to read through it every now and then. It is best to know early on if there may be any contractual, technical, or content-related restrictions that could get in the way of your game launching. Better to find out right away than after six months of working on it.

Most of the guidelines are straightforward: Apple will reject apps that crash, apps that exhibit bugs, apps that do bad things with people's personal information, etc. But there are some rules in there that may come as a surprise, such as the rejection of apps that mention other mobile platforms, or of apps that unlock or enable features or functionality with mechanisms other than the iTunes Store. Be sure to review the guidelines to make sure that both your content and your technical requirements are actually allowed on the iTunes Store.

Almost no "adult" material will be allowed on the iTunes Store. Things such as bad language or sexually explicit content will more than likely result in your game being rejected during the review stage. A few apps have made it through review by hiding such content, only to be removed at a later date when word gets out about it. Be aware that trying to hide anything from Apple is a very bad idea—one that may easily get your developer account banned for life.

1.3.2 Designing Your Controls

With touchscreen input, implementing a successful control system can be a difficult thing to do. For example, a *first-person shooter* (*FPS*) running on a console system might employ all of the buttons on the game controller, as well as one or more analog joysticks, and perhaps even a digital gamepad. A desktop-based shooter has several key controls for the user to aim, fire, move, lean, activate, throw, and manipulate the game environment and weapon systems quickly, as well as rotating the main game camera based on mouse input. How can these types of controls be carried over to a mobile touch-based platform? It just isn't practical to fill up the screen of an iOS device with buttons and virtual joysticks, so perhaps multifunction buttons are called for, or gesture commands. If you are playing a fast-paced action game, however, how much sense will it make in the middle of a firefight to have to move away from controlling the character to swipe around and gesture something to get the game to perform an action?

Another consideration with touchscreen is obstruction. When users have to perform on a touchscreen interface, their fingers obscure the part of the screen that they need to touch. If your game involves reaching up to buttons at the top of the screen, for example, think about what might be covered up as the user moves a hand up to reach them. Will the game area be obscured? If so, consider what kind of impact this may have on game play. A good control scheme takes into account the fact that touchscreen input is not as simple as a replacement for a mouse.

Finally, on the subject of designing a control system, once you have finished designing your control system, think about whether or not a left-handed person could use it. Is it as easy as offering a method to flip the controls, or does a left-handed user break it?

Perhaps your game could use some of the features of iOS to improve on the main conventions of its genre, or maybe even change it completely. Until recently, touchscreen and accelerometer control systems were hard to come by, which means that we are still getting a grip on the language of these newfangled input methods. You can find methods that will complement your game or, in some cases, give users new and exciting ways to explore the game world. You will almost always need to experiment—a well-worked-out control system on paper can easily turn into a nightmare on the iOS device; the only way to find out is to try it.

Prototype your controls, test them on other people, get feedback, and iterate until you are happy with the result.

1.3.3 Unity Control Systems

The *Standard Assets* (*Mobile*) Unity package (provided free-of-charge as part of Unity iOS) contains several different options for user control, already coded and ready to be integrated into your projects. All you have to do is import the Standard Assets (Mobile) package and you have almost everything you need. Just add game play!

Next, we take a brief look at each available option, with a little background on what each one does and some suggestions on where to use them.

Thumb sticks. In the absence of a physical joystick on iOS devices, it is quite common to see virtual joysticks instead, where the user holds a thumb or finger on the screen and, still applying pressure, moves around as if controlling a joystick.

When a finger is placed on the screen, the angle between the center of the onscreen representation of the joystick and the point of finger contact is used to calculate where the joystick should be. The center remains at a fixed point on the screen.

Thumb sticks are most commonly found in arcade-style games, such as platformers or *shoot 'em ups.* The main difficulty is in positioning the joystick overlays as far away from the onscreen action center as possible; otherwise, you may find users covering up the action when they're trying to turn in a particular direction or shoot. A control scheme that blocks up too much of the screen will result in a frustrating experience for users, and they will most likely reject it.

Touchpads. Touchpads are similar in functionality to thumb sticks, but differ in their presentation. A simple touchpad has a touchable area onscreen, and users are free to make contact anywhere within that area. From initial contact, the direction of the finger movement is used to calculate a movement within the game world (rather than the direction of a virtual joystick).

To date, touchpads appear to have found a home in mobile first-person shooter gaming. Due to their more freeform nature than the rigidly located thumb sticks, touchpads are perfect for action games such as first-person shooters.

Accelerometers. One of the great things about an iOS device is the accelerometer. Accelerometer-based controls have opened up a huge new bag of fun for game developers and users alike. We can access the data from the accelerometer to offer users the option to control virtual worlds simply by tilting the device. When iOS first launched, the novelty of the accelerometer meant that there were games using it that had no business being controlled this way. Horrendous control systems were commonplace as each app developer tried desperately to cash in on the new phenomenon and shout out the accelerometer as their gimmick.

Steering with the accelerometer can be as intuitive as a steering wheel. I have used this method both to drive cars and to steer a virtual skateboarder. In Chapter 5 of this book, the game project will use the accelerometer to establish the lean and tilt of the device and move a ball around a maze. The accelerometer is perfect for these kinds of controls, and Unity makes it a breeze.

1.3.4 Practicing

Just because you have a control system that feels natural to you, that doesn't necessarily mean that it will feel natural to everyone else. It should go without saying that you need to test your control systems thoroughly, not only on yourself, but on as many other people as possible. Controls can make or break a game and often there may be more than one ideal offering for your users, as it can be a matter of personal preference. Some iOS games offer a multitude of different control methods, such as turning by leaning the device or by using an onscreen virtual steering wheel or a joystick. If it is possible to give your users the choice, add a controls section to your Options menu and let them decide which method is most suitable for them.

Don't fall into the trap of thinking that you need to use particular controls because of the nature of the device; there are too many titles on the iTunes Store using controls as their big gimmick. As the accelerometer is a relatively new technology, the temptation is to feel as though you have to use it to be different or up with the latest technology. This is just not the case and you can easily find games that would have benefited from other control systems such as thumb sticks or tap input. Don't feel like you have to use any particular method for technical reasons or to show off. Go with your gut and remember that you need to make intuitive, not always revolutionary, controls.

1.3.5 Tips and Tricks

There are often subtle things going on in a game's control system that may not be immediately apparent, such as a variable amount of sensitivity based on the speed of the main character, or the slight damping of accelerometer input based on a difficulty setting. Be creative in making your controls feel intuitive. Your control system needs to support the game world and the game experience just as much as any other element does.

1.4 Clear Out Your Clutter

Once you start bringing your ideas together, remember to keep an overall focus on just a couple of key concepts. As you add new elements, build *around* those concepts in an effort to reinforce them, support them, and grow them. A theme or a unified vibe should run through everything you do and everything that goes into making the game. Game development is an organic process that can't be put together entirely by feature lists or specifications, and a good game designer will recognize the vibe and work with it.

Try not to fall into the trap of what I call "design by checklist." That is when your design document takes an existing concept and just adds a whole bunch of new features to it in an effort to make it "better." The biggest culprit for design by checklist is the designer that plays a lot of games but lacks the understanding of how games are made. He or she plays a number of console games in the same genre and puts together a checklist of elements from each game, with the idea that hammering them together into one will make a great game. Feature quantity for its own sake usually leads to a cluttered mess. Take inspiration from other games, not feature lists. Every single feature, graphic, or sound should reinforce the main themes and the vibe of your game. Stick to the things that make your game fun, focus on them, and build around them, as opposed to padding the game with features. Throw away any unnecessary ideas and stay on target.

1.5 Stay Grounded in Reality

Teams of over one hundred people often put major game productions together over the course of two years or more. To the independent, this might seem like an unrealistic process, and perhaps even the product of a bloated machine. An independent looking at a title often leads to an "I could do better" cry, followed by several months of work that ultimately lead to an abandoned project. To try to get an understanding of how much work your potential project is going to be, the best place to start is with a high-level breakdown. I like to split a project up first as a whole, then break down each component within that until I have a complete task list.

Let's take a brief look at a *massive multiplayer online* (*MMO*) game project commonly underestimated by newcomers and try to get a high-level view of some of the work involved. On the surface, it may seem like a relatively straightforward undertaking, especially having an awesome tool like Unity in your toolkit paired with some of the available third-party networking solutions. A breakdown, however, can shed a little light on how things can get extremely complicated very quickly.

- *Client application* (this is the executable file downloaded by the user and runs on his or her system). Some features of this are as follows:
    - characters walk around, colliding with the game world;
    - users chat through pop-up windows;
    - a character's current animation state, position in the game world, and chat data are sent out to a server;
    - characters pick up objects and weapons;
    - characters visit a store to buy virtual goods; and
    - characters fight through a turn-based combat system.

- *Server* (the back-end system required for MMO capability). Some features of this are as follows:
    - it handles characters' information (positions, chat, and animation data);
    - it stores current character information in a database (name, current inventory items, cash, position, and stats such as strength, current level, or XP); and
    - it processes payments for buying virtual goods or hooks into an external payment system for buying virtual goods.

At this highest level, we already have some questions that need answering:

- Do you have a server solution capable of dealing with the required functionality?
- How can you minimize the amount of data being passed from the client to the server? and
- What are your predicted bandwidth costs from your hosting company or ISP?

If you have 10,000 users on a server, you will only want information for perhaps 20 or so users to be passed to your client application, otherwise you will run the risk of grinding your client's computer to a halt as you process the huge amount of incoming data.

Have you considered the implications of storing user data within a database on your server? To start, you will need to address hosting costs, bandwidth costs, lag caused by a high volume of users hitting the database at the same time, security issues, or any legal issues with the types of information you are allowed to store and how you store it.

How will your payment system work? Does a third party somehow hook into your server code to process payment transactions, or do you need your own merchant account? How will you store purchased items in your database and make sure that users don't lose purchased items if your server is too busy to deal with the database interaction at the time of purchase? Legally, how are you covered if your server is hacked or if there is a problem with the payment provider? How will you go about backing up the user database? Are there legal implications with how you store users' data offline or restrictions as to what you can do with it?

There are potentially hundreds more issues just like these. The only way to find them is to break down your project and actually assess each individual component until you have a complete picture of your project. Once you know what you need, you may be able to find a third-party solution that will make your project easier. After producing a project breakdown, you may even find that your own custom solution is going to make production easier than a third-party solution. Until you ask the questions, there is no way of knowing. Guesswork will only get you so far, and if you find out midway through production that your third-party server solution doesn't actually do what you need, it can be a costly lesson that could kill your project entirely.

The MMO is quite an extreme example, but it is one that I've chosen because I see so many new game developers believing that such a project is a good fit for a first game. I stress that almost all sizes of game will benefit from a breakdown like this before any production actually starts. Even the simplest *Invader* clone has quirks that will need working out.

If making games were easy, everyone would do it and be rich from doing it. Making games is hard work. If you are new to this, don't be afraid to start small and build up.

1.6 Preproduction

You don't need to write a GDD, build spreadsheets, mind map, create *Gantt charts*, or use project management systems to make a game. You could just as well put together an iOS masterpiece with only Unity and your Apple developer account. The level of planning that you go into during preproduction will be determined by your own preference or that of your team or investors. Planning and preproduction is about making preparations for completion, so if you are happy that you have enough information to build your project and finish it, you may well have enough. There are no rules—literally. I've seen million-dollar projects made from four-page GDDs and iPhone games made from just a few sketches on a single piece of paper.

On the other hand, planning is a great way to assess just how viable your game idea is and whether or not it is a concept that you could realistically carry through to launch. On longer-term projects, having a solid plan and timeline can be a huge motivator. It can also provide a solid structure to the production and help outside parties to understand progress. If you are acting as a producer, or you intend to have someone else act as a producer, you will need a plan. Thankfully for those of us who do like to plan, there are some incredible low-cost, open source, or free tools available to help out.

1.7 Mind Mapping

Representing words, ideas, or tasks around a central theme can be difficult. That's why some bright spark came up with *mind mapping*. Mind maps are a particular form of diagram that are an incredible way of studying and organizing information such as ideas or story elements. The core concept is usually at the center of the diagram, with ideas or linked concepts working out from there. See Figure 1.1.

Mind mapping is a great way to get your thoughts from your head and into something visual. Microsoft has its own mind mapping software, or you can find free or open source alternatives such as CMapTools or FreeMind.

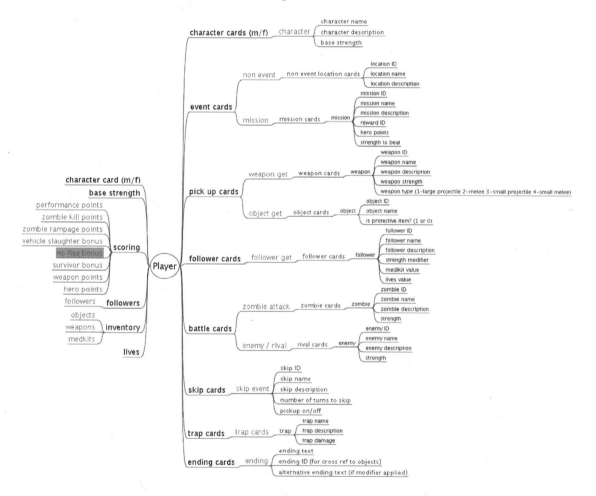

Figure 1.1. A mind map diagram made with FreeMind.

The Institute for Human and Machine Cognition provides free versions of CMap-Tools for both PC and Mac.[1] FreeMind is an open source mind mapping system for PC and Mac, available for free download from SourceForge.[2]

1.8 Scripting and Storyboarding

If you are writing cut scenes, storyboarding, or setting out audio requirements for your project, you could opt to use specialist media preproduction software such as Celtx.[3] Celtx is an easy-to-use free solution (with an optional premium version available for a fee) that will help you to keep track of components, elements, or characters and to format your plans to industry standards.

Whereas a regular word processor might require you to format your documents manually or perhaps find templates to work from, Celtx takes care of doing things like centering text for dialog or capitalizing the names of speakers. Having this extra help means that you can spend more time writing and less time fiddling around changing fonts, setting text sizes, or worrying about text justification settings.

1.9 Gantt Charts

Gantt charts are commonly used in management to represent the development path and components that make up a project. It is a diagram that illustrates a project's timeline with

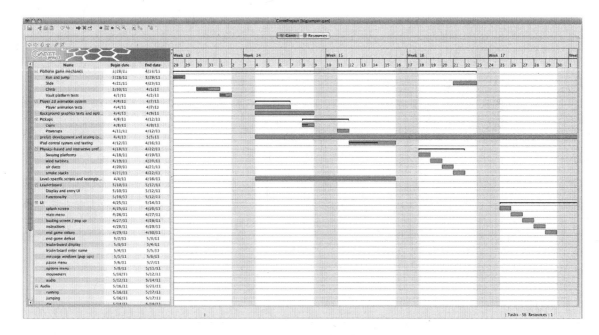

Figure 1.2. A Gantt chart taken from GanttProject.

---

[1] http://cmap.ihmc.us
[2] http://freemind.sourceforge.net
[3] http://celtx.com

blocks representing each task; each block's width is representative of the allocated time. See Figure 1.2 for an example.

Alongside paid options, there are some fantastic open source and free programs such as the GanttProject.[4] Larger project management systems tend to be based around Gantt charts to represent the project, extending them to include features such as resource management, automatic email and report generation, and progress monitoring. If you have your own web server or a hosting account that can support it, you may also want to take a look at the web-based dotProject[5] or Achievo.[6]

1.10 Task List Management

Writing task lists is the simplest form of project management, though not exempt from having dedicated software programs to help. Programs such as Anxiety[7] computerize the process, allowing managers to add or remove items quickly or even integrate with calendar software such as iCal or Mail.

The biggest advantage of using computer-driven task lists is that your list is always available and easy to access as you work, resulting in quick gratification as you check each task off from the list with the minimum amount of time between completion and checking. And who doesn't like gratification?

1.11 Software for Word Processing and Writing

OpenOffice[8] is a great open source solution for word processing and office administration, including presentations and spreadsheets. It is compatible with the common file formats we associate with office productivity. For writing GDDs, OpenOffice provides all the functionality you need and more to write and present them professionally.

Some writers prefer to have little or no extra features. Beside the OS-provided options such as Notepad on Windows or TextEdit on the Mac, there are many paid options such as Notepad++ for PC[9] or Smultron for Mac.[10]

Writing should not be limited to your desktop system, and there are several iOS apps available on the iTunes Store to provide you with text editing on the go. SimpleNote[11] and PlainText[12] are two of the most well known of the iOS text editors. Both use DropBox to sync to your desktop machines, making it easy to access text files from outside of the iOS device.

1.12 Writing Game Design Documents

As with most things within the games industry, there is no standardized method for documenting or planning a game project. The amount of information you will find in a GDD will vary wildly depending on the company, the size of the project, and the author.

[4] http://www.ganttproject.biz
[5] http://www.dotproject.net
[6] http://www.achievo.org
[7] http://www.anxietyapp.com
[8] http://www.openoffice.org
[9] http://www.notepad-plus-plus.org
[10] http://www.peterborgapps.com/smultron
[11] http://simplenoteapp.com
[12] http://www.hogbaysoftware.com/products/plaintext

In development, some companies will follow a GDD rigidly, whereas others will change it along the way. In too many cases, the document only gets written out of necessity and becomes something that gets tossed in the trash once actual production starts.

A good GDD should provide a team with information about the overall ideas and goals of the project, give a rough guide to how the game play will work, and give an idea of the technology behind it. In a large-scale GDD for a commercial title, it is commonplace to find descriptions of every single component and game mechanic. In a puzzle game, for example, each puzzle piece would be listed out in detail along with breakdowns of piece functionality, scoring, and, in some cases, even concept art. Smaller studios often stick to just a few pages of information about the game and leave the detail for later; whether or not this method is successful depends on the team, as it can lead to more time spent prototyping and trying to find core *mechanics* (the key play elements that make the game work), but if a studio employs prototype-centric practices, this could in fact become a winning method. A GDD should always be present, but bear in mind that it only needs as much detail as will be useful to you and your team.

The actual length of a GDD can be anything from just a few pages to over a thousand pages and beyond. If you do choose to write something detailed, do not be afraid to stray from the original path if you know that it will make for a better game. The GDD should always be taken as a fluid part of the game development process, and you should expect it to change, grow, and evolve as your game progresses. Great games are not made on paper and it is almost a certainty that your project will go through a number of changes, which may take it far away from the original draft of the GDD. I've seen games end up in completely different genres from the original GDDs by the time they reached completion. Although this is an extreme example of what might happen, some deviation from the GDD is a normal part of the creative process; making games is an organic process and you will need to remain flexible and open to revision.

Having detailed documentation early on in a project can never really be a bad thing, regardless of how much of it actually makes it through to the final release. At the very least, a detailed GDD can help a team to take the time to consider many of the smaller points that may not have been obvious from a birds-eye view, addressing potential problems prior to or early in production. In a way, it can be a great risk-assessment document.

In this section, we are going to look at what it takes to write a GDD suitable for a small- to medium-sized studio or game project. I have compiled several different design styles and formatted them into this single style. Feel free to use just a little or all of this formatting style to produce your own GDD; just remember that at the end of the day our goal here is to reach completion—whatever works for you is more important than anything you read in a book or on a website. You are the game designer, this is a creative process, and all I can do is offer you the tools I have. It's up to you to make them your own and to make them work for you.

1.12.1 Writing an Overview

Many of the projects that I have worked on began as proposals—that is, single-page documents made up of an overview of a game concept and a brief description of what the game will have in it. Those proposals would usually go off to a client for sign off and, if all went well, would form the first part of a full GDD if the client wanted to take the project further. At the proposal stage, the objective is to make the game sound exciting and sum up all the best parts within a relatively small number of words, so it makes an ideal start to the GDD because we want our readers to also get excited before we start in on the details.

The overview is a bird's-eye view of the game, designed to give readers the right information about it without requiring too much of a time commitment. The first part of your overview is a brief description, similar to what is known in the film industry as an *elevator pitch*—that is, a paragraph or two of text to describe the game in an exciting way, all within the time it takes for an elevator to reach its floor (hopefully a floor near the top of the building!). Try to create an exciting mental image of the game within a few short sentences:

Brief Description

Soccer-O-Tron 9000 is a fast-paced twitch game with the action in 2D, top-down. The sounds of the crowd roaring and gasping along to a thumping soundtrack orchestrate this experience, designed to provide a fun, arcade-like barroom game for real soccer fans.

The game is a recreation of the classic soccer tabletop game where users spin bars to rotate small models of footballers to hit and deflect a small soccer ball into an opponent's goal. Powerups bring the game into the modern day, offering exciting gameplay features such as flaming balls and bullet-time slow motion. Unlockable content also includes different playfields in a variety of styles; real excitement and replayability comes from both single-player and multiplayer modes.

In the second part of the overview, we go into more detail as to how the game will work. The text in this section may take the form of a full story or perhaps some of the features that increase *replayability*—those new additions to the concept that will keep players returning to the game.

The overview should try to answer the key questions that define the entire project, such as what the appeal of the game might be, what the player's role will be, why this game should be made, and what the main focus points of the game are.

It would also be a good place to include images and illustrations, such as concept art or sketches, both to add some sizzle and to demonstrate the game concepts as clearly as possible:

Soccer-O-Tron 9000 brings much needed life to a tired genre. This includes both multiplayer- and single-player-based game modes that bring new concepts to the game:

- *Battle mode.* Play head-to-head against an opponent.

- *Breakout mode.* Play head-to-head table soccer in a race to break through a wall in the center of the play area. Knock out bricks with each hit of the ball to break through.

- *Invader mode.* Table soccer ... with invaders! Use the ball to blast the invaders back to planet Soccertron before they land.

Sounds and particle effects will set a realistic tone for the game, taking it beyond a simple tabletop game and into a full-on immersive soccer experience. The game is aimed at giving soccer fans an arcade-like experience within a virtual environment they can recognize that is fresh, fast, and fun.

Following the overview is a good place to build up a list of design goals. Design goals can go a long way to explain how the game will be designed, who the target audience of the game will be, and what the developers hope to achieve with the game.

Visceral Goals

Air hockey is a two-player tabletop game found in amusement arcades worldwide. *Soccer-O-Tron 9000* tries to recreate that visceral experience. An electronic high-tempo audio track aids the arcade ambience.

Art Goals

This game should try to recreate an overload-of-the-senses atmosphere that an amusement arcade has by using bright, interesting visuals and many particle effects to act as aesthetic rewards throughout the game.

Novelty Goals

Users may also unlock play areas by completing the tournament mode, which should serve to provide extra replay value. The new game modes will draw in both younger and older users who have experienced air hockey before and are looking for something different.

Casual Goals

The game must be able to be played in short, satisfying sessions. A Save Game feature in tournament mode ensures that users can pick up and put down whenever it suits them without losing game progress.

1.12.2 Writing about Key Features

The Key Features section should take the form of a list of the features that will stand out as your game's biggest selling points, with a single paragraph for each one to explain, in simple terms, what each feature means. If you are making a racing game and your most interesting feature is *artificial intelligence* (*AI*), you should start with this feature and highlight what is going to be different about your approach. This section demonstrates that you understand what is important in your game and that you have considered the competition and how you can offer something fresh to the market.

Key Features

Air hockey powerups need to be charged by holding two fingers on the charge zones. Once the selected powerup is fully charged, the user needs to make the correct gesture to fire it. The action doesn't stop, so trying to squeeze in the powerups and keeping the puck in play is a fun and exciting challenge.

Levels are procedurally generated, resulting in an almost infinite amount of playfields to keep up the replay value and to bring something new to the game. Just when you think you've seen it all, try another level and see how the whole dynamic changes!

Users can challenge friends over Facebook Connect and post scores to Twitter. A You-Tube replay system will capture the action and give users the ability to upload the most exciting game highlights for the world to see!

Bluetooth and Wi-Fi multiplayer games bring up to four friends together to play a variety of never-before-seen ways to play, including capture the flag and other game modes, adding a new slant to traditional air hockey.

1.12.3 Writing about Background

The Background section contains any extra information that a reader of your GDD might need to know. This might include a particular technology, an existing game engine, a previous game (if this is a sequel), or anything else that affects the decisions made later on in the document.

Background

The *Soccer-O-Tron 9000* game engine is currently in its first version. Built in Unity3D, the current browser-based game will provide a solid technical base for this iOS-based title.

This version will add new features to the existing engine, such as enhanced visuals, improved physics, the ability to upgrade characters to improve performance, new 3D assets, and a Career mode.

This new game will offer a more advanced game flow, giving users a store to purchase powerups with virtual money and a Career mode where pitches and skins are unlocked and made available to play in quick-game mode.

1.12.4 Writing about Genre

This section is a single paragraph outlining the genre of the game and, if anything, what new aspect this game might bring to the genre. Is there any particular reason for choosing this genre? Write it here.

1.12.5 Writing about the Platform

This section contains a paragraph or two that explains which platforms the game is going to be released on and what benefits or challenges the platforms offer.

1.12.6 Writing about Core Game Play

This section contains a few paragraphs explaining what the core game play elements are and where the focus for game design needs to be in order to make the user's experience a good one. This is different from your key features and genre definitions in that it should focus on actual game play, such as powerups, upgrades, or jumps—any kinds of game elements that will help to enforce the type of experience you want to achieve.

1.12.7 Writing about Walkthroughs and Game Modes

Some people like walkthroughs, some people don't. Personally, I like to have walkthroughs to both try and define the experience and to provide a first-person perspective of how the game might work. My walkthroughs usually start just after the game loads and take readers through the menu system and to the actual game or feature I am attempting to demonstrate.

Walkthroughs help me to visualize the game and all its menu screens, step by step. As I write them, they sometimes give me new ideas on game flow or new features. Walkthroughs are also a great tool for exploring and discovering any potential logic flow problems at a stage where it doesn't cost anything to fix them. Here is an example for a single-player battle.

Description

In this single-player battle mode, players battle against an AI computer opponent to propel the ball offscreen on the opponent's side. When a player (AI or otherwise) manages to score a goal, one point is scored. The objective of the game is to achieve ten points. The first player to get ten points wins the game.

There are three difficulty levels available. Difficulty levels affect the accuracy and speed of the AI opponent and likelihood that an AI player will be able to attain powerups successfully.

Walkthrough

From the menu, the user will select single-player mode.

The user will then be prompted to select an easy, medium, or hard difficulty level.

At the end of the game, the entire play area will explode.

A popup window will display final game scores, with options to return to the main menu or play again.

Here is an example for a multiplayer battle.

Description

Multiplayer battle mode allows two users to go head to head. The only difference between this game mode and the single-player battle mode is that the opponent is another human player as opposed to an AI computer player. Powerups are present in this game mode, and the objective is to push the ball past an opponent to score points.

Walkthrough

From the menu, the user will select multiplayer battle mode.

Any player can first select a playfield.

At the end of the game, the entire play area will explode.

A popup window will display final game scores, with options to return to the main menu or play again.

1.12.8 Writing about Game Play Elements

Whereas our Core Game Play section listed out the core parts that make up our game, the next section of your GDD takes the form of a breakdown of all elements—a game play shopping list, if you will. This should include every item that the character can pick up, interact with, talk to, shoot, swap—all of the individual elements that make up the game.

A short paragraph should explain what each item is, what it does, and how it is used. In some cases, you may need to list out any *dependencies*, or other elements that may be impacted or combined to make something else.

Writing a list like this can help to define your game, brainstorm new elements, and provide a to-do list during production. Having a breakdown of each game play item helps in producing realistic development timelines since your team can go through each one line by line, applying time predictions to each one before reaching a complete timeline.

Ball

The ball is heavier than a ping-pong ball and it should have a good degree of inertia when a soccer player hits it. The ball should be smaller than a ping-pong ball and similar to its real-life counterpart, which would be made of rubber. We should try to give the regular game ball similar levels of restitution and friction in its physics properties.

The ball can be modified by various powerups, so its code needs to be structured in a way that allows for easy modification of its physics properties and potentially caters to the addition of extra visual or audio effects like particles or fire.

Bars

The bars are steel and immovable except for a single axis where users are allowed to slide them up and down. The sliding movement velocity is slightly smoothed out to allow for jittery input methods such as accelerometers. Users can rotate the bars around their x-axes, with the rotational velocity slightly smoothed out, but not so much as to impede upon the required feeling of real-world inertia. Bars have soccer players arranged at uniform positions.

Soccer Players

Soccer players are arranged uniformly across bars. They add a small amount of inertia to the rotation of a bar, but carry little weight and present a very small amount of drag. The soccer players are made from tough plastic, which will give the ball a hard surface to hit. The bottom of each player is constructed in a wedge shape to allow for extra control of the ball.

Pitch

There are a number of pitches of various shapes and sizes. The pitch is a hard surface that offers little traction and maximum bounce. The walls of the pitch will be coated in a number of different materials depending on the level style being played:

- *Cloth.* A thick cloth coating will slow the ball slightly, acting as a minor penalty for hitting the walls, dampening impacts with the edges of the pitch.

- *Metal.* A smooth, shiny metallic surface will allow the ball to bounce off the sides of the pitch with little impact on its velocity.

- *Rubber.* Rubber-coated walls will allow the ball to bounce off at either its inverse velocity or at a slightly accelerated inverse velocity.

The sides of the pitches are decorated with different sponsors, logos, and advertisements just above the play area walls.

Powerups

Numerous powerups will appear at different positions on the pitch, at random times, depending on the chosen game mode. In single-player mode, powerups appear from the center of the pitch. In multiplayer mode, powerups appear from multiple points on the pitches.

In a multiplayer game, some powerups only affect the ball when it is on the opposing player's side of the table. (This is true for any powerup that negatively affects the other player.)

Please see the section on powerups in this document for a full breakdown of each available powerup and its effects.

1.12.9 Writing about Asset Listings

In the games industry, we refer to graphics, sound effects, models, etc. as *assets*. Here, we list out all of the assets required to complete the project. These listings should be split into relevant groups, such as graphics, sound effects, 3D models, animations, and any additional required notes.

If you are working with a third party, note that the more detail you can add to the Asset Listings section, the easier it will be to put together a realistic quote and timeline—especially for creative assets such as music or graphics.

1.12.10 Writing about Concept Art and Reference Images

This is the place to include all of the concept art, sketches, character outlines—essentially, anything graphic that will help a reader to understand how the final product might look or the kind of visuals it might have.

If you don't have concept art, that's okay. You don't have to have expensive concept art to get the message across and you will be okay to use images from existing games, images from other sources, or stock pictures. The goal of reference images is that they should collectively represent the overall aesthetic of the game. For example, you might choose pictures of landscapes to represent color schemes that you expect to see in your game's environments. You could use photographs of wooden surfaces to show the types of textures that you would like to aim for in your menu screen graphics. This section should be jam-packed with whatever it takes to communicate the overall sensations, colors, or ambience you want for your game.

1.12.11 A Final Note on Game Design Documents

As you complete the first draft of your GDD, don't forget to include a title page containing contact details and perhaps a copyright message. Again, let me stress the importance of being flexible. Our goal is to do everything we can to reach completion, not to write the best game document in the world or to shatter the conventions of modern gaming. If you think it contains everything you need to complete the project, move on to the next phase of production.

If you intend to send out your document to potential investors (or anyone else, for that matter) you should be sure that you do this safely. Although in most cases, your game concepts will be perfectly safe and there will be no cause for concern regarding copyright issues, if you are unsure about it, before sending anything you should seek legal advice from a registered legal professional.

Try to have fun picturing your game as a finished project as you write it and enjoy exploring all of the amazing possibilities of your game universe!

1.13 Why Project Manage?

For every project, someone should wear the hat as its manager, regardless of whether or not that person takes on a dominant position. Holding on to the level of motivation seen at the start of production may be impossible, and any project will inevitably have its high and low points for all involved. It is at those points where seeing tasks disappearing from a master task list or having a percentage progress value can be a big motivator. The ability to see that there is an end to a project, and even an estimate as to how far away the end is, should not be undervalued! It can literally keep your project alive. When motivation starts to lag, a little project management can go a long, long way in helping everyone to remain motivated and focused on the tasks at hand.

1.14 Project Management for Guerillas

First up, let me be clear on this: you don't need to plan your project like a military operation. You probably don't have a huge army of hundreds of developers or a billion-dollar budget, so let's keep our management expectations realistic. Some people like to go nuts and use advanced software to have everything down before even a single line of code is written; others prefer to use task lists, and there are a surprising number of developers who are happy just to use a pen and paper to draw sketches and jot down ideas as they go. Personally, I recommend some kind of planning, regardless of the extent or the system you decide to go for, but the only way to find out what works for you and your project is to try on the different hats and see. Don't let anyone tell you that you are doing it wrong if it works for you and if it helps you to reach that all-important finish line.

As your project progresses, there are several things that you can do to keep things on track:

- Have the ability to track progress and report progress to your team at regular intervals.

- Be able to check off completed tasks (a very satisfying activity!) so that you can easily and quickly measure progress and find and assign new tasks as each one ends. This helps the project to remain fluid and to keep moving along toward the finish line.

- Keep project communication at a high enough level so that you and your team-mates work together, even if you are in separate geographical locations. I would recommend a minimum of a weekly ten-minute call, no matter how painful it is for the team. It doesn't even matter if there is nothing to report, just as long as your team keeps talking to each other and has the opportunity to raise issues on a regular basis.

- Maintain realistic expectations of what everyone involved is willing and able to commit to.

- Whenever clients, investors, licensors, agencies, or branding are involved, you need to maintain their expectations and keep them in touch with your project's pulse. Clients often require a minimum of a weekly status update, which takes the form of a quick call or perhaps a working build.

- Attempt to keep a working version of the game at the end of each week, even if it is unstable and missing features. Where clients are involved, try to keep this playable version away from them as much as is possible. Sadly, it is unlikely that clients will understand any technical issues involved or the production process. They may well want to see a demo build each week, but this more often leads to feature creep and too much time spent tackling issues to please the client week by week rather than focusing on completing the game.

- Where clients are involved, schedule regular demonstration builds for them to play and comment on. Try to keep this down to either a biweekly or monthly occurrence to maintain development focus and avoid wasting too much time reacting to "demo feedback."

- Deal with problems head on. If an issue has any chance of escalating, pick up the phone right away. It can be scary and difficult dealing with problems such as late assets or artistic or contractual disagreements, but if you don't, it could be at the expense of the project. Don't think about how it might go, just pick up the phone without thinking and start talking. Direct communication is almost always the best way.

I use a small whiteboard for my daily tasks and either a Gantt chart or simple to-do list software to hold my master task list. I like the whiteboard because of the physical gesture of getting up from my desk and wiping tasks away. Wiping small tasks off the whiteboard feels like progress, and having that physical gesture adds drama to it. When

I wipe off a task, I step back, look at the new space on the board and enjoy the feeling of progress!

To estimate your timeline, break your project up into sections and then break up those sections into tasks. If you can break down those tasks into subtasks, go ahead. Put rough time estimates on each item until you have a ballpark idea of how long your project is going to take. Once you have an idea of how long the project may take, double it. Okay, that's not a very scientific solution, but you would be surprised by how many times I have seen this technique work!

1.15 Set Work Time and Stick to It

The key to making games is commitment. It takes a lot of work and involves working sometimes when you might not feel like it. If you work from home, it is important to set times to work and to stick to them. Tell your family that you are working during that time and ask kindly that you are allowed to do so. Regardless of how you are feeling, it is important to commit to spending a regular amount of time to your project. That time should be set aside as work time, and you should treat it as such.

There are an infinite number of distractions all around us (from social networking to funny cat videos to procrastinating by finding odd jobs around the house that you have been meaning to do for a while now); working on day-to-day or, indeed, week-to-week tasks will help keep you focused on the project and should help to keep distractions at bay.

1.16 Tasks Lists

Even on small projects where I don't feel that full project management software is required, the minimum technology I employ to keep track of things is a task list program. I use a free program called Anxiety by Model Concept.[13]

Don't underestimate the mental encouragement that you will get from checking off items. When going into a project, it's easy to be enthusiastic and feel as though nothing will stop you from finishing your game. Six months in, when you've been awake all night trying to debug some mystery crash bug, you will thank me for this little tip.

1.17 Stay Healthy

When you are knee-deep in code, 3D models, and sound effects, it's easy to lose track of the real world and submerge yourself completely in your game. This can be a good thing until it becomes unhealthy. Sometimes having so much to do can make neglecting your health and well-being an easy thing to do.

1.17.1 Food

The stereotypical image of the programmer is the overweight guy with bad skin, furiously hitting the keys while clawing for mouthfuls of chocolate, pizza, and soda. In reality, the junk food will only keep you going for so long, and the crash down from all of the chemicals in prepackaged food is going to devastate productivity. Trying to avoid junk

---

[13] http://www.anxietyapp.com

food and eat healthily is an obvious thing to do, even though taking breaks and working fewer hours may sometimes seem counterproductive.

When you get hungry, start by having a glass of water to see whether your body is asking for food or refreshment. After your water, wait a short while and see if you are still feeling hungry. If you are, try to avoid the unhealthy snacks and opt for more healthy alternatives such as carrot sticks or fruit. Schedule breakfast, lunch, and dinner breaks and stick to them. Your metabolism will be more stable this way and it will force your work sessions to remain at reasonable lengths.

When you get thirsty, water is the best option to keep your body hydrated and reduce caloric intake. Try to avoid drinking sodas or energy drinks. That stuff is not good for you and it isn't good for your work, either. Too many energy drinks can place a strain on your heart and many energy drinks will give you a boost followed by a crash. Stick to one or two sodas a day at the most to avoid any adverse effects.

1.17.2 Physical Habits

Unhealthy working practices will manifest in the physical world. Aside from common conditions often resulting from frequent keyboard and mouse movements (such as carpal tunnel syndrome, wrist tendinitis, or repetitive sprain injury), staying in one place for a long period of time each day can have a negative effect on other parts of the body, too—in particular, the back and neck. Just a few simple changes to your routine will make a big difference in the long run. Taking a quick stretch or a short walk every 20 minutes will keep the blood flowing in all the right places and help your mind to avoid becoming overloaded. You may be on a deadline, but it is not worth risking your health over. Work for 20 minutes, take a break and stretch, move around a little, then go back to work.

1.17.3 Clutter

It may seem like the coolest indie way to code, but keeping your desk cluttered up with soda cans, junk food wrappers, and layers of dirt is a sure fire way to get yourself sick. Clean your desk regularly and try to keep things as tidy as possible. Clutter on your desk may clutter your thought processes.

1.17.4 Stress

It is too easy to get frustrated when things go wrong. Stress is bad for everyone and bad for your project. If you find yourself cursing the computer, *walk away*! Go for a walk outside, do some exercise, or do something away from the computer, then look at it again once your mind is clear and you feel calm again.

The culture of being a game developer carries with it the misguided image of developers as people who enjoy working long hours. The industry has come to accept this as the norm, resulting in some developers being forced to work extended hours with little or no compensation for doing so. Since game developers are known as people who enjoy working themselves toward an early grave, it makes financial sense for companies to perpetuate and encourage the culture of overtime and crunch time to continue. Cheap workers who will work for days straight and never leave the office may help save dollars now, but, in the long run, they will produce work of a lower quality than those in a more comfortable working situation. It is in everyone's interest to try and avoid working excessively or avoid perpetuating the culture of exploitation within the games industry. Don't be pressured into working unhealthy numbers of hours for a project; no matter how important it may seem at the time, your health is more important.

In the words of Shigeru Miyamoto, "A delayed game is eventually good, but a rushed game is forever bad."[14]

1.18 Keep Communication Going

Whether you employ messaging software, regular VOIP calls, face-to-face meetings, or just emails, you absolutely need to communicate with other team members regularly. I can't stress this one enough. Communicate. Discuss. Work together!

If at all possible, at the start, midway through, and at the end of the project, try to arrange a face-to-face meeting. This could be a trip to the pub, a walk in the park, or just hanging at someone's house. Keeping everyone together *after* the project is just as important too, especially if you want to work with them again in the future.

Schedule a weekly call. Sure, some weeks you may have nothing to talk about. Those nothing calls will be paid back by the times when someone raises an important issue or lets you know when they are going on vacation.

A quick question over instant messaging can quickly turn into an episodic adventure in typing skills. Try to avoid extended messaging sessions, as typing out messages can easily get out of control. If something takes more than two lines to explain, pick up the phone and talk about it instead.

1.19 When Good Games Go Bad

Sometimes games just go wrong. Don't be afraid to cut back on features if you have to, but you should still try to clear a path to the finish line regardless of how broken you think things may be. If you are being held up by something, you can always cut it, finish the game, and return to it later. Cut out enough content to give you time to focus on making a better game play experience, finish it, and ship it. A short game is better than no game and if you can get the game play working nicely, your customers will probably forgive you for a shorter experience.

If your problem is in coding, it may be worth looking at third-party solutions to see if there is anything available on the market that could solve the problem for you. If that is not possible, prioritize programming tasks based on importance and break the tasks required to solve the problem down into their smallest components to form an extensive task list. This will help you to identify a viable solution (and, since you are breaking it down into small components, it will help you to think the solution through thoroughly) as well as provide motivation. If you are not the lead programmer, try to be as understanding as possible and remember that programming is the core of the project, bringing together all of the artistic aspects and harmonizing them into a game. It is not an easy task, and there is always a lot more going on under the hood than you think. Debugging is inevitable (*all* projects have bugs and *all* projects go through a debugging process), so, by all means, keep on top of it, but remember that it is a part of

---

[14] http://www.miyamotoshrine.com/theman/quotes/index.shtml

the development process. It can sometimes take longer than expected, not because of a bad programmer or bad code, but because of the nature of such a creative endeavor.

You may find that you or your programmer feels as though the only option is to scrap a large section of the code and start again. This is a common occurrence, usually referred to as *coding yourself into a corner*. Most code can be salvaged and fixed up with some patient debugging and a relaxed attitude, but if you or your programmer are absolutely sure that the code cannot be salvaged, go ahead and make the call quickly, rewrite it, and move on. Thankfully, these things are always easier the second time around. Just try not to dwell on it too long and keep moving forward. While it is not uncommon to end up rewriting code, be sure to avoid rewriting it more than perhaps two or three times. Consider the following:

- How broken is your project? Are you reacting emotionally to several smaller issues, or are there really enough issues to cause you to shut it down completely?

- Can you get any help? Is there a programmer who could get involved and help out with the programming, or perhaps an artist who could make some extra graphics?

- Can you scale back? If your initial idea was just too big for you or your team, think about ways that you could lose some of the extra content or focus on finishing the game with whatever you have finished so far. A smaller, higher quality game is better than a larger game devoid of any fun. In many cases (especially iOS), you will be able to launch updates with new content at a later date if you need to. Focus on making a good game above anything else, even if it means cutting out half of the content you planned during preproduction.

- Is there any third-party library or third-party code that can help you reach completion? Sprites-rendering code, level-building tools, or even stock 3D models are available online from several different sources. Perhaps you could buy in some code and modify it, or buy in some 3D models and retexture them to suit your game. Unity3D's own asset store is usually a great place to start and it could help to save your project. Even if the asset you buy isn't an exact fit, reaching completion of the project is far more important than a small consistency problem, and you can always go back and fix it later. (Not wanting to chant the golden rule in every paragraph, but completion is everything!)

- Are you asking too much from your team? Perhaps you are looking to recreate commercial-level quality in too short of a time? Consider that commercial titles often take more than six months for a casual game or more than two years for console titles. Get feedback from your team as to what is realistic and keep in the back of your mind that it will probably take double the time you expect. I once knew someone who would work out a schedule then multiply it by three to get the final numbers. Oddly, he was almost always right!

- Are your expectations too high? It may not always be possible to reach your expectations and sometimes you may just have to settle for less. The good thing is that your audience most likely won't even notice. Finish the project first and polish it later.

- Are there too many bugs? You need to take some time to stop adding new features to the game and fix what you have. Put a hold on adding new graphics, sounds, or anything else until the game is back to a more stable place. Take a few days and concentrate on the biggest problems first, working your way down to the trivial bugs until the game is in a good place again. Remember to be patient and strong in resisting the temptation to do anything other than bug fix your game. Many bugs will end up being fixed once the game is finished and you reach an Alpha build. (Alpha is usually described as the build having everything in it, but there's a good chance that most of it will be broken. This is the perfect time to iron out any major problems.) It is very important, at some stage before Beta, that you lock down features and stop building new functionality to concentrate on fixing what you have.

In game development, there is almost no problem that cannot be creatively solved in one way or another.

1.20 Testing and Quality Assurance

In the industry, testing is generally referred to as *quality assurance*, or QA. The common setup is to have a QA Lead, who is someone that coordinates and targets the testing procedures and is responsible for the categorization of bugs and making sure that they are communicated successfully to the developers. The QA Lead is also responsible for making sure that testers have the right equipment and tools to be able to provide reproducible bug reports and clear descriptions, as well as ensuring that developer queries make it back to the testers and receive helpful responses.

In most cases, a QA team will have some kind of bug-tracking database to log bugs in. Common bug-tracking systems include facilities to upload files such as video clips (to show visual bugs), sound clips, or crash logs, and a good bug-tracking system will allow users to track bugs, change their status, categorize them, and query the person who logged a bug if more information is required.

For low-budget or single-developer games, testing could mean recruiting friends, family, random people from online forums, or the family dog. Acknowledging your testers in the final game credits is a great way to reward them, and many people will be happy to play your game for free. Consider posting Works in Progress links publicly, or if you want to keep testing closed, you could consider recruiting testers from a community such as the one found on the Unity forums.[15]

If you work with inexperienced testers, before any real testing begins, you should set aside some time to try to describe and emphasize suitable ways to categorize, prioritize, and provide the right information when they find issues. There will almost certainly be useless bug reports (I can't recall a single project I have ever worked on where there were no useless bug reports), but you will need to try to be understanding about it. There may be times when a useless bug report over something trivial comes at the worst possible time, or a bug report keeps coming back even though you have fixed it as much as it is ever going to be fixed. It can sometimes become frustrating, but during testing your mantra needs to be, "They are trying to help."

---

[15] http://forum.unity3d.com

Try to keep in the back of your mind that QA testers play an important part in making a better end product. If they don't find the issues, your customers almost certainly will—and I know which one I would rather have. Thanks, QA guys!

1.21 What Bug Reports Should Include

To be a good tester or QA Lead, you must be sure to log bugs that are reproducible and include steps to reproduce the bug reliably. Often when a bug is logged without *repro steps* (steps to reproducibility), the developers will either have to spend a great deal of time trying to make it happen again (wasting precious development time) or choose to ignore it. Since development time is often limited, the latter is usually the case. Bug reports containing statements such as "It's broken," "It crashed," or "This doesn't work" are completely useless and frustrating for anyone working on the project. They don't help and they don't make anyone feel good about it. Repro steps need to include as much detail as possible as to how to repeat the issue not just what it is, for example:

Start the game normally.

Walk to the end of level 1, near the level exit.

Walk to the vending machine on the right.

Try to push the vending machine towards a wall.

Notice that the vending machine goes through the wall a little.

It is helpful to include a little write up as to what the expected behavior should be, for example:

Expected Behavior

The vending machine should not clip through the walls.

If it proves difficult to explain with text, a screenshot or a video clip can often speak a thousand words. Additional media is particularly helpful when dealing with graphical or collision issues. Describing a location within an environment can sometimes be difficult to do with words, and in those situations, the tester should provide video or images.

1.21.1 Organizing Your Bug Reports

On smaller projects, you may be able to get by by simply emailing bug descriptions to the project manager or lead developer. If this is the case for you, I would recommend at the very least copying reports out of the emails and into some kind of task list, or at least into a separate document so that you can monitor them and keep tabs on what has been fixed. It is easy to lose track of or miss emails, so keep a close eye on your bug list and be sure to remove fixed items as you go.

Emailed bug reports can easily get out of control. When you receive multiple reports of the same issue, or when a single email contains five or more reports in one, it

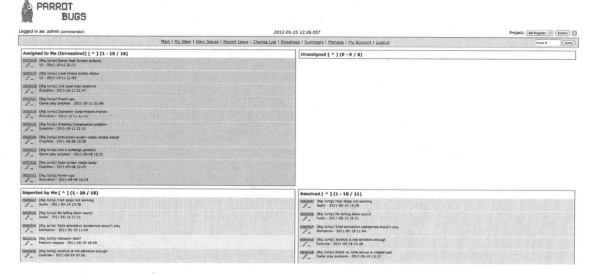

Figure 1.3. Mantis bug tracker.

becomes easier to lose track. If you anticipate a situation like this or you find yourself beginning to slip, then it may be time to look at some of the tools of the professionals. Professional issue- or bug-tracking software such as Mantis (Figure 1.3) or Bugzilla offer more than just the ability to store and retrieve information about bugs. Categorization, tester communication, regression, and task assignment management are just some of the features you would find in a typical bug tracker.

1.21.2 Categorizing and Prioritizing Bug Reports

Setting up categories for your bugs will be an important aspect of your testing cycles. For a start, bug categories may often be used as a pointer for a particular department or developer to pick up on. For example, perhaps your project has an audio category that is handled by a specific audio engineer.

As the team searches through the bug database looking for the next bug to fix, what they spend their time on will also usually be dictated by the category of bug they are looking for. Effective testing not only means finding and describing faults, but categorizing and prioritizing them in a way that is in the best interest of the project, saving as much time as possible.

With the exception of bugs that cause the game to crash completely, many of the problems that seem important to the testers may be trivial to the actual success of the project. Consider a tester who sees a minor collision fault that causes a visual problem, such as two 3D models clipping into each other. To a tester who is more focused on the visuals, it may be vitally important that an issue like this gets fixed. In the eyes of the programmers, on the other hand, a bug that freezes the game will be of a much higher priority and will be more likely to get fixed before any visual problems (and rightly so).

You should try to keep categorizations down to as few choices as possible. If you have dedicated programmers, 2D designers, 3D designers, and sound engineers, you should base categorizations around those departments and the most common tasks within them (such as 3D modeling, GUI, HUD, music, sound effects, etc.). Project workers coming into the bug tracker will be able to quickly see which bugs are related to their work without having to read through individual reports.

Prioritization is always tricky, depending on your project lead. It's especially tricky if you have a client who is actively involved in the production process, as everyone on the team will have their own particular bias or requirements based on their skill sets and their own interests. For example, a client may be obsessed with problems with the visual aspect of a sponsor's logo, whereas a sound engineer may be biased toward the way the music fades out. That is why it is so important to try and set out solid rules for QA early on that are based on the overall interests of the project (rather than any of the individual disciplines that go to make it).

Here is an example of prioritizations:

- *Crash* (level 1—the highest level of bug). Crash bugs trump any other type of problem. All other bugs are considered secondary until the crash bug is eliminated.

- *Freeze* (level 1). Freezes are as problematic as crash bugs because they impede any further progress through the game. A freeze is generally caused by something different to a crash, so they should be categorized differently to help programmers understand the issue and get to it quicker. If you are going to be generating reports based on types of bugs at the end of the project, it is important to separate the two types.

1.21.3 Other Game Breakers (Level 1)

Major game breakers are at the highest level of priority. This includes anything that truly stops the project from launching, such as a failing control system, a screen blackout, unacceptable loading times, or anything that would mean that Apple would reject the game during the review phase.

1.21.4 Sticky Collision Faults (Level 2)

Sticky bugs are where the character becomes stuck in the environment and cannot move. This is usually caused by collision problems that, in many cases, may be an issue for 3D artists when they provide collision meshes within the model files. Since this impedes further progress for the user, it has to be highly prioritized.

There is no set time for when testing starts, and there are strong arguments for starting to test both early and late in the production cycle.

1.21.5 Collision Problems (Levels 3+)

Collision problems may often be as trivial as some minor clipping between 3D models, or as devastating as dropping the character through the environment to its untimely death.

1.21.6 Audio, Visual, or Other Problems (Levels 3+)

Aesthetics are important in making a good game, but they are secondary to finishing a game. Get all of the game breakers out of the way before looking at anything else.

CHAPTER 2

Getting Set Up for iOS Development

The best part about iOS development is the relatively low cost of entry versus the potential returns. You have to bear in mind, however, that you will need some specific hardware and software to begin with. If you are used to PC development, it's time to get used to the command key and some funky mouse action—iOS is a strictly non-PC zone. Apple has made it so that you must use a Mac for iOS development. That doesn't mean you can't develop games in Unity and then transfer them over to a Mac for publishing, but you will need a Mac to build to the device, test with the device, or publish to the iTunes Store.

For many, this may mean the purchase of a Mac. Prior to building iOS games, I had only ever used a Mac during the early 1990s for desktop publishing, and the thought of shelling out my hard-earned cash for something I had little or no understanding of was quite daunting, to say the least. Having suffered a lay off from a job in the games industry, I wasn't exactly down with the idea of spending a huge chunk of cash on a gamble for iOS, so I opted for the cheap and cheerful route (a low-end, used system) until I actually started making enough money to buy something more powerful.

The great news is that you don't need a brand new Mac to be able to develop for iOS. A three- or four-year-old system, as long as it is Intel-based, will in most cases be powerful enough to accomplish what we need, as iOS (in terms of processing power or graphical complexity) is still quite limited compared to what we are used to seeing on our desktop computers. As long as your Intel-based Mac graphics card is capable of rendering 3D, and as long as you meet Unity iOS minimum specs, the nature of iOS development is such that you don't need to spend a fortune. One hiccup may be the operating system, however. Make sure that you can do everything you need on the OS your Mac is running, or at least check that you can upgrade your Mac's OS to the latest OS X. Most systems should be capable of running OS X 10.6+, which is enough for Apple's development tools, but you should check before buying, if you have any doubts.

My first iOS game, where I acted as lead programmer and co-game designer, was made for next to nothing in my basement on the cheapest system I could lay my hands on. Here is the ghetto dev shopping list (pricing is approximate):

- older Mac mini from eBay: $300;

- Apple Developer Program membership: $99; and

- a Unity3D iOS basic license: $400.

My total set up cost was a little over $800 after taxes.

2.1 Which Version of Unity Do You Need?

As mentioned in the introduction of this book, you will need a Unity iOS-specific license to start producing for iOS. You cannot build iOS games with Unity alone, and to produce games for iOS, you will need to own Unity (free) or Unity Pro and a copy of either Unity iOS or Unity iOS Pro. To help you understand the various licenses and decide which one you need, here are some brief descriptions of each one and why you may or may not need them.

2.1.1 Unity (Free)

The cheapest option is to download Unity for free and purchase the most basic license (Unity iOS) at around $400 at the time of writing. The free version of Unity is just that—a free version of their desktop engine that is fully functional for games development, but lacking some of the more advanced features such as soft shadows or the culling engine. You will be surprised as to how much Unity you get in the free version; they have been extremely generous with it and there really is enough functionality in the free version to make commercial-quality games.

2.1.2 Unity Pro

Unity Pro is the paid alternative, offering extra functionality such as audio filters, build size stripping, no splash screen, batched object rendering, and a profiler (to help optimize performance). Unity Pro is available for a free 30-day trial from the Unity website,[1] which means that you can try it out in full before you buy. If you are unsure as to whether or not you need Pro, download Unity free and try it first. Later on, if you find that your projects require the extra features, you can easily upgrade to Unity Pro.

2.1.3 Unity iOS

Unity iOS is the most basic version of Unity that you'll need to be able to make iOS applications or games. It offers a full suite of tools for game development and everything you need to get cracking on that great idea you have. The main limitations of Unity iOS

---

[1] http://unity3d.com

are that your build size will be larger than a Unity iOS Pro build, your game will have a Unity splash screen before it loads, and you won't be able to optimize your game as much as you could with a Pro license. Don't be fooled into thinking that you need Pro from the start, though. This version is still just as powerful as any of the other commercial game engines out there for iOS.

2.1.4 Unity iOS Pro

Unity iOS Pro is the choice for larger projects or larger studios. If your company (or incorporated entity) has a turnover in excess of $100,000 in its last fiscal year, you will need to make the Pro purchase. Some of the Pro advantages include render-to-texture effects, occlusion culling, *lightmapping* with global illumination (although lightmapping without global illumination *is* available in the lower-cost Unity license), the ability to generate smaller-sized builds, and multiplayer capability. Take a look at the feature comparison tables below for more information.[2]

Having the luxury of occlusion culling and build size stripping is a big deal. You can bring down your memory footprint significantly and take a load off of the processor, which leaves a whole lot more room for effects or extra game play elements that you may not have been able to squeeze in with the budget alternative.

General	Unity Pro	Unity	iOS Pro	iOS	Android Pro	Android
Physics	✓	✓	✓	✓	✓	✓
Audio (3D positional and classic stereo)	✓	✓	✓	✓	✓	✓
Audio filters	✓		✓		✓	
Video playback and streaming	✓		✓[3,4]		✓[4]	
Multiplayer networking with RakNet	✓	✓	✓	✓	✓	✓
Full-fledged streaming with asset bundles	✓		✓		✓	
May be licensed and used by companies or incorporated entities that had a turnover in excess of $100,000 in their last fiscal year	✓		✓		✓	

Deployment	Unity Pro	Unity	iOS Pro	iOS	Android Pro	Android
One-click deployment	✓	✓	✓	✓	✓	✓
Web browser integration	✓	✓	✓			
Custom splash screen	✓	✓		✓	✓	
Build size stripping	✓	✓		✓	✓	

[2] Source: http://unity3d.com/unity/licenses
[3] Streaming from the net is not supported on iOS devices.
[4] Video playback can only occur fullscreen on iOS and Android devices, playback as a texture on a surface is not supported.

Graphics	Unity Pro	Unity	iOS Pro	iOS	Android Pro	Android
Optimized graphics	✓	✓	✓	✓	✓	✓
Shaders (built-in and custom)	✓	✓	✓	✓	✓	✓
Lightmapping	✓	✓	✓	✓	✓	✓
Lightmapping with global illumination	✓		✓		✓	
Dynamic batching	✓	✓	✓	✓	✓	✓
Static batching	✓	✓	✓	✓	✓	✓
Terrains (vast, densely foliaged landscape)	✓		✓		✓	
Render-to-texture effects	✓		✓		✓	
Fullscreen postprocessing effects	✓		✓		✓	
Low-level rendering access	✓		✓		✓	
Occlusion culling	✓		✓		✓	
Real-time shadows	✓					
Deferred rendering	✓					

Code	Unity Pro	Unity	iOS Pro	iOS	Android Pro	Android
.NET-based scripting with C#, JavaScript, and Boo	✓	✓	✓	✓	✓	✓
Access to web data through WWW functions	✓	✓	✓	✓	✓	✓
Open a URL in the user's browser	✓	✓	✓	✓	✓	✓
.NET socket support	✓	✓	✓		✓	
Native code plug-ins support	✓		✓	✓	✓	✓

Editor	Unity Pro	Unity	iOS Pro	iOS	Android Pro	Android
Integrated editor	✓	✓	✓		✓	✓
Instananeous, automatic asset importing	✓	✓	✓		✓	✓
Integrated animation editor	✓	✓	✓		✓	✓
Integrated tee creator	✓	✓	✓		✓	
Profiler	✓		✓		✓	✓
External version control support	✓		✓		✓	
Script access to asset pipeline	✓		✓		✓	
Dark skin	✓		✓		✓	

2.2 The Apple Developer Program Subscription

Although you can still build games in Unity iOS without a subscription, you will need a subscription to the Apple Developer Program in order to have access to the iOS development tools software and also to be able to build anything to an iOS device or distribute your game to the iTunes Store.

The hardware you use for Apple development will need to be registered with the *Apple Developer Center* (your portal to everything Apple offers) before you will be able to build any of the projects or samples in this book.

As a fully paid-up member of the developer program, you will also get access to something called Apple iTunes Connect. The iTunes Connect website is your gateway to the iTunes App Store itself and is where you will be able to set up how your games look in the store, upload your game files, check your sales, and do just about anything related to the business part of being an iOS developer.

2.3 Choosing the Right Developer Program Subscription

There are a few different types of developer accounts, and it is important to choose the right one for your needs. Once you reach the developer site,[5] at the time of writing there is a link right on the main page entitled Join the iOS Developer Program. Clicking here takes you through to a page showing basic information about the program and, perhaps most importantly, a nice clear Enroll button.

Transferring accounts between users or companies is prohibited, so be sure to get everything set up correctly the first time around.

2.3.1 Individual

The Individual subscription is intended for an individual developer to create commercial and free apps for distribution on the iTunes Store. Note that this type of subscription is intended for a single developer and only allows for development from a single Mac. If you intend to publish to your iOS devices or publish builds for distribution from more than one Mac, this subscription is not going to allow you to do it.

2.3.2 Company

The Company subscription is for a company with a team who will be creating commercial or free apps for distribution on the iTunes Store. This will allow you to publish to your iOS devices or publish builds for distribution from more than one Mac. It is intended for multiple developers working as a team. Applicants must be a company and able to provide the necessary paperwork for financial and tax purposes.

2.3.3 Enterprise Program

The Enterprise subscription is intended for companies who build apps for distribution to its own employees or members. Applicants must be a company or organization with a DUNS number (Data Universal Numbering System, available from Dun & Bradstreet D&B) to qualify for this program.

---

[5] http://developer.apple.com

2.3.4 University Program

The University Program subscription is for qualified, degree-granting, higher-education institutions. Under this type of free subscription, instructors and professors can create a development team with up to 200 students.

2.4 A Summary of the iOS Developer Setup Process

The first step is to download and install *Xcode* onto your system from the Mac App Store (see Section 2.5). Next, download and install certificates required for development: an iOS Development Certificate and the *Worldwide Developer Relations* (*WWDR*) Intermediate Certificate. From there, certificates must be generated for the application itself (your game) called *development provisioning profiles.* These profiles contain information about the application and which devices your application will be allowed to run on during development. Until your game is approved by Apple and becomes available on the iTunes Store, an Ad Hoc provisioning profile is required for nondevelopers to install your game onto their iOS devices. As the game reaches completion and you are at a stage where you are ready to distribute the build to Apple, you will need to create, download, and install Distribution Certificates.

Note that all of the steps shown in this chapter are made under the assumption that you will be using a single-user admin account, not a full-team admin account.

2.5 Developer Tools

Apple's choice of development language for both Mac OS and iOS is called Objective-C, which is a derivative of the C programming language. As part of the Apple Developer subscription, users are granted access to all of the required tools for programming, compiling, and debugging Objective-C applications, most of which are contained within the integrated development environment (IDE) called Xcode. As a Unity iOS user, knowledge of Objective-C is entirely optional. When Unity compiles, it builds an Objective-C project for you and can open it up in Xcode and begin the build process.

Xcode is available from the Mac App Store, which is installed as part of OS X 10.5 and higher. To find Xcode and download it, open up the App Store and click on the Categories button at the top. Find and click on the Developer Tools section, or go directly to the Xcode link.

Xcode is a serious development toolkit, weighing in at several gigabytes, so prepare for a long wait as it downloads. This is a good time to put the kettle on, if ever there was one.

2.6 Basics of the Apple Developer Center

When you log in to the Developer Center,[6] a lot of options will be available to you on the main *homepage.* It is here that you will find all downloads you will need as well as links to the other parts of the Developer Center we'll be looking at later on in the chapter. This is the mother ship. This is, metaphorically speaking, the big, impressive, shiny spaceport where you get to all the other ships.

---

[6] http://developer.apple.com/devcenter/ios

If this is your first visit to the Developer Center, you need to get that download started and get Xcode and the iOS SDK onto your Intel-powered Apple Mac. Scroll down the main page to the Downloads section and look for the Download Xcode button. Once you click the button, you should be taken to a separate page that lists the available related downloads. From this page, buttons are provided that link to the Mac App Store (the app store now included as part of OS X) and allow you to download Xcode. Start the download and prepare for a long wait. Perhaps on a fast connection, by the time you finish reading this chapter, you could be ready to go.

2.6.1 iOS Provisioning Portal

From the main developer page, look for the iOS Developer Program box on the right. There will be four or more options available to you: Provisioning Portal, iTunes Connect, Apple Developer Forums, and Developer Support Center. Select Provisioning Portal.

The *Provisioning Portal* is where you tell Apple about your applications, devices, and other details required to create certificates and provisioning profiles that need to be downloaded to your system to allow your Mac to talk to iOS devices. You may end up spending some time here, so let's go through each section one by one in the hope that you can use this to set things up for the first time and then hopefully as a reminder or troubleshooting guide in the future.

2.7 Overview of the Apple Developer Center Areas

2.7.1 Certificates

All of your Development and Distribution Certificates can be found in this part of the portal. Here, you will create, manage, and download certificates (Figure 2.1). See Section 2.8 for more information.

The Distribution section is where you create and download certificates for either distributing builds to test devices or submitting to the iTunes Store. The two types of available certificates in this section are App Store and Ad Hoc.

Figure 2.1. Apple Developer Center certificates.

2.7.2 Devices

Regardless of whether your target device is an iPod, iPhone, or iPad, as your device is running the same OS, getting your build from your Mac onto the device follows the exact same procedure. After building into an Xcode project from Unity iOS, Xcode builds the application for use on whichever devices are defined in the provisioning profile (see Figure 2.2).

Again, as the OS is the same on each device, we will follow the same procedure regardless of exactly what the device is.

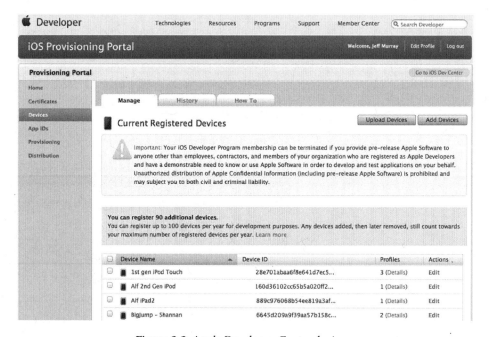

Figure 2.2. Apple Developer Center devices.

2.7.3 App ID

Every application demands a unique bundle identifier. The provisioning profile will contain a part or all of this identifier so that the application may be tied to the profile during the build and distribution processes.

The identifier you will use in Unity is usually something along the lines of `com.CompanyName.GameName`, but in the Apple Developer Center it will be displayed with a prefix (such as `16Q34CZ12B.com.psychicparrotgames.myownfarm`). This structure may vary based on your geographical location. Development accounts tend to have wildcarded bundle identifiers, meaning that as long as your profile starts correctly (as per the provisioning profile), you should be able to use anything you like in the `GameName` part without having to register it in the Developer Center.

When you are building your game for distribution, the build will need to be made using a distribution profile. Distribution profiles require an exact match between the bundle identifier in your game and the one registered in the profile in the Developer Center.

2.7.4 Provisioning

In this tab, you can edit, download, or remove provisioning profiles. We will visit the functions of this tab in Section 2.8.

2.7.5 Distribution

The Distribution section only contains information (and step-by-step guides) on preparing and submitting your iOS app for delivery. Distribution profiles are generated through the Provisioning section, and a Distribution Certificate is generated in the Certificates section. (We will cover this in detail in Chapter 9.)

2.8 Setting Up the Certificates You Need for Development

All applications to be sold on the iTunes Store or to be installed onto iOS devices must be cryptographically signed using an iOS Development Certificate, which is a small file generated by the Apple Developer website and downloaded onto the development machine. Without that file, the developer will be unable to build iOS-ready applications.

To create an iOS Development Certificate, we first need to generate something called a *Certificate Signing Request* (*CSR*) using a program called Keychain Access, which comes preinstalled on your Mac.

A quick note about certificates is that they are only valid for one year from their date of issue. An app will no longer run on any of your development or test devices if its associated certificate expires and, according to Apple, it is best to reissue a certificate prior to expiry rather than letting it lapse and creating a new one. That's just something to keep in the back of your mind, for now. You can keep an eye on certificate expiry dates via the provisioning portal section of the Developer Center.

2.8.1 Generating a Certificate Signing Request

Using Finder (or the magnifying glass search tools on your Mac, if that's your thing), find the Keychain Access tool. It is installed in Applications–>Utilities. Launch the program and you should see something like Figure 2.3.

1. Click on the menu Keychain Access–>Preferences. Set the Online Certificate Status Protocol (OSCP) and Certificate Revocation List (CRL) to Off.

2. Choose the menu Keychain Access–>Certificate Assistant. From there, click Request a Certificate from a Certificate Authority.

3. The Certificate Information demands that you enter a name and email address. (We can ignore the CA [Certificate Authority] email address field, as it will not apply to this process.) Fill in those two fields, but be sure to use the same information that you submitted when you registered your developer account. The name and email address must match with those associated with your iOS developer subscription, or your certificate will not work.

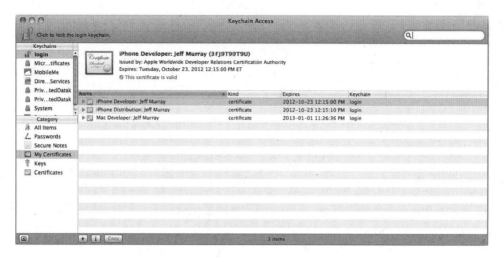

Figure 2.3. The Keychain Access tool.

4. Click on the Saved to Disk option from the radio buttons and, if prompted, select the Let Me Specify Key Pair Information option.

5. Click the Continue button.

6. If the Let Me Specify a Key Pair was selected, specify a filename (I recommend saving to your desktop so that you can find it easily later; wherever you save it, make sure that you can easily get to it when you need it) and click Save.

7. The Key Pair Information window lets us set up the details of the keys we are using to generate our certificate request.

8. Select 2048 as the key size and ensure that the Algorithm box is set to RSA.

Congratulations! The Certificate Signing Request file will now be saved. We can use this to upload to the Apple Developer Center to generate our iOS Developer Certificate.

2.8.2 Submitting the Certificate Signing Request for Approval

Once you have a Certificate Signing Request file, you are ready to upload to the Developer Portal and to generate an iOS Developer Certificate.

1. Open the iOS developer site in your web browser (on your Mac) and click on the Provisioning Portal link on the upper right of the page.

2. On the left side of the window, click on Certificates to bring up the Create iOS Development Certificate page.

3. Click on the Choose File button. This will allow you to navigate your way to the Certificate Signing Request file we generated earlier. Find the file and select it.

4. Click on the Submit button.

The certificate will need to be approved before it can be downloaded. Once created, the status automatically begins at "awaiting approval." Thankfully, it is you or your team who need to approve it, not any third party or Apple representative. Note that if your developer account was set up as an individual rather than a company, then you will be the only user and will have all the rights to approve the certificate. If your account was set up as a company, different roles may be assigned (such as team admin) to different users. Only those with team admin rights will be able to approve a certificate.

The certificate should have the "waiting approval" status. Go ahead and click on the Approve button. Sometimes it can take a little while to update its status, and you may have to refresh the page a few times before the certificate enters an approved state. Once approval is complete, a new link to download the certificate should appear. Download the certificate.

2.8.3 Installing the iOS Developer and WWDR Intermediate Certificates

Open the iOS Developer Center in your browser and click on the iOS Provisioning Portal link at the top right of the page. On the left side, find and click on Certificates.

Beneath your developer certificate is a message that reads "If you do not have the WWDR Intermediate Certificate installed, click here to download now." Go ahead and click on the link to download the certificate. Once the file has downloaded, open it on your Mac. The Keychain Access tool should launch and install the certificate.

Now that we have the WWDR Intermediate Certificate, we need to go ahead and grab that iOS Developer Certificate. Staying on the Certificates screen of the Provisioning Portal, find your certificate in the list (the one we created and approved earlier) and click on its Download link. Double click on the newly downloaded file to open Keychain Access and install it.

Assuming that you get through those steps error-free, congratulations! You managed to get through the hardest part of the setup. If you have trouble, Apple has an extensive help system and great support. Don't be afraid to fire off an email to them if you are struggling.

Note that if you are part of a team, team members can only download their own iOS Developer Certificates. The Certificate Signing Request keys we generated earlier are unique to each machine, which means that your iOS Developer Certificate will only work on your machine. Other team members will be required to follow the process to make their own certificates.

2.8.4 Dealing with an Expired Development Certificate

Development Certificates are only functional for a limited time and you should keep an eye on the expiration date shown in the Certificates section of the Provisioning Portal. To continue development without interruption, you need to revoke the development certificate before it expires. To do this, go to the Apple Developer Center and click on the Provisioning Portal, then click to the Certificates area. Next to the expired certificate there will be a Renew button. Click it. The certificate will move to the "pending" status, so wait for a minute or so and then refresh the page. You, as team admin, can approve the request, which means that after the page refreshes, the status should change to "active" and you should be able to redownload and install it to your development machine.

2.9 Setting Up iOS Devices to Use for Development and Testing

Apple restricts you in allowing installation of your apps only to devices registered through the iOS Provisioning Portal (on the Apple Developer Center), which means that you have to first find out your device IDs before you can proceed with any installation.

Each device has a unique ID number, referred to as a *universally unique identifier* (*UUID*). For any devices you want to install to prior to uploading to the iTunes Store, you will need to get their UUIDs and enter them one by one into the Devices section of the Provisioning Portal (see Section 2.9.2).

2.9.1 Adding Devices to the Developer Center Automatically for Generic Development

If you are adding your own devices, it is possible to automate the process of registering the device and updating provisioning profiles right from within Xcode. Xcode can do a lot of the work automatically when it comes to getting set up for basic development. By setting Xcode to use Automatic Device Provisioning, it will set up a generic development provisioning profile and add any plugged-in devices straight to the Developer Center.

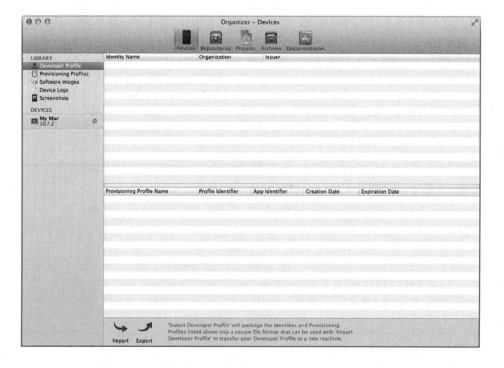

Figure 2.4. Xcode Organizer window.

To add a device to your provisioning profiles without actually have to open the Developer Center, first open up Xcode and bring up the Organizer:

1. Click the menu Window–>Organizer.

2. Click the Devices icon at the top of the window.

3. In the Library section to the left of the window, select Provisioning Profiles.

4. At the bottom of the window is a *checkbox* for Automatic Device Provisioning. Make sure that this is ticked (Figure 2.4).

5. Plug in the device you want to add to the computer via USB cable.

6. Click the Use For Development button, and the device should be added automatically. If this is the first time you have done this, a profile named "Team Provisioning Profile" will be created, which can be used for development and testing on the devices.

Xcode will also copy the provisioning profile over to the device automatically. If this is your first time going through this process, the device you added is ready for you to build to and run your applications on, and the development provisioning profile is there to develop with.

2.9.2 Adding Devices to the Developer Center Outside of Xcode

Before you can register the device in the Developer Center, you are going to need to find its UUID code. There are two ways to do this. If you have access to the device and you are able to plug it into your development system, we can get to the UUID via Xcode:

1. Click the menu Window–>Organizer.

2. If the Device section is not already showing, click on the Devices button at the top of the window (shown underneath an icon that looks like an iPhone). Your device should be shown on the left of the Organizer window.

3. Click on your device from the list. The main part of the window should now show some useful information, such as the capacity of the device, the model, and its identifier. The long string of letters and numbers next to the word "identifier" make up the UUID.

4. You can easily right click this and copy the UUID to the clipboard for pasting into an email or straight into the Apple Developer Center.

Since most of your testers won't have Xcode installed, a second method uses iTunes to get to the UUID. Although this process is relatively straightforward, it can be confusing for new users and may cause some support time for you and your fellow developers. Be patient with your testers and remember that they are usually working for free—look after them!

1. First, start iTunes and connect the device via USB cable.

2. On the left side of the iTunes window there is a list of connected devices. Click on the device to highlight it and show more information in the main part of the window.

3. Near the top of the window, notice the serial number. Click on the actual words "serial number" and they should change to become the word "identifier."

4. The long string of letters and numbers to the right of this make up the UUID.

5. At this point, it is not necessary to highlight it; you can just press CTRL + C (Windows) or CMD + C (Mac).

2.9.3 Adding the UUID to the Provisioning Portal

To add a device to the Developer Center, follow these steps:

1. Log in to the iOS Developer Center and click on the iOS Provisioning Portal.

2. Click on the Devices link on the left side of the page.

3. Click the Add Devices button and enter the UUID of the device you want to add.

4. The Devices page shows you all of those devices that are currently registered to your developer account. Apple places a restriction on the number of devices you can add to this list (most likely to prevent developers from bypassing the iTunes Store and giving away or selling apps). There is a yearly limit, which at the time of writing is at 100 devices.

Note that although there is a way to remove devices from your device list, removing does not lower your total device allowance. Once a device is added, it counts as a device from your allowance and remains that way until the list is reset. For most users, the restriction isn't much of an issue. It may not sound like a lot, but the current limit of 100 is more than enough for most developers. To keep tabs on it all, this page provides a running total, telling you exactly how many devices you have left on your account.

Here's a tip: as you consider a device name for the Add Devices section, make sure that this will be a name that will be easily identifiable in the future. My suggestion for a good naming convention is one that includes a company name or the name of the device owner, followed by the device type (e.g., PsychicParrot Games iPad, PsychicParrot Games iPod, or Steve Murray iPad2). Once you have added devices to the Developer Center, before you build again, you will need to create new provisioning profiles that will include the new devices.

There are two other sections on the Devices section of the Provisioning Portal website, available through the tabs at the top of the window. The History section helps you to keep track of what has been added or removed and when it occurred. If you accidentally remove a device, you will find its ID here if you need to put it back. The How To section guides you step by step through the process of assigning devices for development. It tells you about finding the IDs, adding them, adding devices in bulk, removing and editing devices, and installing iOS with Xcode.

2.10 Setup and Download Provisioning Profiles

We will be going through each section of the Provisioning Portal, but first, let me tell you about something called the Profiling Assistant. This is a wizard-style set of questions and *drop-down menus* that will easily create and install the profiles and certificates that you need to build and install to iOS. I would recommend this as a starting point; by running through it, you could very well be ready to build to your device in under an hour.

On the main Provisioning Portal page, look for the Development Profiling Assistant section and click on Launch Assistant. You should be greeted with something similar to that shown in Figure 2.5.

Figure 2.5. Profiling Assistant.

2.10.1 Choose an App ID

Click on the Continue button of the Introduction page to get to Choose an App ID. An app ID is required for everything you build to the iOS, as it is tied to your profile and is used to grant your application access to the keychain. Essentially, you need an app ID to be embedded into the Development Provisioning Profile, which is why the first step of the assistant is to set one up.

Choose the option Create a New App ID and hit the Continue button to get to the stage where you can choose an actual ID (as shown in Figure 2.6). In the textbox, enter a suitable name. I usually use the actual name of the game I'm working on here, or at the

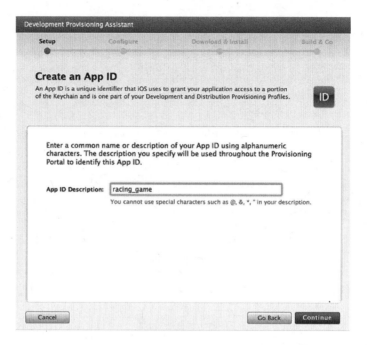

Figure 2.6. App ID.

very least, something closely resembling the name of the game. When you are happy with the name (note that no one else will see this; it's purely for development) click that Continue button to move on to the next stage.

2.10.2 Choose an Apple Device

We need to tell Apple which iOS-enabled devices you are going to be using to test with. The IDs of your devices form another part of the Development Provisioning Profile, and you will only be able to install your games and apps to those devices associated therein.

On the Choose an Apple Device screen of the assistant, you can use a device previously registered here on the developer site, or choose the Assign a New Device option. At this stage, we assume that this is your first visit to the site and that you have no devices registered already. Go ahead and click on the Assign a New Device option, then hit the Continue button to reach the Assign Development Device section.

There are two text-entry boxes on the Assign Development Device screen. One is for you to enter a description of the device, and the other is where you need to enter the device's UUID number. The description can be anything, but you should try to be specifc enough to identify this easily at a later date. A description of "iPod" could be bad; something more along the lines of "Sarah Taylor's iPod" would be more descriptive. Once your iOS development career takes off and you have more testers or developers, the list of devices can get pretty long. It's important to make sure that your descriptions make sense.

We need the UUID number to describe our device to the profile. If you need additional help to get this, refer back to Section 2.9.2. I hate to break up this party, but if you need to grab your device ID, you should go and do that now. We'll rendezvous back here once you have it.

Assuming that you went away, grabbed a device ID, and came back here, you can now go ahead and enter the device ID into that second Device ID text-entry box. Hit the Continue button once you are done to move on to the next part of the assistant.

2.10.3 Name Your Provisioning Profile

We're getting close to the end now, so you should be feeling pretty good about yourself having made it this far. This section of the assistant shows a summary of what you've entered so far and prompts for you to enter in a description for the provisioning profile. Go ahead and name this. Try to describe this in a way that you will easily be able to identify—use the name of the project and any other identifying features you think might help later on if you ever get to the stage where you have a lot of different projects and profiles.

Click on the Generate button once you are happy with your profile description. The profile should be generated within a couple of minutes and the window updates the process. Once it is done, you should see a message telling you that the provisioning profile has been generated and the Continue button should be available to click. Go ahead and click on it.

2.10.4 Download Your New Profile

Congratulations! You have just made your first provisioning profile, and now it is time to download and install it onto your Mac. This is a huge step toward making iOS-based games, so try to pat yourself on the back without putting your shoulder out.

Click on the Download button to begin downloading the profile.

2.10.5 Installing Provisioning Profiles onto Your Devices

Once the provisioning profile has been downloaded to your Mac, it will need to be copied onto the device before you will be able to build anything that will run on it.

1. If not already connected, connect your iOS device into the Mac via USB cable now.

2. Open Xcode.

3. Click the menu Window–>Organizer to show the Organizer section of Xcode. Your profile should appear in the Provisioning Profiles section within the Summary tab of the Organizer window.

4. Simply click and drag the profile onto your device to install it.

CHAPTER 3

Setting Up Unity and Your Mac for iOS Development

3.1 Introduction to Unity

Although I highly doubt that you've come this far without knowing about Unity, I feel our story would not be complete without a little background as to its superpowers. The first time I came across Unity was when I was searching for a game engine capable of taking on a racing game within a short turnaround time for a project commissioned by an advertising agency. The brief specified Mac and PC download with a possibility of going to console at a later time. When I spoke to the guys at Unity (known back then as Over The Edge), it looked as though the Unity engine could do everything I needed with bells on. The downside was that Unity authoring was only possible on a Mac. The studio didn't have a Mac and introducing a new technology that only ran on systems we didn't have was challenging, to say the least. The racing game project never materialized and, at that time, I was unsuccessful in convincing anyone that this amazing new game engine was the way forward.

When Apple launched the iPhone, I was lucky enough to get my hands on an early version of Unity iPhone, and my developers were able to use it to make one of the first titles to launch on the iTunes Store for release day. The game was a huge success, and finally Unity found a home within the company.

Today, Unity is capable of powering games for just about any platform you can think of—iPhone, iPad, iPod, Android, Nintendo Wii, Xbox360, Playstation 3, web browsers, Mac, PC, and even more devices through Unity's own Union scheme. In-house, Unity developers have ported games to a number of different platforms, and if there is a specific requirement for a particular device or OS that they don't sell on the website, they may have already ported it privately. If you have any questions, support@unity3d.com is always a good place to go to find friendly and helpful Unity staff.

3.2 Setting Up Unity to Work with Your Apple Developer Profile

Before we go ahead and build anything to iOS from Unity, there are some important bits of information we need to give it.

The first thing we need to do here is to open up Unity and navigate to Player Settings. Open Unity, click on the menu File–>Build Settings. The Build Settings window (Figure 3.1) shows a list of scenes included in the build, the currently selected platform, and any platform-specific settings. In the Platform section, ensure that iOS is selected before continuing. The selected platform will determine how assets are imported and compressed by the engine, so it is important to have this set correctly early on. Once you are sure that iOS is selected as the target platform, click on the Player Settings button at the bottom of the window.

Here you will find (amongst other things) the name of your company, your game name, your game's icon, and some important things that we need to tell Xcode to be able to install our game onto our devices—some pretty important things! In actuality, most of the settings in Player Settings can be left at their default values for the first run. There are just four things that need their default values changed and are essential to the build, but we will take a look at the rest of the Player Settings since there are some things that you will inevitably need in the future, and it will help to know where they are.

3.2.1 Company Name

If you have a company name, put it here, or perhaps use your own name if you don't have a company. Unity will use this to form a filename when it builds a Preferences file (used to store your game's preference data). Be sure to change this from its default value.

3.2.3 Product Name

When you see your app on the home screen of your iPad, iPhone, or other iOS device, an icon will be displayed and the product name is the name shown under it. We usually use the name of the game as the product name. Unity also uses this as part of the Preferences file filename. Be sure to change this from its default value.

3.2.4 Default Icon

This is the icon that will appear on all platforms (such as desktop Mac/PC builds or iOS builds). It can, however, be overridden with specific icons for specific platforms later, which is useful when you need to do things like have a smaller icon for iPhone and a larger high-quality icon for iPad.

3.2.5 Per-Platform Settings

The first thing we need to do here is to open up Unity and navigate to Player Settings. Open Unity, click on the menu File–>Build Settings. As shown in Figure 3.1, the Build Settings window shows a list of scenes included in the build, the currently selected platform, and any additional platform-specific settings. In the Platform section, ensure that iOS is selected before continuing so that iOS-specifics are shown from here on. The selected platform will also determine how assets are imported and compressed by the engine, so it is important to have the platform set correctly early on. Once you are sure

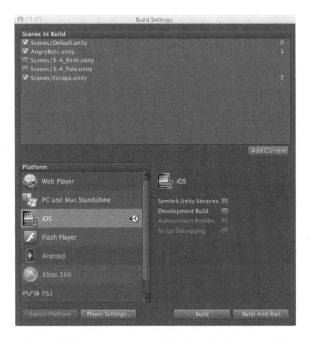

Figure 3.1. Build settings and platform settings in Unity.

that iOS is selected as the target platform, click on the Player Settings button at the bottom of the window.

3.2.6 Resolution and Presentation

- *Default orientation.* Which direction on the device is initially up?

- *Use animated autorotation.* Should we use that native rotation animation when users change the orientation (the one that makes the screen spin around to match the new orientation) or should the screen just flip around?

- *Allowed orientations.* In some cases, you may not want users to be able to rotate the screen to a particular orientation. For example, if we build our UI to only fit into a portrait orientation, we will need to disable landscape. Use these checkboxes to check which ones to allow Unity to automatically turn to.

- *Status bar.* iOS has a status bar showing things like battery charge, the time, signal strength, or carrier. We can choose whether or not to hide this when users are playing a Unity game. Unity also provides us with a drop-down to specify the style of the status bar as the application launches.

3.2.7 Icons for iPhone, iPod Touch, and iPad

The splash image is an image to be displayed when a user launches your project. Note that the free version of Unity always displays a Unity3D logo during the initial loading sequence and this section is only applicable to Pro licenses, as shown in the table below.

Splash Image Type	Splash Image Description and Resolution
Mobile splash screen	Specifies a texture that should be used for iOS splash screen. Standard splash screen size is 320 × 480. (This is shared between Android and iOS.)
High res. iPhone	Specifies a texture that should be used for iOS fourth-generation device splash screen. Splash screen size is 640 × 960.
iPad portrait	Specifies a texture that should be used as iPad portrait orientation splash screen. Standard splash screen size is 768 × 1024.
iPad landscape	Specifies a texture that should be used as iPad landscape orientation splash screen. Standard splash screen size is 1024 × 768.

3.2.8 Other Settings

There are only two values in the Other Settings section that you will need to change when you make a build for the first time. The bundle identifier and target platform settings will need to be set, but you should also take a quick look at the SDK Version and Target iOS Version settings.

3.2.9 Static and Dynamic Batching

When Unity draws objects on the screen, it has to send out what is known as a *draw call* to the graphics system (OpenGL). Each draw call has a cost in terms of performance, so we need to keep the number of calls down as much as possible. By cutting down on draw calls, the system doesn't have to work so hard at processing them and our game will run faster. Unity provides two batching methods.

- *Static batching.* This is a Unity Pro-only feature for performance optimization. This is the process whereby Unity combines a number of immoveable objects (models or meshes) at runtime, then rather than sending out draw calls for each object, the engine combines them wherever it can into a single draw call. In a nutshell, the fewer draw calls, the better performance we will get. We will look at batching some more in Chapter 9.

- *Dynamic batching.* Nonstatic objects (things that move!) can go to the batch party, too! Simply by having the "dynamic batching" checkbox checked, any objects that share the same material may be batched automatically into a single draw call. The downside is that this only applies to objects containing less than 300 vertices, as batching actually begins to degrade performance on objects that have more than that.

3.2.10 Bundle Identifier

Whenever we build to iOS, our source files need to include something called a *bundle identifier*. Sounds scary, but it's just a fancy name and Unity will take care of the hard part once we tell it what to include. The bundle identifier is a string, similar to a web URL in format, that ties your build to an application ID you register through the web-based developer portal. In essence, it ties your application to the one that you are telling Apple about. Your profiles will contain these identifiers, and if the one in your game doesn't match up with the one in the profile, Xcode will give you errors when you try to put it onto your devices.

In Section 2.9, we covered everything you needed to get set up through the Apple Developer Center, including setting up the application ID. Refer to that section to set up an app ID. You will need it now.

3.2.11 Target Device

This drop-down provides options for all of the available iOS-based platforms. Treat the iPod as the same device as the iPhone—there are very little differences between the two in terms of what Unity can do with them.

3.2.12 Target Platform

This area provides a drop-down so that you can select which processor architecture your game will run on. If you don't know what *ARM* is or much about processor architectures (and why would you be expected to?) you don't need to be alarmed.

3.2.13 ARMv6 (OpenGL ES 1.x)

This is for iPhones and iPods. Newer graphics capabilities are not supported under this platform, such as features supported by OpenGL ES 2.0.

3.2.14 Universal ARMv6+ARMv7 (OpenGL ES 1.1+2.0)

This creates a build that will work on both older devices and newer, including the iPad and new Retina display-capable iPhones.

3.2.15 ARMv7

This target creates a build that works on iPads exclusively, relying on the capabilities of the ARMv7 architecture.

3.2.16 Target Resolution

- *Native (default device resolution)*. The default resolution of the device will be used when you choose this option.

- *Standard (medium or low resolution)*. The standard resolution setting is the lowest you can get, the same as the original first-generation iPhone: 480 × 320.

- *HD (highest available resolution)*. This setting uses the maximum resolution allowed on the device.

There are several different screen resolutions that need to be supported across iOS platforms. When Apple brought in the retina display, it meant higher-quality images for the user, and more work for us to support them. If you are working on a 2D-based game, this may present more of a problem in terms of making a 2D system that is scalable and does not distort or tear when exposed to differing aspect ratios. Games that use a 3D *user interface* (*UI*) generally translate easier, as most can be supported by a simple change of camera position or orthographic height. Third-party libraries such as EZGUI[1] make it easier to produce 2D UIs that translate between resolutions, but you should try to approach your designs carefully and formulate scaling strategies early on.

For simple menus, you can use Unity's built-in GUI class along with the *graphical user interface* (*GUI*). Matrix function to scale the UI to the current resolution. Due to the performance impact of the GUI system, this option should only be applied to instances where highly optimized performance is not a goal.

At the time of writing, the resolutions on iOS devices are listed in the following table:

iPhone 4, second-gen. iPod Touch with retina display	960 × 640
iPhone 3G/3GS, first-gen. iPod Touch	480 × 320
iPad	1024 × 768
iPad 2	1024 × 768
iPad 3	2048 x 1536

3.2.17 Override iPod Music

If this checkbox is checked, any music that the user is playing through the device will be paused when the game launches. Once the game is closed, the music should resume.

3.2.18 Requires Persistent Wi-Fi

If your application requires a Wi-Fi connection (for example, a Wi-Fi–based multiplayer game), you can check this box to ensure that iOS keeps any current Wi-Fi connection open throughout the game.

3.2.19 Exit on Suspend

Several iOS devices are capable of multitasking, which means that you can keep an application open and switch to another one then back again without the original application losing its place. If this "exit on suspend" checkbox remains unchecked, Unity will hold on to session data so that users can switch out and back again; otherwise, session data will be lost and the game will exit whenever users try to switch.

3.2.20 API Compatibility Level

As iOS users are often paying for bandwidth, or at least trying to limit how much bandwidth they use, it makes sense for us as game developers to try and keep our file sizes down as reasonably as possible. Unity gives us some great tools to reduce sizes such as image optimization and compression, audio compression, mesh compression, and even

---

[1] http://www.anbsoftware.com

asset size profiling. One extra boost in cutting down the file size is to use reduced *.NET libraries.*

Using a subset of .NET means that you cut out a lot of the uncommon functionality and leave in place all of the main parts of .NET used in most Unity games. This will cut down the overall file size dramatically as well as cut down the memory footprint your game makes as it is running on iOS devices. .NET 2.0 includes the full .NET Mono libraries. The .NET 2.0 Subset only includes a smaller subset of libraries, to reduce file size.

3.2.21 AOT Compilation Options

AOT stands for "Ahead of Time." AOT compilation is the act of compiling an intermediate language, such as Java bytecode or .NET Common Intermediate Language (CIL) code, into a system-dependent binary. The binary, in our case, is the app file itself—the file that gets run by the iOS device and makes up your iOS game.

3.2.22 SDK Version

With Unity, there should be no real reason to worry about this setting. It refers to which version of the Apple iOS SDK that Xcode will use to compile your app with. There are options here to compile to the Simulator, which, sadly, at the time of writing is still not something that Unity can actually do.

There are too many options in here to go through one by one, but the ones you will use most are

- *iOS Latest.* Uses the latest iOS only. For most cases this is the best and easiest option; and

- *Unknown.* Xcode will manage the SDK version, not Unity. This is for advanced users only.

3.2.23 Target iOS Version

Even though iOS has gone through so many changes and seen so many different versions, it is still possible to build versions of your game that will run on older versions, which is useful to us in supporting those iOS device owners who may have chosen not to or are unable to update their OS to the latest version. There may be features missing from older versions, but we usually want to at least try our best to support them.

Setting this to Unknown is usually enough. When you build your project, Xcode will use its default settings and you should be able to go ahead and compile without any trouble.

3.2.24 Stripping Level (Pro Feature)

If you are not a Unity iOS Pro user, you can skip this section. It's not much of a party, though, so try not to feel left out. Only Unity iOS Pro offers the opportunity to strip out some of the unused (or least-used) libraries from your build, reducing the application file size substantially.

For extra information on this (such as how to put together a per project custom stripping black list), take a look at the "Optimizing the Size of the Built iOS Player" section[2] in the Unity documentation.

As a quick heads up, if you ever start seeing strange errors you should disable any stripping options before starting to debug. Although Unity handles stripping really well, it may on occasion cause problems that might not have obvious causes, so it's always a good thing to rule this out early on. Don't let that scare you off, of course, since stripping is a fantastic way to reduce the download size and memory footprint of your games.

The three settings for stripping are:

- *Strip assemblies.* Script byte code is analyzed and classes and methods that are not referenced from scripts are removed; essentially, this cuts out the bits of the engine that you aren't using. Be aware that this may, occasionally, get it wrong. If your scripts use reflection, this can be a common area for the stripping to fail.

- *Strip byte code.* .NET DLLs are stripped down to metadata only. This substantially reduces file size. Note that this will not affect performance, but will make for a smaller download.

- *Use micro mscorlib.* With this setting, several of the least-used components are removed from the core .NET libraries. If your code uses System classes (such as System.XML), you should use this option carefully. Most of the basics you need to achieve in Unity will be there, but if you're getting heavy and you're having troubles, you might want to keep an eye on this.

3.2.25 Script-Call Optimization

There are two options for script calling. One is used during testing and debugging to make sure that errors are caught and reported, and the other is used in a final release. The Slow and Safe setting means that errors are usually caught, but scripts may be slightly slower than the alternative option—Fast but No Exceptions, which is the option you want selected when it is time to build and send your game to Apple.

3.3 Downloading and Installing Apple Developer Certificates

In Chapter 2, we covered setting up and downloading the required provisioning profiles and certificates using the easiest method, the Development Profiling Assistant. Here, we are going to look at generating and downloading profiles outside of the assistant, which will help later on if you need to add any extra devices or redownload the certificate and provisioning profiles.

3.4 What Is the Unity Remote?

Using the keyboard and mouse to test iOS games doesn't make sense, and it would be a long, slow process to fine-tune controls if you had to build and deploy to the device

---

[2] http://unity3d.com/support/documentation/Manual/iphone-playerSizeOptimization.html

each time you wanted to test the game. That's why the Unity guys went ahead and built the fantastic Unity Remote, which is an application that you install onto your iOS device to be able to interact with your game as it plays within the editor, as if it were running on the device.

The remote uses your Wi-Fi network to stream a video feed of your game from your Mac to the device. All of your touches, taps, and movements, picked up by gyroscopes and accelerometers, are also fed back to the editor so that your game can react to them accordingly.

Many people make the mistake of thinking that the video feed is how things will look when they build the release version, but don't expect this to look much like the final result—it is low-quality video. As this is a substantial amount of data we're streaming and we need information to flow back and forth from the device to our editor as quickly as possible, the quality of video is purposefully set low and should only be used as a rough guide to where things will be, not as any kind of a reflection as to the final graphics quality. Since you will still be able to see the full-quality game preview in the Unity editor on your Mac, you don't have to rely on the video stream alone.

How responsive the Unity Remote is will no doubt depend on the speed of your Wi-Fi network. There is inevitably some lag from time to time, but on the whole, the remote is a great way to test your game right from within the editor without having to wait for a build every time you want to tweak the controls.

3.5 Installing Unity Remote onto the Device

They couldn't have made this part any easier. You can grab the Unity Remote application from the iTunes Store, completely free, and download it straight to your iOS device. Open up the iTunes Store on your device, search for Unity Remote, and install.

If you prefer to build and install the Remote yourself, the source project is provided on the Unity website for you to download.[3] The project is set up and ready to go, although in some cases you may need to change a few values to be able to build it.

Before you attempt to install the remote, you will need to download and set up the provisioning profile as per Section 3.3.

Once your provisioning profile is set up, you need to extract the Unity Remote project to a directory on your Mac. The compressed file contains an Xcode project, which is opened with the Xcode application downloaded from the Apple Developer Center. Xcode then compiles the source and transfers the build to your device. Don't worry if you are unfamiliar with Xcode; when you are using Unity iOS, most of the work is already done. Unity creates an Xcode project similar to the one you download for the Unity Remote, which is then compiled and transferred in the same way.

Double click "UnityRemote.Xcodeproj" in the "UnityRemote" folder. This will launch Xcode, where we can build and install it to your device via USB cable. Once Xcode has launched, you should see something similar to Figure 3.2.

The Run button, in the top left of the Xcode window, should compile the project and automatically go ahead and try to install the built Unity Remote to whichever device is connected via USB. In many cases, this is all you need to do to successfully set up and install the Remote. As long as your device is successfully connected to the same

---

[3] http://unity3d.com/support/resources/unity-extensions/unity-remote

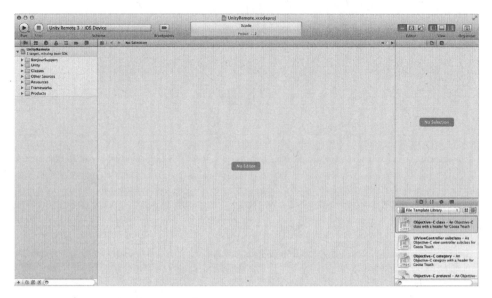

Figure 3.2. The Unity Remote project in Xcode.

Wi-Fi network as your Mac, you should be able to launch the Unity Remote on the device and select your computer from the list. When the Unity editor is running on the Mac and in Play mode, you should be able to use your device as a remote control. You can unplug the USB cable now to use the Unity Remote wirelessly if you like. (Again, let me reiterate the point that what you see on the remote is not full-quality resolution. The video streaming to the device is just a low-quality preview.)

If you hit trouble as Xcode attempts to compile the remote project, it may be the case that the default bundle identifier is incompatible with your provisioning profile. In this case, you can manually set the identifier to match the one you set up on the Program Portal on Apple's Developer Center when you set up the provisioning profile earlier in Section 2.9.

3.6 Naming Profiles Properly

Perhaps an obvious point to make, but a very important one all the same, is to name your profiles appropriately. When you have one or two in the system, this may not seem like a very big deal; two years down the line when you have several projects on the go and your profiles begin to expire (they have a limited lifespan before they require renewing), you will be thankful for well-named profiles.

Include the client name (if there is a client involved), the name of the game, and perhaps even go so far as to include your company name. There is no need to include the date, but if you think that it may help you to know exactly what the profile is quickly, go ahead. At the end of the day, there are no rules, but descriptive naming is for your own benefit and peace of mind!

CHAPTER 4

Basics of the Unity Editor

4.1 What Makes a Unity Project?

In this chapter, we're going to start out by looking in detail at the parts that make up a Unity project. Knowing what goes into a project will help you to understand the interface, as well as manage everything when we reach Chapter 6 and start making an actual game. Chapter 6 isn't that far away now, but try not to skip ahead just yet!

4.1.1 Scenes

The easiest way to imagine a scene would be to think of it in terms of a scene within a play. It contains everything to tell the story for a single scene, such as actors or props. *GameObjects* (your game elements) may be brought in from external sources, such as from disks or the Internet; however, the scene is a place where the game exists.

There is no set way to use scenes. The way in which you use them depends on your preferences and sometimes on the project requirements. Some games will have a scene per level; some may have all of the menu screens in a single scene and the game play in another; others may even have a single scene with everything all in it or everything instantiated dynamically.

4.1.2 GameObjects

GameObjects are, in essence, empty objects to which all parts that go to make your game elements are attached. A GameObject has a transform used for setting its rotation, scale, and position. A GameObject may also contain components, such as scripts or components that define physics, audio, or camera properties, and more. If we refer back to the analogy of the scene as a theater stage, the GameObjects may be thought of as the actors, props, or anything else that will make up the content of the play itself.

4.1.3 Materials and Shaders

Materials allow you to adjust properties and assign assets to *shaders*. A shader contains everything Unity needs in order for it to render something on the screen, and a shader defines which properties or assets are used when a mesh is rendered to the screen. The language Unity uses for coding shaders is called ShaderLab, and it is similar in style to CgFX and Direct3D Effects .FX languages.

Unity ships with over 30 shaders at no extra cost. There are shaders available for transparencies, reflections, and all kinds of particle effects. Have a look at the shader drop-down menu on any material to see the different options Unity provides you with.

4.1.4 Models

In a Unity game, its *models* or *meshes* are rendered with a *renderer*. When you import the mesh and drag it into the scene, the renderer component (a mesh renderer) is automatically added to the GameObject. The renderer displays the mesh at the GameObject's position and its appearance is controlled through the renderer's materials.

4.1.5 Transforms

Every object in a scene has a *transform*, used to store and manipulate object properties such as position, rotation, and scale. If a transform is parented to another transform in the Hierarchy View, it will be affected by the parent's transform properties. This means that you could, for example, have several objects affected by the scale factor or rotation of its parent object(s).

Be aware that modifying the scale of a transform via code in real time (as your game is running) is not recommended, as it can negatively impact performance. When you modify the transform scale, it can mean that the mesh information needs to be sent to the GPU and the CPU multiple times. In most cases, the difference is negligible, but it is certainly bad practice to work this way.

4.1.6 Scripts

Unity supports three different languages for scripting: Boo, C#, and UnityScript. UnityScript is a custom language with ECMAScript-inspired syntax and is the language usually referred to by Unity users and in the documentation as *JavaScript*. Even though UnityScript is not technically JavaScript, it is very similar, and most JavaScript syntax can be applied without issue.

Having such flexibility in its supported scripting methods has no doubt helped Unity reach such a wide range of users, making it easy to transfer existing skills. Reading through the official Unity forums or chatting in IRC, it is not too difficult to find arguments over which language is better; but I say ignore all that and go your own route. Each language has its pros and cons. There are even converters available on the Asset Store to convert between C# and JavaScript.

It is entirely possible to use a mix of scripts from C#, UnityScript, and Boo, although I would recommend trying to stick to one because of issues with compilation order and complications that arise when you need one to talk to the other. Unity 3.5 did introduce a fully customizable compilation order system, but I prefer to let Unity take care of all that and stick to a single language.

Unity scripting is built on an open-sourced .NET implementation called Mono.[1]

4.1.7 Sounds

The engine supports a number of audio formats to use for your game sounds. It is recommended that you bring in all of your audio as uncompressed .wav format files and allow Unity to take care of the compression. On iOS, you will need to use compressed audio as much as possible to avoid filling up the memory unnecessarily.

The biggest drawback to using compressed audio on an iOS device is that the decompression process may eat up valuable CPU cycles, resulting in performance degradation. For incidental sound effects such as laser blasts or impact sounds, choose uncompressed audio to avoid slowdown.

Finding the balance between resources (CPU and memory) and quality is never an easy task. Ensuring that your game runs smoothly on iOS may sometimes mean that you have to compromise on the audio quality here and there. You and your audio engineer should be prepared for this.

4.1.8 Textures

Textures are images that wrap around your 3D objects, and Unity is extremely flexible in the formats that it supports and how they can be manipulated once inside the engine.

4.1.9 Unity Packages

A Unity package is a collection of files and components (scripts, etc.) wrapped up into a single file with the extension .unitypackage. A .unitypackage file could contain anything from scripts to materials to sounds to 3D models—anything that we can use in Unity. You can make your own unity packages to distribute or import into other projects, and all of the purchases made from the Asset Store will be delivered as packages wrapped as .unitypackage files.

We will be looking at some of these fantastic freebies in more detail in Chapter 6 when we build out our first Unity iOS game. Unity and Unity iOS gives you a whole bunch of free code examples and things to get you started like character control rigs, control schemes for iOS, scripts, and more, all wrapped neatly into .unitypackage files and ready to import into your project.

Notice that when you create a new project, the editor brings up all of the available unitypackages provided by Unity so that you can start a new project with those assets already in place and automatically imported.

4.1.10 Prefabs

A *prefab* is a type of asset made from a GameObject. Prefabs are reusable; they can be used in any number of scenes, multiple times per scene. When you add a prefab

---

[1] http://www.mono-project.com

to a scene, you create an instance of it, but it continues to be linked to the original prefab object. Changes to the main prefab will effect those changes to all instances in all scenes.

Prefabs are commonly used for interactive objects such as characters, pickups, or vehicles. We usually create a complex set of GameObjects in the scene, such as a car rig with suspension, wheels, collision body, etc., and then create a prefab of it and delete the original objects from the scene. Whenever that type of object is needed in the game, the prefab is instantiated into the scene. A good example as to why you might use a prefab in this way would be a racing game where each scene contains an environment for cars to race around. Rather than have to copy all of the cars into each scene, we instantiate cars as needed. That way, to change all cars we only need to change the prefab, alleviating any need to update all scenes that have cars in them whenever the car needs to change.

To create a prefab, the easiest way is simply to drag the root GameObject from the Hierarchy window down to into the Project window. You can also use the menu Assets –>Create–>Prefab.

4.2 Finding Your Way Around

4.2.1 Scene View

The Scene View is where you will do most of your work on each scene of your game, such as rotating or positioning GameObjects (Figure 4.1). Unlike the Game window, the picture you see rendered by the Scene View is not specifically indicative of what

Figure 4.1. The Scene View of the Unity editor.

the final game will look like, and elements such as lighting or GUI may be turned on or off to allow for easier editing. The Scene View camera is set up for you to move around freely (using the keyboard shortcuts, the gizmo, or mouse and key combinations) and is intended to be used during the working process; that is, wherever you leave, it has no effect on the final game.

The top left of the Scene View provides a drop-down menu containing a number of different rendering options:

- *Textured* shows all meshes in the scene with textures on.

- *Wireframe* shows all meshes drawn in wireframe with no textures.

- *Tex-Wire* shows all meshes drawn in wireframe with textures.

- *Render paths* is supported by Unity for several different paths, but the only ones of interest to us, as mobile developers, are the Forward Rendering and Vertex Lit entries. There is a great section in the documentation provided with Unity explaining how these work.

- *Lightmap resolution* is used to represent the resolution of lightmapping. It should be used as a guide in estimating whether or not the resolution is correct.

The next drop-down menu at the top of the Scene View window is Render Modes. Its default setting is *RGB* (*red, green, blue*), and there are several other render modes available:

- *RGB* renders the scene normally.

- *Alpha* renders only alpha values in the scene for checking and tuning transparency or effects using alpha.

- *Overdraw* renders the scene in wireframe, but with red rectangles representing how much of the screen is consuming overdraw time. The more overlap you see between the boxes, the more time is being spent by the engine rendering things that are not even in view. Occlusion culling (a Pro-only feature) will go some way to reducing this load in the actual game environment.

- *Mipmaps* show how mipmapping is affected by texture sizes. Red areas mean the textures are too big for mipmapping at that distance; blue areas mean a texture is too small. I don't see it having much use for iOS development at the moment, as we need to keep textures as small as possible regardless of mipmapping. That said, if you need to fine-tune mipmaps, this is probably a good place to visit.

To the right of the Render Modes drop-down are three buttons (Figure 4.2).

- *Scene lighting* toggles between the very basic, easy-to-see-everything default lighting setup and the game lighting setup (whatever lights you have in the scene).

Figure 4.2. Scene View buttons in the Unity editor.

- *Game overlay* toggles on or off some elements that are only normally shown in the game window, such as GUI elements or skyboxes, in the Scene View.

- *Audition mode* makes AudioSources play as though the game were playing. This is great for testing out environmental sounds (such as background machinery, bleeping computers, or perhaps ambient animal sounds like birds' song) and making sure that they are positioned correctly in the environment to provide the intended effects.

4.2.2 Game View

When Unity is not in play mode, the Game View shows the view from whichever camera within the scene has the highest depth (Figure 4.3). When you hit play, the Game View changes to show what the player will see. You cannot navigate the scene through the Game View; this is your preview window into the game world, through its cameras only.

The Game View has a number of parameters and features to make your game development easier:

- *Viewport aspect ratio.* In the top left of the window of the Game View, you can select an aspect ratio for the viewport. The aspect ratio is the ratio of the viewport's width to its height (for example, a 4:3 aspect ratio means that the width of the window will be four units to the height's three—these units are arbitrary

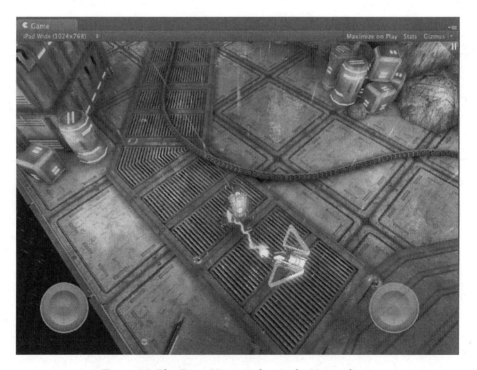

Figure 4.3. The Game View window in the Unity editor.

at this point). Affecting the Game View aspect ratio does not affect the game camera or Game View in any way, and the settings here will only affect what you see on the screen during editing. Click on the Aspect Ratio drop-down to see the aspect ratios available to you. Notice that there are several platform-specific settings such as resolutions and ratios suitable for iOS development both in landscape and portrait orientations.

- *Maximize on Play button.* When this button is checked, the Game View viewport will stretch to fill the editor window whenever the editor enters play mode.

- *Stats.* The Stats window contains a host of very useful information. As an iOS developer, you will no doubt pay the most attention to Draw calls, Tris, Verts, and VRAM usage.

- *Gizmos.* The Gizmos drop-down allows you to change the way in which gizmos are displayed in the Game View viewport. Gizmos are iconic representations of game elements, such as lights, cameras, or custom icons for objects such as AI waypoints or proxy objects. At the top of the drop-down, you can change the size that gizmos are drawn at; moving down, you should see a list of available gizmos. To toggle gizmos on or off, simply click on its icon to hide it or click the checkbox to hide or show the gizmo itself.

4.2.3 Hierarchy View

The Hierarchy View includes all of a scene's cameras, models, sounds, particle effects, and UI elements—everything you use to make up a scene (Figure 4.4). It is shown in a Tree View–based style (text based, with children of objects shown as branches), although things are never too difficult to find in complex scenes, thanks to the handy search function.

You can create GameObjects for your scene by using the Create button at the top of the Hierarchy View. After clicking on Create, you are shown a list of the types of objects you can create. Click one of these and Unity adds the new object to your scene.

4.2.4 Project Window

The Project window has everything that makes up your project: all of the materials, textures, meshes,

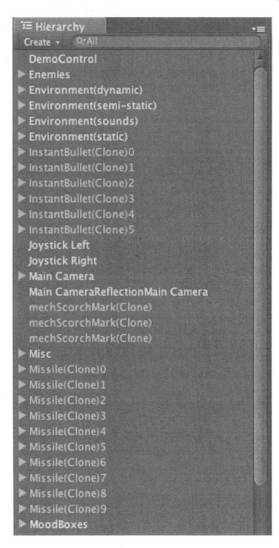

Figure 4.4. The Hierarchy View in the Unity editor.

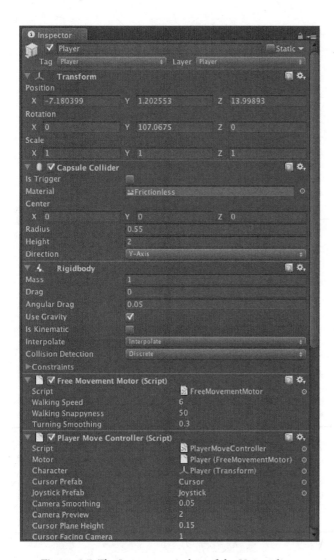

Figure 4.5. The Inspector window of the Unity editor.

prefabs, animations, and just about anything else you can think of that might go into a Unity project. The Project window is your gateway to content, and you will find yourself spending a lot of time dragging things out of here and into your scenes.

4.2.5 Inspector Window

Whenever you select a GameObject, its properties will appear in the Inspector window (Figure 4.5). This window contains the selected objects' properties, and you can easily modify values as per regular text input boxes for numeric values or similar, well-established regular UI methods.

To alter numeric values quickly, Unity gives you the option to do this through a drag-and-drop method. Click on the text next to the numeric value and the icon changes to something resembling two arrows. Once you see this, you can hold and drag left or right to change the numeric value. Hold down the shift key as you drag to change values faster.

4.3 Navigating the Game Scene

You will most likely spend a lot of time moving around the game scene, placing and manipulating objects within your scenes. The editor is extremely intuitive and offers some great methods for getting around the scene, such as keyboard shortcuts to center objects in the viewport or grid snapping.

- *Zooming.* You can always zoom in or out using a mouse wheel or a trackpad.

- *Movement.* Use the arrow keys to move around. Hold down the SHIFT key to move faster.

- *Focusing/framing.* To frame (or center) a selected object in the viewport, press the F key. The object's pivot point will appear in the center of the view.

There are shortcuts to orbit, move, and zoom around your scenes as well as a super useful method of orbiting around the currently selected object. You will be spending a lot of time orbiting, moving, and zooming around the scene. To find the best method for you, try out the shortcuts as well as the standard methods:

- *Orbiting.* Hold the ALT key and hold down the left mouse button and drag to orbit around the currently selected object.

- *Zooming.* Hold the ALT key and the right mouse button and drag to zoom in or out of the view. On a single button mouse, hold down ALT + CTRL (ALT + CMD on a Mac).

- *Moving.* On a three-button mouse, hold the ALT key and the middle mouse button and drag to move the camera. On a mouse with only two buttons, hold ALT + CTRL (ALT + CMD on a Mac) and hold down the left mouse button to move around. On a mouse with only one button, hold ALT + CTRL (ALT + CMD on a Mac) and hold down the left mouse button to move.

4.3.1 Scene View Toolbar

The Scene View is your playground. It is where you will spend most of your time in the editor, manipulating objects and moving around your game scenes. The Scene View Toolbar (shown in Figure 4.6) is your gateway to the Scene View, providing several methods to navigate and manipulate objects.

Figure 4.6. The Scene View toolbar in the Unity editor.

4.3.2 The Hand Tool

To enter the hand tool mode, press Q or click on the hand icon from the toolbar. With the hand tool selected, click and drag anywhere on the scene with the left mouse button to move around.

From the hand tool, you can easily switch to orbit and drag modes with the following keyboard shortcuts:

- *Orbit.* Hold the ALT key and click and drag with the left mouse button to orbit the camera around the scene.

- *Zoom.* Hold the CTRL key (CMD on a Mac) and click and drag with the left mouse button to zoom in or out of the scene.

- *Translate tool (hot key W).* The translate tool is used to move objects around in the scene (this is the one that looks like four arrows in a + shape). In this mode, when you click on a model, the currently selected object will have a tool handle appear (the handle looks a bit like the scene gizmo) by default at the object's pivot point, which is set in the 3D modeling package, or in the case of primitive objects, will be at the object's center. Up above the Scene window, there is a toggle button to switch between the object's pivot point and its center. This makes it easier to manipulate objects, which may have pivot points off-center.

- *Rotate tool* (*hot key E*). The rotate tool allows you to rotate objects around in the Scene window. In this mode, a rotation tool handle will appear over the object and you can click and drag to turn it. Above the Scene window is a toggle button to switch between local or global rotation.

- *Scale tool* (*hot key R*). The scale tool is used to alter the scale of objects in a scene. When selected, a scale tool handle will appear over the object and you can click and drag to set sizes accordingly. By clicking and dragging in the center of the tool handle, you will uniformly scale all three axes.

4.3.3 Flythrough Mode

Moving around the 3D world can sometimes be tricky, particularly when an interface does not follow conventions or offer any kind of navigation system you may be used to. Unity offers several alternatives, and its many combinations can likely be put together to provide something of satisfaction to most users.

The *flythrough* mode works in a similar way to how flying is sometimes represented by games. The camera will fly around in first person, controlled by the arrow keys and with a "mouselook" system to rotate the camera.

To fly through, click and hold the right mouse button. As you continue to hold down the button, you can move around using the W, A, S, and D keys to move left, right, forward, or backward, respectively. The Q and E keys move up or down. As with the rest of the Unity navigation system, you can hold down the SHIFT key to move faster.

4.3.4 The Scene Gizmo

A fast way to change the angle of view is by using something called the scene gizmo (Figure 4.7). You will find it in the top right corner of the Scene View. Click on the various axis arms to move around. The cube in the center of the gizmo toggles between using a perspective or an orthographic camera for the viewport.

I find the scene gizmo is most useful when trying to align objects. By clicking on the *x*-axis, you can immediately see a side view of the object you are attempting to align. The gizmo may then be used to switch around other angles to align the object on all three axes.

4.4 Finding Objects in a Scene Quickly

When you are dealing with complex scenes, reading through the hierarchy to find what you want and then using F to focus it within the Scene window can be long winded. Even when you focus on a particular object, you may find that you have so many things within a small area that it becomes difficult to distinguish between meshes. To alleviate this, you can use the search box at the top of the window.

When you enter something into the search box (Figure 4.8), the first thing that Unity does is try to find all objects that match your search term and to fade out all of the

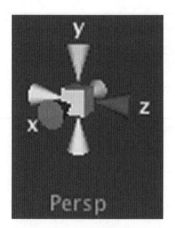

Figure 4.7. The scene gizmo in the Unity editor.

Figure 4.8. The Unity search box.

others in the background. Any matches are easy to see right away, and as you continue to type, the search gets narrowed down toward an exact match.

As your search narrows down in the Scene View, notice that the hierarchy also narrows down to show only those objects shown in the viewport. Click on an item in the hierarchy, then move your mouse over the Scene View and press F on the keyboard to move the camera to focus on your chosen item.

4.5 Unity Physics: PhysX

All versions of Unity include the NVIDIA PhysX physics system as native to the engine. That is, you have a fully functional, commercial-level physics engine all ready to go out of the box. PhysX is a proprietary real-time physics engine that deals with the simulation of physics objects and their collisions, meaning that you can concentrate on making great games and leave all of the complex simulation code for the engine developers. By adding physics components to GameObjects, you tell the engine what types of physics objects you need and Unity deals with making it happen.

The main type of object you will see most of, in a game project, is called a *rigidbody*. The scientific description of a rigidbody is a little hard hitting in this context, so let's say instead that we can think of a rigidbody as a physics "thing" that will react to and act upon the world of other physics "things" around it. Static objects (for example, models that you might use as walls or a floor) do not need to be rigidbodies. We simply give them a *collider* and rigidbodies will react accordingly when a collision occurs.

Making an object become a rigidbody is as simple as highlighting it and clicking on the menu Component–>Physics–>Rigidbody.

4.5.1 Properties

On a rigidbody, there are a few properties available to set through the Inspector window (see Figure 4.9):

- *Mass.* To keep your physics simulation stable, you should try to keep to values between 0.1 and 10.

- *Drag.* Drag will slow down an object over time. Higher values slow the object quicker.

- *Angular drag.* Angular drag slows angular velocity over time. It can be used to reduce spinning of a physics object (we use this value to help control the

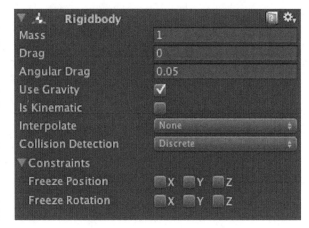

Figure 4.9. Rigidbody properties in the Inspector window.

spinning and turning of our karts in Chapter 6 when we build a kart-racing game).

- *Use gravity.* By default, all physics objects are affected by gravity. You can change this if you are either going to deal with gravity yourself or to simulate an object floating through space.

- *Interpolate.* When the movement of your physics object is interpolated, its movement will be smoothed out. This is particularly useful when your frame rate fluctuates, as interpolation will hide this, and its use is recommended for main characters or vehicles. Other objects should not be interpolated, wherever possible, to avoid unnecessary additional math calculations eating up valuable CPU cycles.

4.5.2 Interpolation

There are three options in the Interpolate drop-down menu:

- *None.* No interpolation.

- *Interpolate.* The visible representation of the physics object will lag behind the simulation a little (by a barely noticeable amount), but this will produce a smoother effect than extrapolation.

- *Extrapolation.* When this is set, the rigidbody's position will be predicted from the object's velocity.

4.5.3 Collision Detection

Three collision detection modes are provided by Unity and accessible through this drop-down menu:

- *Discrete.* Continuous collision detection is off.

- *Continuous.* Continuous collision detection for colliding with static mesh geometry.

- *Continuous dynamic.* Continuous collision detection for colliding with static and dynamic objects.

In almost all cases, the default setting of Discrete will be sufficient for standard collision detection.

4.5.4 Constraints

Constraints are used to constrain a rigidbody on one or more chosen axes. In Chapter 6, we look at how our example kart-racing game used constraints to hold the x-axis and z-axis of a car in place as the race countdown begins, leaving the y-axis unconstrained so that gravity can still do its thing.

4.5.5 Colliders

Unless you are somehow dealing with collisions in your own code, objects in your scene will need to have collider components applied to them. The shape of the collider need not be a complete representation of the shape of the object it is attached to, meaning that you may sometimes choose to represent a complex model by a simple box collider or perhaps a sphere. The shape of the object remains the same, but how the physics engine deals with the collisions will be different.

There are several different types of collider available, meaning that you can choose to represent your 3D objects in the physics world in a number of different ways, depending on your specific requirements. The way that your collider is shaped will affect how friction affects the movement of your rigidbody (objects with more surface contact will encounter more friction), how collisions are resolved, and how weight is distributed. The weight of your rigidbody will be distributed within the volume of the collider, meaning that if your collider is large, the weight will be spread across a larger area (and vice versa).

The complexity of your collider may also affect performance, which means that wherever possible you should try to use basic shapes.

There are several available colliders:

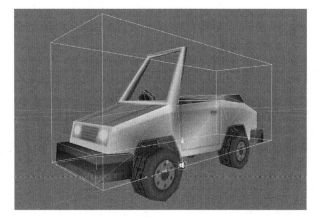

Figure 4.10. A box collider in the Unity editor.

- *Box collider.* For simple collisions, the box collider is usually the best option (Figure 4.10). It is a fast, efficient way of dealing with simple box-shaped physics representations. When you create one of Unity's built-in primitives, such as the cube available via the menu GameObject–>Create Other–>Cube, a box collider will be automatically added to the object it creates. The plane primitive (GameObject–>Create Other –>Plane) also uses a box collider, with a low number in its *y*-axis within size.

- *Sphere collider.* The sphere collider (Figure 4.11) is commonly used to represent spherical objects, although it may also be used for other shapes that need to roll, slide, or contact surfaces (for low friction). When you create a sphere primitive in the editor through the menu GameObject–>Create Other –>Sphere, Unity will automatically add on the sphere collider.

- *Mesh collider.* For complex collision shapes, a mesh collider is available (Figure 4.12). The mesh collider takes mesh data and forms a collision area from it. The resulting collision will be most realistic, representing the visual object with an identical collision area. As the mesh collider uses mesh data to build

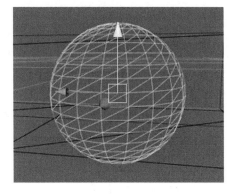

Figure 4.11. A sphere collider in Unity.

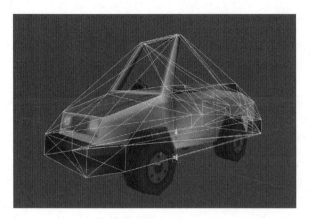

Figure 4.12. A mesh collider in the Unity editor.

with, be aware that a more complex mesh will result in more calculations during physics updates. If in doubt, use a primitive collider, such as a box collider, instead.

A mesh collider can also be a convex mesh. This essentially creates a collider that is shaped similar to how wrapping paper might be wrapped around an object, not tucking into any holes or entrances. This is useful for detailed meshes that are too complex for mesh colliders but still require accurate collisions. Simply check the checkbox in the Inspector window with a mesh collider selected in the editor.

Another property available in the Inspector window with a mesh collider is the "smooth sphere collisions" checkbox. This will use interpolated data on the mesh surfaces, rather than actual polydata, which can result in a smoother roll when a sphere collider moves over it. The effect is similar to smoothing out the mesh, but the movement of the sphere collider may sometimes appear unnatural.

4.5.1 Tips and Tricks

You can modify the positions of windows to whatever suits your personal way of working and then save the layout for later. Once you have saved a layout, you can access it and switch between layouts at any time using the Layout drop-down in the top right of the interface. Personally, I find this really useful for dealing with cross-platform iOS games and I like to have one custom layout for working with iPad and another one specifically for iPhone.

Get used to highlighting objects in the Hierarchy window and using the F key to focus them in the Scene View. This is by far the fastest and easiest way to manipulate objects in a scene.

Try to get to know the navigation keyboard shortcuts, such as those that switch the mouse drag between panning and rotating. You will save a lot of time if you can master them!

CHAPTER 5

Building a Game in Unity iOS: The Roll-a-Ball Game

5.1 Game Overview

In this chapter, we will be building a simple ball-rolling game (Figure 5.1). The idea of the game is to roll the ball around a maze to reach a finish point, avoiding obstacles along the way.

Users will control the ball using the accelerometer on the iOS device. The camera looks down from above, as though the device contains a maze with a ball in it. Users

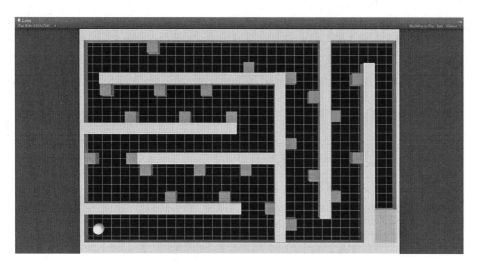

Figure 5.1. The Roll-a-Ball game.

lean the device and gravity carries the ball in the direction it would go if in a physical maze.

This is a simple skill-based game that requires us to look at some of the basic concepts of Unity and iOS games. By using some of the scripts and components that come with Unity, we will explore the accelerometer, collisions, simple scripts, and triggers.

5.2 Controls

The control system for this game is straightforward. As the game is top-down, we can assume that users will hold the device flat and look down as though they were looking down into the game's world. To move the ball through the maze and to the finish, the user must tilt the device as though it were a wooden puzzle, and the ball should roll around as though it were resting inside it.

To make the control system work, we need to take input from the device's accelerometers to find out how much the user is tilting. The actual script we will use to move the ball around is provided free of charge by Unity as part of the Standard Assets included with the engine, which means no programming required!

5.3 Making the Game

Let's get started by opening up Unity and creating a new project. I call this project "rollaball." Not the most exciting name, I know, so feel free to come up with something more dramatic if that floats your boat. (I think "Ball Roller" is probably a good idea for my project, since my other naming ideas were terrible: "Ball Escape Zone X," "Ball's Revenge," and "Balls Gone Wild.")

5.3.1 Set Up the Scene

First, we will set up a basic Unity project and a simple scene that will form the basis of our game. You can find a completed scene in the example files for this book (in the "rollaball_base" folder) or go through the steps below. If you choose to skip ahead and open the example files, before you try and build to the device, you will need to set the bundle identifier (as discussed in Section 3.2.10) to one suitable for your own Apple Developer account.

1. Create a new, empty project containing the iOS Standard Assets (Mobile) (Figure 5.2).

2. Go into Build Settings and select iOS. As we are setting up the way in which Unity will put together the build, we should go ahead and set up a few more parameters so that we can publish straight to the device. Click on the Player Settings button to bring them up in the Inspector window.

3. Now click on the Other Settings section and click on the Bundle Identifier field. Fill this in with a valid bundle ID (e.g., "com.yourname.thisprojectname"). This field needs to be filled in correctly in order for your builds to work on the device, so be sure to get this right.

4. Enter your company name (if required), followed by a name for your game into the Product Name field.

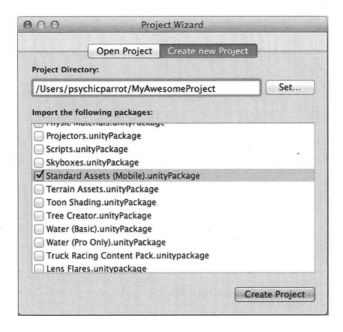

Figure 5.2. Creating a new project with the Standard Assets (Mobile).unityPackage.

Now that we have the basic parameters set up for the build, we can go ahead and get started with the scene. By default, your new project will already have a scene, but it won't be saved until you actually visit the menu File–>Save Scene (Figure 5.3).

Add a plane for the ground by going to the menu GameObject–>Create Other –>Plane (Figure 5.4). The plane we just added will eventually form the ground for our game, so we can leave it right where it is. The only problem with this plane is that our play area is too small to be any fun, so let's scale it up. Set the *x* scale to 3, the *y* to 2, and the *z* to 2 (Figure 5.5).

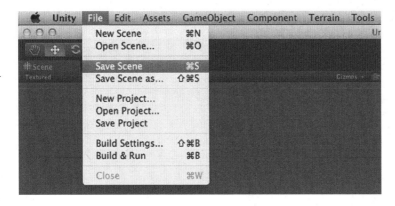

Figure 5.3. The Save Scene window.

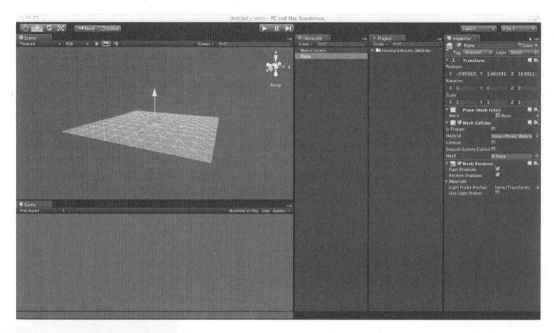

Figure 5.4. A plane added to the scene in the Unity editor.

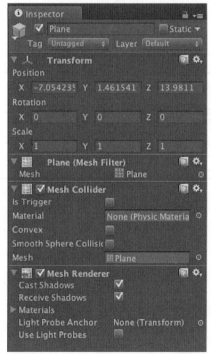

Figure 5.5. Properties of the plane in the Roll-a-Ball game.

We now need a ball to roll around. Unity has kindly provided one free of charge along with Unity iOS Standard Assets. Find the Roll-a-Ball prefab within the "Standard Assets (Mobile)" folder, under "prefabs," and simply drag it in to the scene (Figure 5.6).

The Roll-a-Ball prefab is set up to work with a bigger level than the one we are going to be building, so first we need to change its scale. Select the Roll-a-Ball object in the Hierarchy window then, in the Inspector window, set all three axes (x, y, and z) of its scale to 1. Set the position of the ball to $x = 0$, $y = 0.5$, and $z = 0$.

We are going to need a little more of a visual guide to put the scene together correctly, so the next step is to reposition and rotate the camera so that we have a better idea of how things will look when we play the game.

Select the camera (the GameObject called Main Camera) from the Hierarchy window and, through the Inspector window, position it at $x = 0$, $y = 50$, and $z = 0$.

Change the rotation x-axis to 90. Then, find the Field of View slider and move it so that the value is 50. Your Inspector window should look something like the one in Figure 5.7. Use this as a guide to double check through your position and rotation values.

Figure 5.6. The Roll-a-Ball prefab in the Project window of the Unity editor.

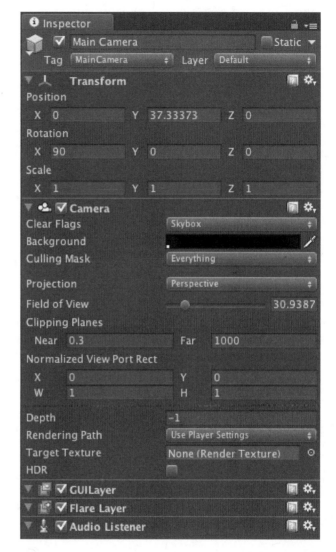

Figure 5.7. The main camera parameters in the Inspector window of the Unity editor.

When you look at the Game window, you can see exactly what the main camera sees. The way in which the view scales depends on the setting of the Aspect Ratio drop-down (located in the top left of the Game window; Figure 5.8), which by default will be set to Free Aspect. To get a better idea of how our game will look on the device, click on the Aspect Ratio drop-down and select the first iPhone Wide setting from the menu.

From this new viewpoint, it is hard to see the ground plane from above and difficult to achieve much of a gauge as to how quickly the ball is moving once we get the game running. We need to help players to associate with some sense of scale.

Adding a texture to the ground plane will solve this (Figure 5.9), so go ahead and find the grid material from the project. Drag the material from the Project window over into the Scene window and drop it onto the plane.

By changing the tiling parameters of the material, we can make this more visually appealing. An *x* value of 15 and a *y* value of 10 should make things look better.

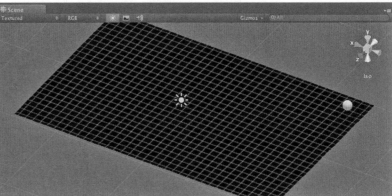

Figure 5.8. The Aspect Ratio dropdown from the Game window of the Unity editor.

Figure 5.9. A texture applied to the ground plane in the Roll-a-Ball game.

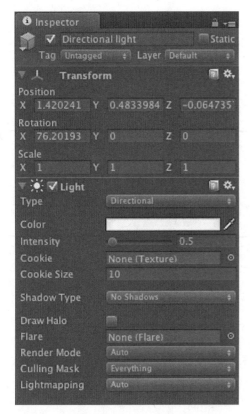

Figure 5.10. The Inspector window in the Unity editor showing properties of the main light in the Roll-a-Ball game.

5.3.2 Lights

On iOS, lights are a precious commodity, and we never want to use more than a couple in a scene. In fact, your performance will benefit most if you leave lights out altogether and just use ambient lighting instead. The ambient light is applied to all materials in a scene, so if you set the ambient to white, it will look as though the scene is lit, though only in its most basic form and the scene will be lit in a flat and uninteresting way. By using lightmapping and perhaps some clever environment modeling, you can, however, still make a scene look incredible with just ambient lighting.

That said, we are going to get fancy and add a directional light. This will give our simple scene a sense of depth.

Click on the menu Game Object–>Create Other–> Directional Light. This will add a directional light to the scene. The light's position and rotation need changing here, so you can use the settings below or feel free to use Unity's rotation gizmo to reach a satisfying effect.

Through the Inspector window, position the light at $x = 0$, $y = 0$, and $z = 0$, and set its rotation to $x = 76$, $y = 0$, and $z = 0$, as shown in Figure 5.10.

If you haven't already started up or installed Unity Remote onto your device, you should do that now. (For full instructions on installing the remote, see Section 3.5.)

Start up the Unity Remote on your (USB-connected) iOS device and press the Play button within the Unity editor. You should see a low-resolution streaming video of the

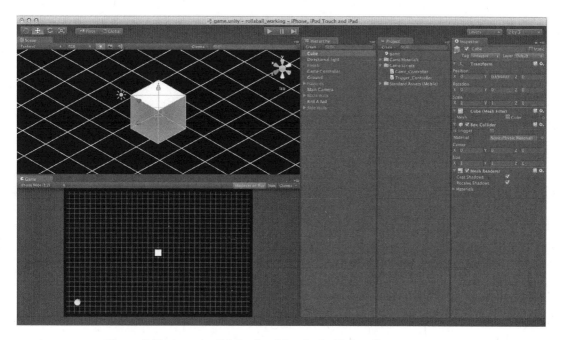

Figure 5.11. A newly added cube object in the Unity editor.

game screen appear on your iOS device. Lean the device around and the accelerometer data will be passed onto Unity, making the ball move around the plane.

As the video that is being streamed is of such low quality and is prone sometimes to lag, it is easier to watch the Unity window than try to control the game by looking at the device. The video is there just as a guide, but don't be alarmed by it—when you build to the device it will look much better!

You should be able to roll the ball around the ground plane now, but what if we roll off the edge of the ground plane? Unless you're the star of a children's animated movie, it's not much fun falling into infinity and beyond, so let's stop that from happening with some walls.

Add a cube by clicking on Game Object–>Create Other–>Cube (Figure 5.11). In the Inspector window, set the scale up to $x = 1$, $y = 1$, and $z = 20$, and the position to $x = 5.7$, $y = -66.4$, and $z = 1.87$. Since we are on a roll (pun intended), let's keep going and make another three walls.

Select the Cube object you just created in the Hierarchy window. Hit CTRL + D (or CMD + D on a Mac) to duplicate the cube. You should see a new cube appear in the Hierarchy window. Move this new, duplicate box to make it appear on the other side of the plane. Don't worry about being exactly in position, just as long as the y position values stay at 0.

Using CTRL + D (CMD + D on a Mac) to duplicate objects, copy the cube another time, and type "90" into the y rotation value in the Inspector window to turn it around and form a top wall. Position it at the edge of the ground plane and duplicate it to form

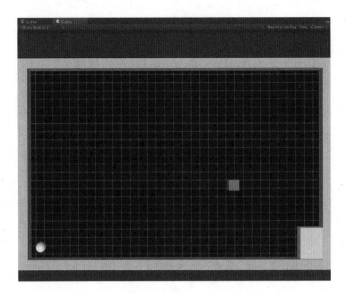

Figure 5.12. The Roll-a-Ball game scene with just four walls.

our final wall. Position this on the other side of the ground plane, and you should have all four walls in place (Figure 5.12).

It is important to remember to save your work regularly. I make it a part of my routine to hit Save (CTRL + S or CMD + S on a Mac) just before I hit Play to test my games, which prevents any loss should the editor crash for any reason. Go ahead and save the scene now either by going through the menu File–>Save Scene or using the keyboard shortcut. If this is the first time you are saving, you will be prompted for a filename. In the filename box, type in *game*. The scene should now appear in the Project window with a little Unity icon next to it.

If you hit Play and roll around some more, notice that the cubes we added already have collision set up on them. The default collision type for a cube, perhaps unsurprisingly, is a box collider. When you create a new cube, the box collider component is automatically added to the Cube GameObject.

5.3.3 Making Some Simple Materials

All of the shaders and materials in our ball-rolling game are very simple and have no actual graphics attached to them, with the exception of the grid we use on the floor plane. All of the other shaders are just simple diffuse shaders with a color set for each one. In our final ball-rolling game, the materials are all within a folder called "game materials," so let's go along with this idea. If you are building along with this chapter, the next thing you need to do is to create a folder in the Project window through the menu Assets –>Create–>Folder. The folder will appear in the Project window, named by default "new folder." Rename it (to do this, just click on its name) to "game materials."

The next step is to build a material for each element in our game. We are going to go ahead and build materials for the ball, the finished box, the walls, and the hazards.

To create new material, go through the menu Assets −>Create−>Material. A new material will appear in the Project window, named by default "new material." Change this name to "ball material" and click, hold, and drag it up into the "game materials" folder you just created, to keep things neat and tidy.

Select the material in the Project window and set the main color property in the Inspector window. Click the main color swatch (a big white box, by default) in the Inspector window, as shown in Figure 5.13. Select the color that you would like the ball to be. I went for a nice light blue, but if you have a preference for another color, go for it!

There are many different shaders available in the Shaders drop-down menu, but this time around we will stick to a simple diffuse.

Next, we need to apply the texture to our ball. Make sure that the ball is in view in the Scene View window (one way to do this would be to select the Roll-a-Ball object in the Hierarchy window, then move the mouse pointer over the Scene View and press F on the keyboard to focus it in the center of the view).

Click on the material for the ball in the Project window and drag it across to the Scene window; don't let go just yet, though. Note that whatever object is under the mouse when you hold the material over the Scene window, the object changes as though it has the material applied to it. This is an instant preview of how the object will look with the new material applied to it. Of course, we need to apply it to our ball, so go ahead and drop the material onto the ball.

The next step is to create materials for the finish, hazard, and wall objects. Follow the same procedure as above, naming the materials and changing their colors as shown below:

- Name the first material "Wall Material." The suggested color is yellow. Apply this material to all of the walls of your maze.

- Name the second material "Hazard Material." The suggested color is red. Apply this material to your hazard objects.

- Name the third material "Finish Material." The suggested color is green. Apply this material to your finish box.

With a bit of luck, your now colorful scene should now look something like the one in Figure 5.14.

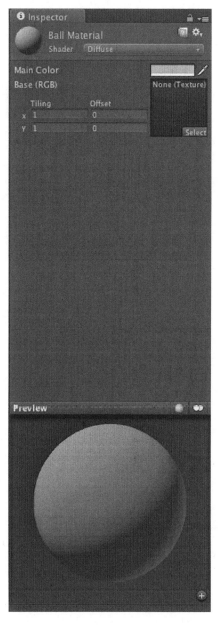

Figure 5.13. The Inspector window of the Unity editor showing the ball material from the Roll-a-Ball game.

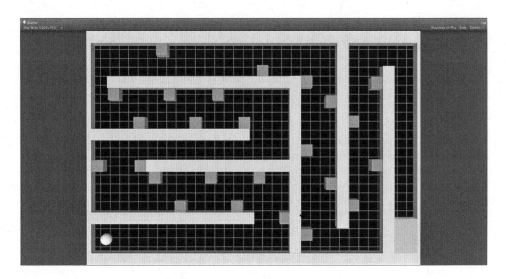

Figure 5.14. The Roll-a-Ball game final level layout.

5.3.4 The Roll-a-Ball Script

Now is as good a time as any to take a quick look at the ball control script to see how it works. It contains, among other things, a few Unity-specific commands or calls that we will need later on in Chapter 6 when we build out the kart-racing game.

```
#pragma strict

var tilt : Vector3 = Vector3.zero;
var speed : float;
private var circ : float;
private var previousPosition : Vector3;

@script RequireComponent(Rigidbody)
function Start()
{
        // Find the circumference of the circle so that the circle can be
        // rotated the appropriate amount when rolling
        circ = 2 * Mathf.PI * collider.bounds.extents.x;
        previousPosition = transform.position;
}

function Update ()
{
        tilt.x = -Input.acceleration.y;
        tilt.z = Input.acceleration.x;

        rigidbody.AddForce(tilt * speed * Time.deltaTime);
}

function LateUpdate()
{
        var movement : Vector3 = transform.position - previousPosition;
        movement = Vector3(movement.z,0,  -movement.x);
```

```
        transform.Rotate(movement / circ * 360, Space.World);
        previousPosition = transform.position;
}
```

At the start of the script we see `#pragma strict`, which tells the compiler to be strict about the syntax and declaration of variables. Put simply, if you have this statement in your script, it tells the compiler to enforce strict programming practices and to make sure that you declare variables correctly and specify the scope of variables.

The next four lines are variable declarations for holding the accelerometer data, the movement speed, ball circumference, and previous position.

The command `@script RequireComponent(Rigidbody)` tells Unity to ensure that there is a rigidbody component attached to the GameObject that has the ball script attached. If the GameObject does not contain a rigidbody component, Unity will automatically add it for us. You can use `@script RequireComponent` for any type of component or script; this is great for making reuseable scripts without having to provide lengthy instructions about other components you may need to set up.

The `Start()` function gets called once in the lifetime of the script. It gets called before any updates run for the first time, but only if the script is enabled. This is a great place to put anything that needs setting up at the start of the level and, in this case, we calculate the circumference of our ball using the extents of the physics object collider and get a first reading for our `previousPosition` variable. This is something we don't need to worry too much about, as it is specific to this application and not something that you will need on a regular basis. In case you are interested, the bounds represent the physical size of the collider our GameObject uses. Here, we multiply π by two and multiply that by the bound's x (width) value to find our ball circumference.

There are two types of functions useful for initializations that get called automatically by Unity:

- `Awake` is called after all objects are initialized, so you can safely speak to other objects or query them, but before any `Start` functions.

- `Start` is called before any `Updates` are called for the first time. It is only called once in the life cycle of the script it is contained within.

Further down in the script, we move on to the `Update()` function. `Update` gets called before a frame is rendered on the screen. There are several main `Update` functions that get called by the engine automatically:

- `Update` is called before rendering a frame. This is where most game behavior code goes, except physics code.

- `FixedUpdate` is called once every physics time step. This is the place to do physics-based game behavior.

- `LateUpdate` is called after all of the `Update` functions have been called. This is the place for code that relies on everything having already been updated and moved.

Our `Update` function starts by getting values from the accelerometer input. It does this by polling `Input` (which is our interface to all input in Unity, including the keyboard for nonmobile projects). We look to `Input.acceleration` to provide the accelerometer reading. Due to the default orientation of the device, we reverse the *y* value.

Once we have copied the *x* and *y* accelerometer input values into our *Vector3* object called "tilt," we can go ahead and apply physics forces to our rigidbody:

```
rigidbody.AddForce(tilt * speed * Time.deltaTime);
```

To apply force to a rigidybody, we simply call `rigidbody.AddForce` and feed it a Vector3 value. In this case, we take our tilt value (accelerometer input) and multiply it by the speed we want to move at then multiply this by `Time.deltaTime`. The reason we multiply the value by `Time.deltaTime` is so that our final value is a time-based movement. If our frame rate drops or the system stalls for any reason, our function will calculate movement based on delta time (the time between updates), and we will see a corrected amount of movement that is unaffected by the stall or frame rate drop.

5.3.5 The Game Controller Script

Now that we have a game environment in its most basic form, we need to look at building it into a game. For this, we are going to need a GameObject that acts as a hazard, one that acts as a finish point, some way to detect when the player hits them, and also a script to react to game events such as the player hitting a hazard or reaching the finish point.

The structure I usually use in my own Unity-based games is one where I have a main game controller script that has its functions called by other objects, such as a player or another type of game element. My game controller script keeps track of scoring, lives, or level numbers, and other game-related data, which leaves scripts such as the player control script to deal with those things more closely related to them (such as moving the character or dealing with collisions).

For this game, we will build a game controller script that will comprise just a few functions. One will be to draw the UI when the game ends; another will be called when the player hits a hazard; and one more will get called when the player finishes the game by hitting the finish point.

Create a new script by clicking on the menu Asset–>Create, then JavaScript. This adds a new blank script to the project (you should see this appear in the Project window) called NewBehaviourScript. Rename the script "game_controller"—it should start out selected and ready to take your new filename, but if you need to select it, do so by single clicking on the scripts' name in the Project window to highlight it then type the new name. Once you have a game_controller script, double click on it to open the default script editor and we will start scripting.

Delete the code already in this script (added automatically by Unity) and replace it with the following:

```
private var didFinish : boolean;
private var isDead : boolean;
private var windowRect : Rect = Rect (150, 90, 200, 150);

public var thePlayerScript : RollABall;
```

```
function OnGUI ()
{
        // enter the matrix
        GUI.matrix = Matrix4x4.TRS (Vector3.zero, Quaternion.identity, new
        Vector3(Screen.width / 480f, Screen.height / 320f, 1));

        if(didFinish)
        {
                windowRect = GUI.Window (0, windowRect, DoFinishedWindow,
                "CONGRATULATIONS!");
        } else if (isDead) {
                windowRect = GUI.Window (0, windowRect, DoDeadWindow, "GAME
                OVER");
        }
}

private function DoFinishedWindow()
{
        GUI.Label(Rect(15,50,200,64),"WELL DONE! YOU MADE IT!");
        if(GUI.Button(Rect(10,100,180,40),"PLAY AGAIN"))
        {
                Application.LoadLevel(Application.loadedLevel);
        }
}

private function DoDeadWindow()
{
        GUI.Label(Rect(35,50,200,64),"YOU DIDN'T MAKE IT");
        if(GUI.Button(Rect(10,100,180,40),"PLAY AGAIN"))
        {
                Application.LoadLevel(Application.loadedLevel);
        }
}

public function finishedTheGame()
{
        didFinish=true;
        thePlayerScript.gameObject.rigidbody.velocity=Vector3.zero;
        Destroy(thePlayerScript);
}

public function playerDied()
{
        isDead=true;
        thePlayerScript.gameObject.rigidbody.velocity=Vector3.zero;
        Destroy(thePlayerScript);
}
```

Let's take a closer look at what's going on in this script. For the UI, we need to know which message to show. We'll use two Boolean variables to keep tabs on this. When the game ends, one of these will be set:

```
private var didFinish : boolean;
private var isDead : boolean;
```

When the player hits either a hazard or the finish point, we will tell the ball to stay where it is so that there is no risk of it rolling around after the game has ended. To do this, we need to be able to talk to the script that controls the ball. To talk to the script, we need to store a reference to it like this:

```
public var thePlayerScript : RollABall;
```

The game control script needs two functions, which will be called from other objects in our game. The first function we need will be called by the player when it hits the finish point.

```
public function finishedTheGame()
{
        didFinish=true;
        thePlayerScript.gameObject.rigidbody.velocity=Vector3.zero;
        Destroy(thePlayerScript);
}
```

In our `finishedTheGame()` function, the first thing we do is set our `didFinish` *Boolean* variable to state that the game has finished. The `didFinish` variable can be set to `true` or `false`, and we will use this to decide which UI messages to draw when the game has finished.

The next line takes the reference to the player script and tells its rigidbody (the physics object of the ball) to stop by setting its velocity to zero.

Finally, we destroy the player script. When we use the term "destroy," don't be alarmed; we are not actually destroying anything. It will just remove the component from our player, meaning that there will no longer be a script attached to the ball to move it around. We do this so that the player cannot move the ball around after the game has finished. It's a quick and simple way of stopping the game.

Since we have a function to trap when the player hits the finish point, we now need to build a similar function to react when the player hits a hazard. Since our hazards are to be evil red squares, this function is named `playerDied`:

```
public function playerDied()
{
        isDead=true;
        thePlayerScript.gameObject.rigidbody.velocity=Vector3.zero;
        Destroy(thePlayerScript);
}
```

Notice that this function is almost identical to the `finishedTheGame()` function we made earlier to trap the event of the player hitting the finish point. The only difference is that we set the variable `isDead` to `true` instead of `didFinish`. Everything else works exactly the same in stopping our physics ball object and in taking away any user control script from it.

Add this new function:

```
function OnGUI ()
{
```

```
// enter the matrix
GUI.matrix = Matrix4x4.TRS (Vector3.zero, Quaternion.identity, new
Vector3(Screen.width / 480f, Screen.height / 320f, 1));

if(didFinish)
{
        windowRect = GUI.Window (0, Rect (150, 90, 200, 150),
        DoFinishedWindow, "CONGRATULATIONS!");
} else if (isDead) {
        windowRect = GUI.Window (0, Rect (150, 90, 200, 150),
        DoDeadWindow, "GAME OVER");
}
}
```

The OnGUI function is where we make the calls to draw any required UI. This particular OnGUI() function will do nothing until either the didFinish or the isDead variable is set to true, at which point it will show the necessary Game Over UI with a button inviting the user to play again.

The first line of the OnGUI function uses the GUI.matrix transformation system to define our UI space as being 480 × 320 (the size of a pre-Retina display iPhone or iPod). Now, whenever the screen size changes (for example, if we were to run this on an iPad), the transformation matrix is such that our UI space will be scaled so that it appears in the same place proportionally. This can lead to some ugly, stretched UIs on larger screens, but it does remove any unexpected behavior as we go from resolution to resolution. In regular production, it would be uncommon to just leave it at this as a solution to multiple screen sizes. In our case, however, it works just fine, and since I don't know what kind of iOS device you will be running this on, I can rest assured that the buttons will be at least big enough to tap on, even if they are ugly!

Next, we check to see if isFinished is true. If this variable were true, it would mean that the player reached the finish point and we need to show the Finish Point Game Over UI. This UI window is displayed by using the GUI.Window command to draw a window.

Our call to GUI.Window defines the dimensions of the window itself, then the function (which we tell GUI.Window about, in this case called DoFinishWindow) contains the actual content that we need to display inside the window. We need to go ahead now and add in some content for our window to display when DoFinishedWindow() gets called:

```
private function DoFinishedWindow()
{
        GUI.Label(Rect(15,50,200,64),"WELL DONE! YOU MADE IT!");
        if(GUI.Button(Rect(10,100,180,40),"PLAY AGAIN"))
        {
                Application.LoadLevel(Application.loadedLevel);
        }
}
```

The GUI.Label displays text on the screen. Again, we use a type of object called a *rect* to describe the size and position of our text label area, and then we just pass the string we want to display.

The GUI.Button perhaps speaks for itself. This is a quick, easy way of displaying a button on the screen. We use it within a conditional to find out whether or not it has been clicked, which means we can display a button and react to it being clicked in just a couple or more lines of code.

If our condition is met and the button is pressed (as this is a Play Again button), the current scene is reloaded.

Under normal circumstances (in a full game), we would probably load in a menu screen or jump to the next level, rather than just reloading this scene. Treat this reload function just as a demonstration as to how we can make a button load a scene. If you go ahead and build a full game out of this, I would recommend building a funky level-selection menu screen and loading that instead.

Going back to the OnGUI() function, the main part of the script checks to see if didFinish is true; if it is not, we go ahead and check isDead instead. If the isDead variable is set to true, we set up a different window whose content is drawn from the DoDeadWindow() this time:

```
private function DoDeadWindow()
{
        GUI.Label(Rect(35,50,200,64),"YOU DIDN'T MAKE IT");
        if(GUI.Button(Rect(10,100,180,40),"PLAY AGAIN"))
        {
                Application.LoadLevel(Application.loadedLevel);
        }
}
```

As you can see, both window content functions are very similar. They both display the same-sized window in the same position, although each one displays a different message about the outcome of game play.

5.3.6 Adding the Hazards (An Introduction to Triggers)

Triggers are extremely useful tools for developing games in Unity. We will be using them here to find out when the player hits upon a hazard or reaches the finish point, and we will use them again in Chapter 6 to build some parts of our kart-racing game.

According to the Unity documentation, a message "is sent to the trigger collider and the rigidbody (or the collider if there is no rigidbody) that touches the trigger. Trigger events are only sent if one of the colliders also has a rigidbody attached." As a very relevant example, in our ball-rolling game, a rectangular-shaped area represents a hazard, and when the ball enters this area, a function is triggered on a script attached to our ball and we can act upon it reaching the finish point.

The types of messages sent by triggers are

- OnTriggerEnter, which occurs once when an object first enters a trigger area;

- OnTriggerExit, which happens once when an object leaves a trigger area; and

- OnTriggerStay, which will be made every frame, for as long as the object remains within a trigger area.

At this stage, your project should contain a ball, four walls, and ground. You should have the game controller script ready to go as per the code in Section 5.3.5. If not, you can open the file "rollaball_noMaze" from the example files provided with this book.

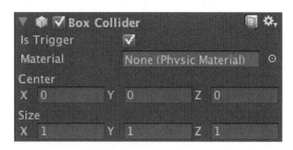

- Open up your "rollaball" Unity project (or the one from the example files).

- Click on the *y*-axis of the scene viewport to get a top-down viewpoint.

Figure 5.15. The Inspector window of the Unity editor with the "isTrigger" checkbox checked on a box collider.

- Click the menu GameObject–>Create Other–>Cube.

- Set the cubes position to 0, 0, 0 by typing the values into the Inspector window.

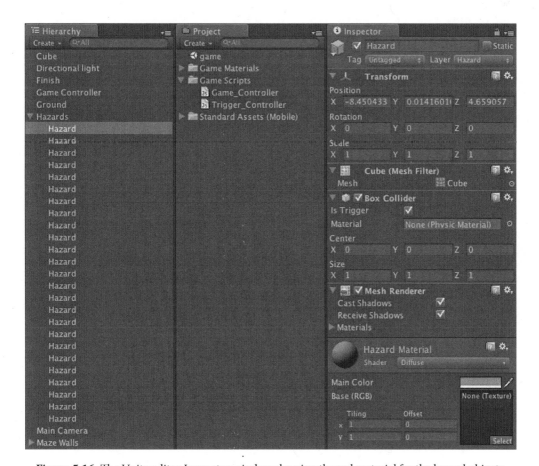

Figure 5.16. The Unity editor Inspector window showing the red material for the hazard objects.

- Move your mouse so that it is somewhere over the scene and press F on the keyboard. This should bring the newly created cube into the center of the window.

- Click into the textbox at the top of the Inspector window where it says "cube" and rename this to "hazard."

- Look for the Box Collider section and notice that there is a checkbox titled "isTrigger." Click on it to put a tick in this box to say yes, this is a trigger (Figure 5.15).

That's all it takes to create a trigger. Triggers provide the perfect solution for situations that require nonresolving collision detection combined with event messaging. When the "isTrigger" checkbox is left unchecked, the collider will act like a regular box collider, and anything running into it will simply bounce off.

Since we're creating a specific type of trigger (a hazard), we need it to look like a hazard, so go ahead and find the hazard material we created earlier and drag it in from the Project window right into the scene and drop it onto the cube to make it turn red (or whatever color you chose to make your hazards; Figure 5.16).

When we are done putting together the hazard trigger, we will be using the same system for our finish point. The finish point will be a trigger that, again, will tell our script when the ball rolls into it. So how do we tell the difference between the two triggers? One way might be to compare names and see if our trigger is named "finish" or not, but that isn't the most efficient method as string comparisons are quite greedy in terms of CPU cycles. If possible, we want to avoid string comparisons and Unity's Layer system provides the perfect alternative.

5.3.7 Layers and Tags

The Unity documentation states that *layers* "can be used for selective rendering from cameras or ignoring raycasts," and they are perfect for this. We can create a new layer called "finishpoint" and one called "hazard," then put our trigger GameObjects onto each applicable layer. When we get the message that we hit a trigger, we can simply compare the layers and find out which one it was. Clean, fast, and simple!

In the Scene window, click on your hazard GameObject. Over in the Inspector window, find the Layer button and click on it to show the Layer drop-down (Figure 5.17).

Our "hazard" layer needs to be added to this list, so click Add Layer at the bottom of the drop-down menu. The Inspector window should change to show the *Tag Manager*.

The Tag Manager shows three different types of elements: tags, built-in layers, and user layers. Tags work in an extremely similar way to layers and are useful for

Figure 5.17. The Layer drop-down menu from the Unity editor Inspector window.

describing particular types of GameObjects. Tags, however, cannot be used for selective ray casting or rendering, as layers can. Also, whenever you use tags you need to provide a string to identify the tag you are looking for, which is not the most efficient method. In a desktop- or console-based game, perhaps this would never become an issue, but we are writing games for very limited hardware where every little bit helps.

Built-in layers are inaccessible layers for specific uses, so in this particular case they are of no use to us. We need to use two user layers.

- Click in the text area next to the label "User Layer 8." Type in the word "Player."

- Click in the text area next to the label "User Layer 9." Type in the word "Finish."

- Click in the text area next to the label "User Layer 10." Type in the word "Hazard."

Your Tag Manager should look something like Figure 5.18.

5.3.8 Adding the Finish Point

The procedure for adding a finish point is the same as it was for adding our hazard, with the exception of a few little things here and there.

- If your view within the Scene window has changed at all, click on the y-axis of the scene viewport to get a top-down viewpoint.

- Click the menu GameObject–>Create Other–>Cube.

- Set the cube's position to $x = 13.3$, $y = 0.46$, and $z = -7.5$ by typing the values into the Inspector window.

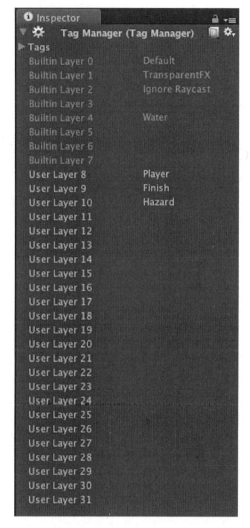

Figure 5.18. The Tag Manager in the Unity editor.

- Move your mouse so that it is somewhere over the scene and press F on the keyboard. This should bring the newly created cube into the center of the window.

- Click into the textbox at the top of the Inspector window where it says "cube," and rename this to "Finish."

- Look for the Box Collider section and notice that there is a checkbox titled "IsTrigger." Click on it to put a tick in this box to say yes, this is a trigger (Figure 5.19).

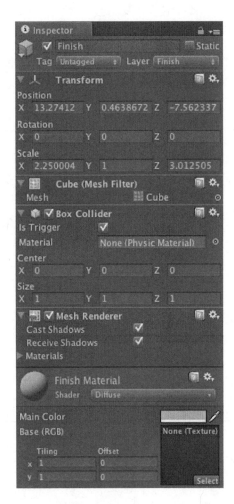

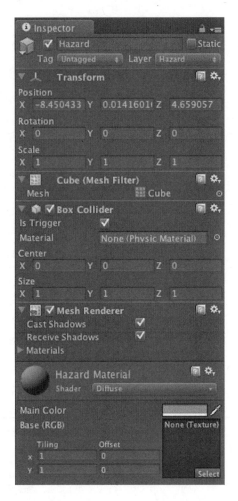

Figure 5.19. The finish object with the "isTrigger" checkbox checked in the Inspector window of the Unity editor.

Figure 5.20. The Hazard object has its layer set to "Hazard" in the Inspector window of the Unity editor.

5.3.9 Setting the Layers of the GameObjects

Earlier in this chapter, we set up three new user layers: "Player," "Hazard," and "Finish." Next, we are going to assign each of our objects to their correct layers.

- Click on your Hazard GameObject in the Hierarchy window.

- In the Inspector window, find the Layer button and click it to show the Layer drop-down menu (Figure 5.17). From the menu, select Hazard (Figure 5.20).

- This sets our hazard to use the "Hazard" layer we created earlier. Now, let's go on to do the same for the next two.

- Click on your Finish GameObject in the Hierarchy window.

- In the Inspector window, find the Layer button and click it to show the Layer drop-down menu. From the menu, select "Finish."

- Click on your Player GameObject in the Hierarchy window.

- In the Inspector window, find the Layer button and click it to show the Layer drop-down menu. From the menu, select Player.

5.3.10 Reacting to the Triggers

If you were to try out the game now, you would notice that nothing happens when you roll through the hazard. The ball will roll right through it without consequence. Our trigger will send out an `OnTrigger` message to the ball (we don't see this happen, but it does), and there is no receiver to receive it or react to it. To pick up the message, we simply need to add a function with a particular name (`OnTriggerEnter` or `OnTriggerExit`) to a script attached to our ball object.

When we put together the game controller script earlier on, there was a function called `playerDied`, which needs to be called when the player enters our hazard area to end the game. Our trigger cannot do this directly, as triggers will notify only the objects involved, so we need to call the `playerDied` function from another script attached to our ball object instead.

Create a new JavaScript script by clicking on the menu Assets−>JavaScript. When the new behaviour script arrives in the Project window awaiting a name, type in "Trigger_Controller." Double click the Trigger_Controller script to open it in the script editor.

Once the script is open in the script editor, delete what is already there and add the following code:

```
public var gameControl : Game_Controller;

function OnTriggerEnter (other : Collider)
{
        // we know that we have just hit a trigger, but now we want to
        // find out what kind of trigger we hit. we do this by looking at
        // the other object (the object that has the trigger attached to
        // it) and finding out what layer it is set to.
        if(other.transform.gameObject.layer==9)
        {
                // finish
                gameControl.finishedTheGame();
        }

        if(other.transform.gameObject.layer==10)
        {
                // hazard
                gameControl.playerDied();
        }

}
```

In the above script, we start out by setting up a reference to our game controller script like this:

```
public var gameControl : Game_Controller;
```

We need this to be able to pass on important messages later, such as an alert to tell the game controller that the player has completed the level or hit a hazard. Once the script is applied to a GameObject, we will need to set this reference up in the Inspector window by dragging the game controller (its GameObject) onto this script.

Following on, we have a function declaration for `OnTriggerEnter`. The `On TriggerEnter` function will be called automatically by Unity when the ball enters the trigger area.

```
function OnTriggerEnter (other : Collider)
```

When the trigger tells us about an event such as `OnTriggerEnter`, it also passes on some extra useful information about what just occurred. It passes in the collider that was hit (the other object in the collision). We can use this to get extra information, such as the other object's name, transform, or GameObject (then, in turn, the GameObject's tag or layer).

Using the collider data to get to the other object's layer is exactly how we determine which trigger has been hit:

```
if(other.transform.gameObject.layer==9)
```

This script will be applied to our player, so when a trigger hit happens, the trigger will be that "other" object and we can do a simple check to find out whether it was a hazard or finish point simply by checking its layer.

Note that we are using a number here, not a string, in determining which layer the other object is on. Since string comparisons are bad for performance (see Section 7.5.2 for more on this subject), we use the index of the layer instead. To find out which numbers are connected to which layers, you can refer to the Tag Manager.

To tell the game controller that an event occurred, we talk directly to the script via the `gameControl` reference we created at the top of the script:

```
gameControl.finishedTheGame();
```

Now, go ahead and try the game (the completed example file for this point is called "rollaball_noMaze"). You should be able to roll around the ball, and when you hit either the hazard or the finish point, the correct popup window should appear and the game will end.

5.3.11 Creating a Maze

As you may well be aware, the game is currently in a very dull place. We avoid the red block easily and roll straight to the green finish point.

Go ahead and create some more walls now by using the Duplicate command (CTRL + D or CMD + D on a Mac) to copy some of those outside walls and drag them

Figure 5.21. The final Roll-a-Ball game.

in to turn them into a little more of an interesting play area. When you are done creating a fun little maze, use the same technique to duplicate some hazards and place them around your level.

Get creative, test regularly, and have fun making a crazy level! To see the final level that I put together, feel free to jump ahead and open up the example file "rollaball_complete" (Figure 5.21).

5.4 Building and Testing the Game on Your iOS Device

You've done the hard work (or perhaps you just went ahead and opened the "rollaball_complete" project from the example files), and our ball-rolling game is as good as complete.

Now that we're happy with how everything works in the editor, we can go ahead and make an iOS build to see how the game translates to the real device.

Open the project in Unity, if it isn't already.

5.4.1 Add Your Bundle Name to the Player Settings

From within the Unity editor, click on the File menu. Now click on Build Settings. Check to ensure that the target platform is set to iOS. If it is not, select iOS from the list of platforms and click on the Switch Platform button.

Click the Player Settings button. Over in the Inspector window, the player settings will appear. Click Other Settings.

In the Identification section of the Inspector window, enter your bundle identifier into the Bundle Identifier box. The Bundle Version number is used to identify your build (bundle) version. Although you can put any number you like in here, it is best to start at a low number, like 1.0. Personally, I keep to 0.x numbers until I hit a release, then move up to a 1.0. With each trivial release, such as bug fixes or minor additions, I increase the bundle version number by .1 until I reach 1.9 (when I move up to version 2), or if something major is updated, such as adding a new level or a new game mode or something like that, I increase the bundle version to the next integer.

Keep your version numbers sensible (as in, don't just go from a version 1 to version 6.2.5 to trick people into thinking you are working harder), because if you try to submit a version of the game to Apple that has a lower bundle version than a previous upload, it will be rejected.

5.4.2 Publishing to Your iOS Device

Now that we have some interactivity, we are all ready to publish to our device. The first steps to take are to make sure that we have the correct information for Unity to build with.

- Click on the File menu in the top left of the screen, followed by Build Settings. In the Build Settings window (see Figure 5.22), check that the game scene appears in the "Scenes in Build" window. If not, find and click the button under Scenes in Build labeled "Add Current." What this does is add the scene to the build so that we can access it when the game runs on iOS. Only scenes in this list will actually be included in the final build, so it is important to check this before spending time building to the device. Another reason to keep an eye on

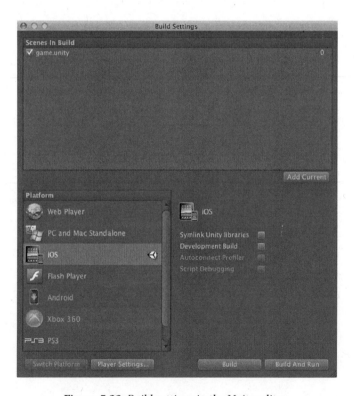

Figure 5.22. Build settings in the Unity editor.

this window is when you intend to load a scene from another scene, since the scene you are loading will need to be included in this list for Unity to recognize it.

- Double check that the platform is set to iOS. If not, select the iOS platform and click the Switch Platform button.

- Click the Player Settings button.

- The Inspector window will change to display player settings. Check that the iOS tab icon (the little iPhone icon) is selected to show iOS-specific settings.

- Click Other Settings.

- In the Identification section, check the box Bundle ID. This needs to match with the one you set up in the Apple Developer Center in Section 3.2.10 (e.g., com.yourcompanyname.yourgame).

- Set the target device to be the same type as your iOS device.

- Check that the Target iOS Version drop-down is reflective of the latest version of iOS. If you are unsure, click Unknown.

- At the top of the Inspector window, type "Hello World" into the Product Name field.

- Make sure that there are no errors in the Console. This will stop a build from being made. To bring up the Console, click the menu Window–>Console, or you can shortcut there with CTRL + SHIFT + C (CMD + SHIFT + C on a Mac).

- Warning messages are generally okay, but anything shown in red needs to be addressed prior to building.

There are a few more questions to consider at this point:

- Is your iOS device connected via USB cable?

- Did you download and install the required software outlined in Chapter 2 of this book?

- Did you set up and download all of the necessary certificates outlined in Chapter 2 of this book?

If the answer is no to any of the items above, refer back to Chapter 2 for setup information and check back here when it is rectified.

If it looks like you have covered everything in our little flight check, click on the menu File–>Build and Run. If this is the first time you have attempted to build, you will be prompted for a name and location to save the build. Choose a suitable location to save the project, noting that it is the Xcode project we are saving here and it should be kept away from your Unity project. Do *not* save your build within the "assets" folder of your project. Put it at the same level as the "assets" folder, or better still, save it into a new, appropriately named folder.

Don't be alarmed if the build process appears to take a while—there is a lot going on. Once it has successfully completed building your project, Xcode should open

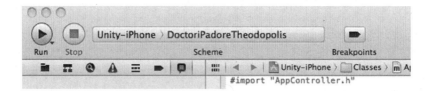

Figure 5.23. The Scheme drop-down within Xcode.

automatically. Once Xcode has finished launching, it should automatically make a build of the project. If Xcode says "Build Succeeded" at the top of the window, we can go ahead and rebuild it for the device.

Before building to the device, ensure that the Scheme drop-down, which appears at the top of the Xcode window (Figure 5.23), is set to the name of your iOS device. The Scheme drop-down may default to the iPhone Simulator, which is, of course, not where we want to build. If this is the case, click on the left side of the Scheme and select Unity—iPhone. If your device is connected via the USB cable and it has been set up correctly for development, its name should appear in the drop-down from the right-hand side of the Scheme box. Click on the right-hand side to see a list of available options and select your device from the list.

Congratulations! You just found out how easy it is to build from Unity to iOS.

5.5 There's Always Room for Improvement

This is a basic game, with really simple graphics. If you were looking to make this into something saleable, there are a few things you might want to consider doing to improve it first. Some worthy improvements might be:

- *Improve graphics.* It perhaps goes without saying that the game is visually quite mundane in its current form. You could liven up the game by using textures or perhaps models purchased from the Unity Asset Store or elsewhere.

- *Add extra levels.* Building extra levels should be relatively straightforward, as you can treat each level as a new scene and load them from some kind of menu scene. Using the Unity command `PlayerPrefs`, you could even build in some way of unlocking levels to give players a progressive game experience.

- *Time the player and record the fastest times.* Using the Time class, you could put together a timer for each level and use the `PlayerPrefs` command to save the best times to disk.

- *Add in pickups for extra time, or say that all pickups must be collected to progress to the next level.* By using triggers in the same way we detect hazards, you could add in some pickups and call `Destroy` on the actual GameObjects as they are hit. Add a counter to the game controller script, and you could potentially add all kinds of cool pickups.

- *Add sounds.* In Chapter 6, we will be looking at some simple ways to manipulate sound effects in Unity. Once you're done making the kart-racing game, perhaps you can come back to the ball roller and add in some cool sounds?

Whether or not you choose to add new features to the game or simply polish up what we have here, the sky is the limit! Perhaps you could take this game example further and move the camera to one that sits behind the ball, turning this top-down game into a 3D game. You could take what we have here and make it into an entirely different game, if you wanted. Go crazy and have fun making games!

CHAPTER 6

//

Making a Kart-Racing Game

Our ball-rolling game was a lot of fun and a fantastic example of how you can build games with little or no programming experience in Unity. In this chapter, we are going to step things up and do a lot of JavaScript programming to bring to life a fully featured 3D kart-style–racing game.

6.1 Game Overview

Although racing video games have been around since the 1960s, kart-style–racing games were popularized largely by the Super Nintendo Entertainment System in the 1980s. Their massive hit *Mario Kart* featured bright, colorful environments and allowed players to pick up powerups that would enhance performance or fire projectiles to knock other players off-course. Its fun, cartoon-like style made it approachable for all ages, and perhaps the biggest draw of all was that the whole family could play simultaneously, via a *split screen*, against each other in races and death-match modes.

In our kart game, tentatively named *iWhiskerKarts*, we will offer a similar racing experience, although for simplicity's sake, projectiles and powerups will not be included. The player will compete against three computer-controlled opponents in a 3D environment (Figure 6.1).

As with any racing game, the objective is to complete a set number of laps on a track before any of the other players. The first one to complete all laps successfully wins the race.

Figure 6.1. The finished kart-racing game.

6.2 Controls

The control system for this game is more complex than our rolling ball game. In this project, due to the extra complexity and extra functionality required, we will be looking at custom control code rather than Unity's out-of-the-box packaged solutions.

To steer the player's kart, we need to take input from the device's accelerometers to find out how much the user is tilting and apply that value to a force against the angular velocity of the vehicle. Acceleration and braking will be controlled by touch inputs, which will be handled by our custom code and passed on to the car physics and movement calculations.

Finding out where touches or taps are currently occurring on the screen is as easy as iterating through `Input.touches` (which contains Touch objects) and looking at each object's touch information. This happens later on in the chapter when we look at the `CheckInput()` function of the Car_Controller.js script.

6.3 Making the Game

You will definitely want to check out the game and familiarize yourself with how it works before continuing. Open the sample files in Unity and perhaps build and play it on your iOS device, too. This will help you to understand how things will work in the final build.

For our kart racer, we will start by investigating common elements in similar games that we will need to bring to life, such as

- basic kart physics,

- a waypoint system,

- a lap counter (and a combined start/finish line),

- a simple computer-controlled car controller,

- race position detection, and

- a simple results display.

This may be a little intimidating, but don't worry too much about the big picture right away. As with everything in project development, we need to focus on the items one by one until we pass the finish line. Once you have the start, the rest is inevitable.

Open the "iWhiskerKarts Base" Unity file. This is the empty shell of our game, containing all of the 3D models, sounds, and graphics that we will need to build our kart racer except for the scripts. Nothing is hooked up (no cameras, no physics, no messages, no menus), and when you hit the Play button of the editor, nothing at all will happen. That part is up to you!

6.3.1 Basic Kart Physics

Although the latest iOS devices will allow for more, we are going to keep the kart physics very simple. As a kart-style–racing game requires only simple arcade physics, we don't need to worry about the more complex problems we would need to solve with advanced physics. There will be no gearing, simulation of RPM (revolutions per minute), or wheel contact surfaces.

Put simply, try to think of the kart for this game as a simple box sliding around on a low-friction surface, like an ice cube sliding on ice. Our car (or kart) physics control script will take care of simulating wheel grip, applying forces to compensate for sliding.

The car controller is the longest and most complicated script in the game, and we will be extending the script right through to completion. Once the basic physics are in place and we are able to drive around an environment, we will build the script out further to include a waypoint system and computer control.

In this chapter, we will put together a basic car script and build on it as we build up the game, which means that the script we build now may look quite different from the final version. The example files included with this book contain a Unity project called "iWhiskerKarts – Kart physics only," which is essentially the result of this section of the book. Let's deal with setting up the player and getting it moving around. Here is the kart player script, "Car_Controller.js," which may be found within the Scripts folder of the project:

```
// car physics and calculations

private var accel : Vector3;
private var motor : float;
private var throttle : float;
private var deadZone : float = 0.05;
private var myRight : Vector3;
private var velo : Vector3;
private var flatVelo : Vector3;
private var relativeVelocity : Vector3;
private var dir : Vector3;
private var flatDir : Vector3;
private var myUp : Vector3;
private var myTransform : Transform;
private var myRigidbody : Rigidbody;
private var engineForce : Vector3;
private var turnVec : Vector3;
private var imp : Vector3;
private var rev : float;
private var actualTurn : float;
private var myMass : float;
private var wheelT : Transform[] = new Transform[4];
private var aGrip : float;
public var horizontal : float;

private var isConstrained : boolean;
```

```
public var id : int;

// user input
public var doUserInput : boolean;
public var deviceTest : boolean = false;

// car transforms
public var front_left_wheel : Transform;
public var front_right_wheel : Transform;
public var rear_left_wheel : Transform;
public var rear_right_wheel : Transform;

// physics
public var power : float = 300;
public var maxSpeed : float = 50;
public var theGrip : float = 70;
public var turnSpeed : float = 3.4;

public var slideSpeed : float;
public var mySpeed : float;
public var lockedInPlace : boolean;

private var gamePower : float;
public var carBody : GameObject;
private var aFwd : Vector3;
private var aRight : Vector3;
private var tempVEC : Vector3;

function Start()
{
        Init();
}

function Init()
{
        // cache reference to our transform
        myTransform = transform;

        // cache rigidbody
        myRigidbody = rigidbody;

        // cache our up direction
        myUp = myTransform.up;

        // cache mass
        myMass = rigidbody.mass;

        // cache world forward vector
        aFwd=Vector3.forward;

        // cache world right vector
        aRight=Vector3.right;

        // call to set up our wheels array
        setUpWheels();

        // start out unlocked
```

```
        SetLock(false);

        // set center of gravity to stop our cube falling over
        myRigidbody.centerOfMass=Vector3(0,-0.01,0);

}

function CheckConstraints()
{
        if(lockedInPlace && !isConstrained)
        {
                myRigidbody.constraints= RigidbodyConstraints.Freeze
                PositionX | RigidbodyConstraints.FreezeRotationZ;

                // set a flag to track whether or not we are constrained
                isConstrained= true;
        }

        // if our rigidbody is still constrained from a lock, release it
        // now
        if(!lockedInPlace && isConstrained)
        {
                myRigidbody.constraints= RigidbodyConstraints.Freeze
                PositionY;
                isConstrained= false;
        }
}

function SetLock(state : boolean)
{
        lockedInPlace=state;
}

function Update()
{
        // update gets called automatically by the engine. this is where
        // we do all of our major updates
        if(!lockedInPlace)
        {
                // if we are locked in-place (such as at the start line
                // waiting) then we update the physics, but not any input.
                // we also constrain the rigidbody on its x and z so that
                // gravity can drop it but it won't slide around

                // if we are a user-controlled car, update input
                if(doUserInput)
                {
                        checkInput();
                } else {
                        // no one is controlling this, so reset the input
                        // vars
                        throttle=0;
                        horizontal=0;
                }
        }

        // update our car physics
```

```
                    updatePhysics();

}

function LateUpdate()
{
        // do unimportant visual-only updates to our wheel graphics to make
        // them move and turn
        updateWheels();

        // check to see if our rigidbody should be held in place or not
        CheckConstraints();

}

function setUpWheels()
{
        //set up wheels
        wheelT[0] = front_left_wheel;
        wheelT[1] = rear_left_wheel;
        wheelT[2] = front_right_wheel;
        wheelT[3] = rear_right_wheel;
}

private var rotateAmount : Vector3;

function updateWheels()
{
        // front wheels need rotating on their y-axis too, for steering
        wheelT[0].localEulerAngles.y=horizontal*40;//=newVector3
        (0,horizontal*40,0);
        wheelT[2].localEulerAngles.y=horizontal*40;//=newVector3
        (0,horizontal*40,0);
        rotateAmount = aRight * (relativeVelocity.z *1.6 * Time.deltaTime *
        Mathf.Rad2Deg);
        wheelT[0].Rotate(rotateAmount);
        wheelT[1].Rotate(rotateAmount);
        wheelT[2].Rotate(rotateAmount);
        wheelT[3].Rotate(rotateAmount);
}

function setUserInput(state : boolean)
{
        // should we allow user input on this car?
        doUserInput = state;
}

private var sensitivity : float = 1.2;
function checkInput()
{
      if (Application.platform==RuntimePlatform.IPhonePlayer || device-
Test) {
                // ------------------------------
                // TURNING INPUT FROM DEVICE
                // we give the acceleration a little boost to make turning
                // more sensitive
                accel = Input.acceleration * sensitivity;
```

```
                    if(accel.y > deadZone || accel.y < -deadZone){
                            horizontal= -accel.y;
                    } else {
                            horizontal = 0;
                    }

                    // if we are holding the phone 'the other way' up, reverse
                    // the input!
                    if(Input.deviceOrientation ==
                    DeviceOrientation.LandscapeRight)
                            horizontal=-horizontal;
                    throttle=0;

                    for (var touch : Touch in Input.touches) {
                            if(touch.position.x>Screen.width-Screen.width/3 &&
                               touch.position.y<Screen.height/3)
                            {
                                    throttle=1;
                            } else if(touch.position.x<Screen.width/3 &&
                                    touch.position.y<Screen.height/3)
                            {
                                    throttle=-1;
                            }
                    }

            } else {
                    // -----------------------------
                    // TURNING INPUT FROM KEYBOARD

                horizontal = Input.GetAxis("Horizontal");
                throttle = Input.GetAxis("Vertical");
            }
}

function updatePhysics()
{
        //grab all the physics info we need to calculate everything
        myRight=myTransform.right;

        // find our velocity
        velo=myRigidbody.velocity;

        tempVEC=Vector3(velo.x,0,velo.z);

        // figure out our velocity without y movement - our flat velocity
        flatVelo=tempVEC;

        // find out which direction we are moving in
        dir=transform.TransformDirection(aFwd);
        tempVEC=Vector3(dir.x,0,dir.z);

        // calculate our direction, removing y movement - our flat direction
        flatDir=Vector3.Normalize(tempVEC);

        // calculate relative velocity
        relativeVelocity = myTransform.InverseTransformDirection(flatVelo);
```

```
        // calculate how much we are sliding (find out movement along our x
        // axis)
        slideSpeed=Vector3.Dot(myRight,flatVelo);

        // calculate current speed (the magnitude of the flat velocity)
        mySpeed=flatVelo.magnitude;

        // check to see if we are moving in reverse
        rev=Mathf.Sign(Vector3.Dot(flatVelo,flatDir));

        gamePower=power;

        // calculate engine force with our flat direction vector and
        // acceleration
        engineForce = ( flatDir * ( gamePower * throttle ) * myMass);

        // ----------------------------------
        // do turning
        actualTurn=horizontal;

        // if we're in reverse, we reverse the turning direction too
        if(rev<0.1f){
                actualTurn=-actualTurn;
        }

        // calculate torque for applying to our rigidbody
        turnVec=( ( ( myUp * turnSpeed ) * actualTurn ) * myMass )* 250;
        // calculate impulses to simulate grip by taking our right
        // vector, reversing the slidespeed, and multiplying that by our
        // mass to give us a completely 'corrected' force that would
        // completely stop sliding. we then multiply that by our grip
        // amount (which is, technically, a slide amount) which reduces the
        // corrected force so that it only helps to reduce sliding rather
        // than completely stop it


        aGrip = Mathf.Lerp(100, theGrip, mySpeed*0.01);
        imp= myRight * ( -slideSpeed * myMass * aGrip);

}

function FixedUpdate()

{
        if(mySpeed<maxSpeed)

        {
                // apply the engine force to the rigidbody
                myRigidbody.AddForce( engineForce * Time.deltaTime );
        }

        // apply torque to our rigidbody
        myRigidbody.AddTorque ( turnVec * Time.deltaTime );

        // apply forces to our rigidbody for grip
        myRigidbody.AddForce( imp  * Time.deltaTime );
}
```

Our script begins with quite a few variable declarations. What we are doing here is relatively complicated and the variables it takes to run our kart are only used during the calculation of our physics forces. I am not going to go through all of the variables one by one, as there are too many of them and their meanings and usefulness will become clear as we go through the rest of the script. Let's move down and start at the `Start()` function, instead:

```
function Start()
{
        Init();
}
```

After the variable declarations, the `Start()` function tells Unity to run the `Init()` function. Our initialization takes place outside of the `Start` function, which was a design choice to keep the `Start` function clean, should we decide to add more later. I like to keep initialization within separate `initialization` functions both to keep scripts tidy and to give me some way of easily reinitializing a scene if that situation ever arises.

```
function Init()
{
        // cache reference to our transform
        myTransform = transform;

        // cache rigidbody
        myRigidbody = rigidbody;

        // cache our up direction
        myUp = myTransform.up;

        // cache mass
        myMass = rigidbody.mass;

        // cache world forward vector
        aFwd=Vector3.forward;

        // cache world right vector
        aRight=Vector3.right;

        // call to set up our wheels array
        setUpWheels();

        // start out unlocked
        SetLock(false);

        // set center of gravity to stop our cube falling over
        myRigidbody.centerOfMass=Vector3(0,-0.01,0);

}
```

When you access a transform, the engine has to first find the transform before it does anything else, which can lead to a performance hit. Keeping a simple reference to the transform in a variable like this will avoid any problems. As we build games for limited hardware, it makes sense to employ little tricks like this wherever we can. Here, *cache* references to the transform, the rigidbody, an up vector, and our rigidbody mass value.

Next, a call to `setUpWheels()` gets the wheels ready. All we do within that `setUp Wheels()` function is to move the references to our wheels into an array so that we can iterate through them easier when we want to update them. The `setUpWheels()` function looks like this:

```
function setUpWheels()
{
        //set up wheels
        wheelT[0] = front_left_wheel;
        wheelT[1] = rear_left_wheel;
        wheelT[2] = front_right_wheel;
        wheelT[3] = rear_right_wheel;
}
```

The `setUpWheels()` function simply takes references to the wheel GameObjects (`front_left_wheel, rear_left_wheel, front_right_wheel`, and `rear_right_ wheel`) and copies them into an array called "wheelT." The array makes it easier and faster for us to update the wheels from our main functions. When you have applied the player script to the vehicle, you will need to drag and drop each wheel into the wheel variables in the Inspector window, otherwise this script will throw an error.

Getting back to, and moving further down, our `Init()` function, we called `Set Lock(false)`, which basically tells the script to start the game with our car unlocked.

`SetLock` is a small function that locks or unlocks our player in place. This is useful for the beginning of the race when we are waiting for a countdown to complete. If we didn't lock the player in place, it would be free to drive away during the countdown, leaving all the waiting AI cars behind. The `SetLock` function itself looks like this:

```
function SetLock(state : boolean)
{
lockedInPlace=state;
}
```

`SetLock()` simply passes its state over to a variable called `lockedInPlace`. You may wonder why we do it this way, and you would be right to ask questions about it. `SetLock` will eventually be accessed from other scripts, outside of our player script, to tell the player when it can or can't move. It is bad practice to set the value of a variable from another script; a much cleaner solution is to build a function to do it. The other script will call in with, for example, `SetLock(true)`, and the player script takes care of the rest.

The actual part of the code that holds the car in place doesn't happen here in `SetLock`, however. We have another function called `CheckConstraints()` that does all the work:

```
function CheckConstraints()
{
        if(lockedInPlace && !isConstrained)
```

```
    {
            myRigidbody.constraints= RigidbodyConstraints.Freeze
            PositionX | RigidbodyConstraints.FreezeRotationZ;

            // set a flag to track whether or not we are constrained
            isConstrained= true;
    }

    // if our rigidbody is still constrained from a lock, release it
    // now
    if(!lockedInPlace && isConstrained)
    {
            myRigidbody.constraints= RigidbodyConstraints.Freeze
            PositionY;
            isConstrained= false;
    }
}
```

The CheckContraints() has a main goal of setting the constraints values of our
rigidbody to reflect whether or not we want the car to be held in place. Our rigidbody
can be constrained to its current position on its x-, y-, or z-axis, or constrained to its
x-, y-, or z-rotation axis. That is, we can hold the rigidbody in place so that the physics
engine no longer allows it to move on the constrained axis.

We don't want to set the constraints every time Update is called, so our conditions
check to see if lockedInPlace is true, then check to see if this player is constrained (by
checking the isConstrained variable—a Boolean). If lockedInPlace has been set to
true, but the player has not yet been constrained, the isConstrained variable will be
false, and we know that we will have to set up the constraints on our rigidbody. On the
other hand, if both lockedInPlace and isConstrained are set to true, we know that
we have already set the constraints to hold the player in place.

Note that the isConstrained Boolean variable is set by our code whenever we
add those constraints to the rigidbody. This is not some fancy system property; it's just
another variable we are using to track the state.

myRigidbody is the cached reference to our rigidbody, as set up in the Init()
function of this script. When we set the constraints of our rigidbody, there are a number
of parameters available to use through the RigidbodyConstraints interface:

- RigidbodyConstraints.FreezeAll freezes both position and rotation on
  all axes.

- RigidbodyConstraints.FreezePosition freezes just the position of our
  rigidbody.

- RigidbodyConstraints.FreezePositionX freezes just the position of our
  rigidbody on the x-axis.

- RigidbodyConstraints.FreezePositionY freezes just the position of our
  rigidbody on the y-axis.

- RigidbodyConstraints.FreezePositionZ freezes just the position of our
  rigidbody on the z-axis.

- RigidbodyConstraints.FreezeRotation freezes the rotation of our rigidbody on all axes.

- RigidbodyConstraints.FreezeRotationX freezes just the rotation of our rigidbody on the *x*-axis.

- RigidbodyConstraints.FreezeRotationY freezes just the rotation of our rigidbody on the *y*-axis.

- RigidbodyConstraints.FreezeRotationZ freezes just the rotation of our rigidbody on the *z*-axis.

- RigidbodyConstraints.None leaves our rigidbody free to rotate or change position on any axis.

It is also possible to chain together constraints by using the | symbol as a separator. In our CheckConstraints script, when we hold the player in place we use the following:

```
myRigidbody.constraints = RigidbodyConstraints.FreezePositionX |
                          RigidbodyConstraints.FreezeRotationZ;
```

When CheckConstraints finds that it needs to release the player's rigidbody, we simply use

```
myRigidbody.constraints = RigidbodyConstraints.FreezePositionY
```

Now, I bet that you are wondering why we freeze the *y* position? Well, it's just easier to do that for this game. Our player never changes height, as there are no hills or jumps, so we keep the player's position constrained. This spares us from having to do anything fancy to stop the car leaving the track (rolling during a crash, etc.). You may want to remove this for your own kart racer to have jumps, but be aware that you will have to implement some kind of system to check when the player is flipped (upside-down or trapped) and to reposition its rigidbody. For simplicity's sake, this was not implemented in our simple kart racer and the decision was made to freeze the position on the *y*-axis instead.

The next part of our car control script is the Update() loop, which is central to everything that happens to our car. The Update loop is called every frame, and all of our main updates are called from it:

```
function Update()
{
        // update gets called automatically by the engine. this is where
        // we do all of our major updates
        if(!lockedInPlace)
        {
                // if our kart is locked in place (such as at the start line
                // waiting) then we update the physics, but not any input.
                // we also constrain the rigidbody on its x and z so that
                // gravity can drop it but it won't slide around
                // if the kart is a user-controlled car, update input
```

```
            if(doUserInput)
            {
                    checkInput();
            } else {
                    // no one is controlling this, so reset the input
                    // vars
                    throttle=0;
                    horizontal=0;
            }
    }

    // update our car physics
    updatePhysics();
}
```

That `lockedInPlace` variable makes another appearance here, as we don't need or want to check user input when the car is being held in place. There's just no need, so we don't do it.

The `doUserInput` variable determines whether or not we run the `checkInput()` function, which is the script we call to control the car with either the keyboard or the iOS device. Most often, we implement a Disable Controls feature like this when we implement AI players. We will be using the same script for them as we do for the human player, only that `doUserInput` variable will be set to false and those cars will get their input from AI functions instead of the keyboard or device. Having a method to disable input is usually a good thing, regardless. You never know when you might want to disable the keys for one reason or another, so it's good practice to include this functionality in your games.

The function `checkInput()` does just that: it takes the input from either the device or the keyboard. The decision was made to include keyboard controls so that the game can be easily and quickly tested within the editor without the need for the remote and without having to build to the device. The keyboard controls are quite different from the device controls, however (accelerometer versus keyboard), so it was important to do a great deal of testing with the device once the basics of the game were in place.

```
function checkInput()
{
    if (Application.platform==RuntimePlatform.IPhonePlayer ||
        deviceTest) {
            // -------------------------------
            // TURNING INPUT FROM DEVICE
            // we give the acceleration a little boost to make turning
            // more sensitive
            accel = Input.acceleration * sensitivity;

            if(accel.y > deadZone || accel.y < -deadZone){
                    horizontal= -accel.y;
            } else {
                    horizontal = 0;
            }

            // if we are holding the phone 'the other way' up, reverse
            // the input!
```

```
            if(Input.deviceOrientation == DeviceOrientation.
               LandscapeRight)
                    horizontal=-horizontal;
            throttle=0;

            for (var touch : Touch in Input.touches) {
                    if(touch.position.x>Screen.width-Screen.width/3 &&
                       touch.position.y<Screen.height/3)
                    {
                            throttle=1;
                    } else if(touch.position.x<Screen.width/3 &&
                            touch.position.y<Screen.height/3)
                    {
                            throttle=-1;
                    }
            }

    } else {
            // ------------------------------
            // TURNING INPUT FROM KEYBOARD

        horizontal = Input.GetAxis("Horizontal");
        throttle = Input.GetAxis("Vertical");
    }
}
```

Our car is driven by two basic values: throttle and horizontal. If one were to drive the car with a joystick, the throttle would be our vertical axis (accelerate and decelerate) and the horizontal would be our turning axis left and right.

If the `doUserInput` variable is false, right now our script simply resets the throttle and horizontal values to 0. If we decide to simply disable the player input when the race finishes, this will stop the car from trying to keep driving and eventually our car will slide to a halt.

The final part of the `Update()` script calls on `UpdatePhysics()`. This is the function that drives the car forward, turns the car, and, among other things, adds physics forces to compensate for sliding. It is core to the player control script and without `UpdatePhysics()`, our car would just sit there doing nothing. We will look at `UpdatePhysics` in detail later in this section, but for now just keep in mind what `UpdatePhysics` does as we look at some of the functions between that and `Update()`.

```
function LateUpdate()
{
        // do unimportant visual-only updates to our wheel graphics to make
        // them move and turn, etc.
        updateWheels();

        // check to see if our rigidbody should be held in place or not
        CheckConstraints();

}
```

The `LateUpdate()` function is called by Unity automatically, after all of the Updates have been called. When `LateUpdate()` gets called, we know that Update has already been fired and that our physics have been updated. In this case, the update of our wheel positions and rotations need to match what is happening with the physics and player input (and, most importantly, match their updated positions and rotations). If we were to do this before the `LateUpdate()`, it could cause jitters as the object positions are updated after we position the wheels.

We also call `CheckConstraints()` here so that our player will be locked in place (or unlocked if need be) for the next frame update.

Now, getting back to updating the wheels, it is important to note that our wheels are only for show. They don't actually do anything other than serve as a visual enhancement. There is no real "contact" with the road surface or any suspension in our kart racer.

```
function updateWheels()
{
        // front wheels need rotating on their y-axis too, for steering
        wheelT[0].localEulerAngles.y=horizontal*40;//=new
        Vector3(0,horizontal*40,0);
        wheelT[2].localEulerAngles.y=horizontal*40;//=new
        Vector3(0,horizontal*40,0);
        rotateAmount = aRight * (relativeVelocity.z *1.6 * Time.deltaTime *
                        Mathf.Rad2Deg);
        wheelT[0].Rotate(rotateAmount);
        wheelT[1].Rotate(rotateAmount);
        wheelT[2].Rotate(rotateAmount);
        wheelT[3].Rotate(rotateAmount);
}
```

The `updateWheels()` function rotates the wheels to make them look as though they are rolling and it also turns the front wheels to provide a visual cue that we are steering the kart.

If you are unfamiliar with *Euler angles*, think of them as the "real" rotation values. Unity uses something called Quaternions to represent rotations internally; this has several advantages, but can be quite tricky to figure out. Euler angles provide an easier-to-understand method of representing rotation with a 3D vector instead (Vector3). All three axes have a rotation value, in degrees, which can be set easily. For simplicity's sake, I prefer to work with Euler angles wherever possible.

Before we go into detail about how the rotations actually happen, we need to understand the way in which our wheels are set up in the scene.

As you may know, every object has a pivot point. It is around this pivot point that all rotations are based, which means that when a pivot point is centered and we rotate the transform around its *y*-axis, it will simply turn. If the pivot point is not centered on the object, when we try to rotate it, we will get some funky results whereby the object turns—not in the way it should. For that reason and to ensure clarity in our calculations, each of the wheels are parented to an empty GameObject. The empty GameObject serves as a pivot point and, as it is simply an empty GameObject with no special properties set up on it, its own pivot point is centered.

By parenting each wheel to an empty GameObject, the wheel's pivot point no longer matters. Whatever happens to its parent will be carried through relatively, meaning that when we rotate the empty GameObject about its *y*-axis, as our wheel model is centered on the empty GameObject, the wheel model will rotate the way we need it to.

Empty GameObjects can be useful for an infinite number of things, not the least of which is correcting pivot points. We also use empty GameObjects to represent starting points for each player on the track, but let's get back to the updateWheels() function now and deal with that later.

The updateWheels() function starts out by rotating the front two wheels to represent our current steering angle. It does this simply by setting the y-axis rotation angle to whatever our steering input value is, multiplied by 40. Note that this value is a made-up number to give a nice effect. It could be 40, 45, or whatever multiplication takes the steering angle and turns it into an angle that makes a big enough visual impact on the wheels to let the user know that he or she is steering. Feel free to adjust it if you wish!

At this point, we've figured out how to deal with input and how to rotate the wheel, but it's time for the real meat in this script: the UpdatePhysics() function. It looks like this:

```
function updatePhysics()
{
        //grab all the physics info we need to calculate everything
        myRight=myTransform.right;

        // find our velocity
        velo=myRigidbody.velocity;

        tempVEC=Vector3(velo.x,0,velo.z);

        // figure out our velocity without y movement - our flat velocity
        flatVelo=tempVEC;

        // find out which direction we are moving in
        dir=transform.TransformDirection(aFwd);
        tempVEC=Vector3(dir.x,0,dir.z);

        // calculate our direction, removing y movement - our flat direction
        flatDir=Vector3.Normalize(tempVEC);

        // calculate relative velocity
        relativeVelocity = myTransform.InverseTransformDirection(flatVelo);

        // calculate how much we are sliding (find out movement along our x
        // axis)
        slideSpeed=Vector3.Dot(myRight,flatVelo);

        // calculate current speed (the magnitude of the flat velocity)
        mySpeed=flatVelo.magnitude;

        // check to see if we are moving in reverse
        rev=Mathf.Sign(Vector3.Dot(flatVelo,flatDir));

        gamePower=power;

        // calculate engine force with our flat direction vector and
        // acceleration
        engineForce = ( flatDir * ( gamePower * throttle ) * myMass);
```

```
// -----------------------------------
// do turning
actualTurn=horizontal;

// if we're in reverse, we reverse the turning direction too
if(rev<0.1f){
        actualTurn=-actualTurn;
}

// calculate torque for applying to our rigidbody
turnVec=( ( ( myUp * turnSpeed ) * actualTurn ) * myMass )* 250;
// calculate impulses to simulate grip by taking our right vector,
// reversing the slidespeed, and multiplying that by our mass, to
// give us a completely 'corrected' force that would completely
// stop sliding. we then multiply that by our grip amount (which
// is, technically, a slide amount) which reduces the corrected
// force so that it only helps to reduce sliding rather than
// completely stop it

aGrip = Mathf.Lerp(100, theGrip, mySpeed*0.01);
imp= myRight * ( -slideSpeed * myMass * aGrip);

}
```

The way in which we control the car produces an unrealistic but fun arcade-like simulation. The physics in our kart racer are extremely basic (in terms of vehicle simulation), and the principles applied here haven't changed in perhaps 15 or 20 years of game development.

To summarize, the actual car physics rigidbody has almost no friction. The only physics properties we apply to it are drag to bring the body to an eventually stop and angular drag to help control how quickly it rotates. Everything else is dealt with by our code (everything else being not that much, actually!). Our rigidbody is, in effect, an invisible block of ice, sliding on an icy surface, that gets pushed around by our script. (If it helps to visualize the effect, imagine the script as our fingers poking at the sliding block of ice to control it.)

```
function updatePhysics()
{
//grab all the physics info we need to calc everything
        myRight=myTransform.right;
```

We start out the UpdatePhysics() function with the caching of our transform's right axis. This tells us, in a 3D vector, which direction is right from our transform. We need this so that we can later work out how much our rigidbody is moving right or left, which in turn tells us how much we are sliding. For now, though, we just find out what right is and store the vector in a variable called myRight.

```
// find our velocity
        velo=myRigidbody.velocity;
// figure out our velocity without y movement - our flat velocity
        flatVelo=new Vector3(velo.x,0,velo.z);
```

Next in the function, we find out the current velocity of our rigidbody, then from that vector now stored in the variable named `velo`, we can find something called a *flat velocity*. Our flat velocity is our velocity without the *y*-axis—in effect, it is flat on the ground with no height. We'll use this to calculate our speed. To understand why we use a flat velocity, think of a car driving at 30 mph along a road. If it is going up a hill, it is still going 30 mph. If we took into account how much the car was moving on the world's *y*-axis when we calculate its speed, we would end up with a speed reading more or less than 30 mph, which (of course) is not what we need for any ground-based calculations or for a speedometer readout!

```
// find out which direction we are moving in
        dir=transform.TransformDirection(aFwd);

// calculate our direction, removing y movement - our flat direction
        flatDir=Vector3.Normalize(new Vector3(dir.x,0,dir.z));
```

Following on from finding our velocity, we look to discover the direction that our rigidbody is currently travelling in. This is again represented by a vector, this time named "dir," which is calculated by getting the `TransformDirection` of the world's forward vector. That is, we take the transform's forward vector and transform it from local space to world space. This will give us our direction vector, no longer relative to our transform but in a world-space vector.

As with velocity, we need to find out what our flat direction is, so in the next line we remove the *y*-axis from the equation and normalize the vector in the process. Normalizing a vector takes away its distance and leaves only a direction. Any value will become either –1, 0, or 1—for example, the Vector3(0, 0, 0.3) would become Vector3(0, 0, 1) and Vector3(–6, 4, 0.2) would become Vector3(–1, 1, 1).

Normalized vectors are exactly what we need in this situation. We don't want to have to deal with uneven length values during our direction-based calculations, so we normalize them.

```
// calculate relative velocity
        relativeVelocity = myTransform.InverseTransformDirection(flatVelo);
```

The `relativeVelocity` variable contains the rigidbody's relative velocity, as calculated by finding the inverse transform of our flat velocity.

```
// calculate how much we are sliding (find out movement along our x-axis)
        slideSpeed=Vector3.Dot(myRight,flatVelo);
```

The float `slideSpeed` contains the amount that our rigidbody is sliding. By finding the dot product of our transform's right (stored in `myRight`) and our flat velocity, `flatVelo`, we find out just how much the rigidbody is moving left or right. We will use this a little further on in the script to apply grip to our icy rigidbody.

```
// calculate current speed (the magnitude of the flat velocity)
        mySpeed=flatVelo.magnitude;
```

From the flat velocity in `flatVelo`, we go ahead and calculate the speed our rigidbody is moving at simply by finding its magnitude. The value here could easily be converted to other units, such as miles per hour or kilometers per hour for a speedometer readout.

```
// check to see if we are moving in reverse
        rev=Mathf.Sign(Vector3.Dot(flatVelo,flatDir));
```

The easiest way to tell whether or not the player is reversing the kart is with some nifty math. We can then use the result of this to swap left and right controls while reversing, or perhaps restrict the speed of the kart when it is going backwards.

```
gamePower=power;
```

Right now, the above line looks a little crazy. Why are we copying the value of `power` into `gamePower`? This will become clear when we add in our AI karts in Section 6.5.2. This line will change later on to make our AI players a little more interesting, as it will modify their power to make each one different to beat.

```
// calculate engine force with our flat direction vector and acceleration
        engineForce = ( flatDir * ( gamePower * throttle ) * myMass);
```

So far in the `UpdatePhysics()` function, we have captured all of the data we need to be able to work out the force to apply to our rigidbody that will act as an engine force. We have a flat direction, the power, and, from elsewhere, the throttle value and mass of the rigidbody. In the above line, we take that and convert it all into a single vector stored in the variable `engineForce`.

At this stage, we have our engine forces, but we don't want to apply them just yet. Unity recommends that whenever you apply a force to a rigidbody using `rigidbody.AddForce` or `rigidbody.AddForceAtPosition`, you should do this within the `FixedUpdate()` function, which is called every fixed frame rate frame.

If we were to add forces to a physics object anywhere other than within the `FixedUpdate()` function, the forces may be added unevenly to the rigidbody, resulting in the game operating differently on different systems, depending on the speed and smoothness of the frame rate. As `FixedUpdate` is updated every fixed frame rate frame, we can be sure that it will be applied the same number of times, regardless. To ensure that our physics are time dependent, however, we do still use `Time.deltaTime` to make sure that the amount of force is going to be constant across the board.

Continuing on, we calculate out the forces required for turning;

```
        // do turning
        actualTurn=horizontal;

        // if we're in reverse, we reverse the turning direction too
        if(rev<0.1f){
                actualTurn=-actualTurn;
        }
}
```

First we copy our horizontal value (the left or right value provided by our Check Input() function) into the actualTurn variable, then we check the current value of rev to see if our kart is moving in reverse. If so, actualTurn becomes its polar opposite and our left/right controls are reversed to match the reverse movement of the kart.

```
// calculate torque for applying to our rigidbody
turnVec=( ( ( myUp * turnSpeed ) * actualTurn ) * myMass )* 250;
// calculate impulses to simulate grip by taking our right
// vector, reversing the slidespeed and multiplying that by our
// mass, to give us a completely 'corrected' force that would
// completely stop sliding. we then multiply that by our grip
// amount (which is, technically, a slide amount) which reduces the
// corrected force so that it only helps to reduce sliding rather
// than completely stop it

aGrip = Mathf.Lerp(100, theGrip, mySpeed*0.01);
imp= myRight * ( -slideSpeed * myMass * aGrip);
}
```

Again, we have the forces worked out, but we don't apply them just yet. Any physics forces, including torque, should be applied in the FixedUpdate() function.

That wraps it up for the Update() function. Next in the script, right at the bottom, we have the final function to make our kart move, and that is FixedUpdate().

```
function FixedUpdate()
{
        if(mySpeed<maxSpeed)
        {
                // apply the engine force to the rigidbody
                myRigidbody.AddForce( engineForce * Time.deltaTime );
        }

        // apply torque to our rigidbody
        myRigidbody.AddTorque ( turnVec * Time.deltaTime );

        // apply forces to our rigidbody for grip
        myRigidbody.AddForce( imp  * Time.deltaTime );
}
```

In FixedUpdate, we first check to make sure that the current speed (mySpeed) of our rigidbody is less than the maximum speed held in the variable maxSpeed. If the kart is going faster than our maximum speed value, we don't want to keep pushing it forward, potentially making it move faster. As long as the speed of the rigidbody is less than the maximum speed, we can apply our force to push the kart forward.

To apply a force to a rigidbody, you can use AddForce or AddForceAtPosition. Using AddForce applies the force to the center of the rigidbody, which is what we use here to simulate engine force being applied to our kart.

Notice that we multiply our engineForce value by Time.deltatime. This is really important, as it means that our game is frame-rate independent. If we simply applied the `engineForce` and the device slowed for one reason or another, our `update` function would be delayed, hence, the force may be delayed too. This difference in speed could result in a game that runs faster or slower depending on the power of the target device.

The `Time.deltaTime` tells us the time (in seconds) that the engine took to complete the last frame. By using this number as a multiplier for our movement values, we can be sure that every object will move the same amount in the same amount of time, on every device.

```
// apply torque to our rigidbody
       myRigidbody.AddTorque ( turnVec * Time.deltaTime );
```

Applying torque to our rigidbody will make it turn. Specifically, we only ever apply torque to the rigidbody's *y*-axis. The force calculated in `UpdatePhysics()` gets applied here with a `Time.deltaTime` multiplier for frame-rate independence.

```
// apply forces to our rigidbody for grip
       myRigidbody.AddForce( imp  * Time.deltaTime );
```

The final piece of our Car_Controller.js script applies a force to compensate for sliding, simulating grip. Remember that the kart is actually a box with little to no friction, sliding around on a surface that also has little to no friction. To stop the kart from spinning and sliding off around the track, the `UpdatePhysics()` function finds out how much the car is moving to its (local) left or right and then creates an opposite force to apply here. To give the kart the opportunity to slide some (like a real kart would), we use the `wheelGrip` multiplier to reduce this force before we apply it.

What we should have at this stage is a fully driveable kart. Take it for a spin, as we move on to the next piece of the game: the waypoint system.

6.3.2 Waypoint System

The waypoint system will do more than just guide our AI players around the track. We will use the waypoints to track who is winning, to make sure that the player is going in the right direction, to reposition players on the track (for when the player gets struck or hits the reposition key), and to count laps. Waypoints hold what might be a surprising amount of value for us, when it comes to working out racing-game logistics.

Step one is to put together some kind of waypoint management system that will help us to visualize the path when we are editing as well as give us the tools we need to utilize the waypoints during game play. The first iteration of this script sat inside the player control script, but it works a lot better as a separate script since we can then chop and change our player physics or player control systems and reuse the waypoint system without having to recode. It also means that our waypoint system is quite portable and may be useful for more than just this project.

The waypoint controller script needs to be able to do several things, such as

- produce a visual representation of the path we want our AI karts to take, to make manipulation of our waypoints in the editor a little easier;

- provide an interface that can allow other scripts to search for the nearest way-point to a given point in 3D space, so that we always have the ability to find a waypoint no matter where we are on the track;

- provide an interface that allows other scripts to get waypoint information from an index number—as our cars go around the track, they have a waypoint counter which could potentially be used with this function to establish where the current, next, or previous waypoints are; and

- provide an interface that allows for other scripts to find out the total number of waypoints—as our cars hold their own waypoint counter numbers, they need some way to ensure that the counters stay within the boundaries of how many waypoints there actually are.

In the editor, create a new JavaScript script and name it "Waypoints_Controller," or open the Waypoints_Controller.js script from the Scripts folder in the example project. The script looks like this:

```
@ExecuteInEditMode

private var transforms : ArrayList;  // ArrayList for easy access to
                                     // transforms
private var firstPoint : Vector3;    // store our first waypoint so we can
                                     // loop the path
private var distance : float;        // used to calculate distance between
                                     // points
private var TEMPtrans : Transform;   // a temporary holder for a transform
private var TEMPindex : int;         // a temporary holder for an index
                                     // number
private var totalTransforms : int;
private var currentPos : Vector3;
private var lastPos : Vector3;

function Start()
{
        // make sure that when this script starts (on the device) that
        // we have grabbed the transforms for each waypoint
        GetTransforms();
}

function OnDrawGizmos()
{
        // if we didn't populate our list of transforms, do that now
        if(transforms==null)
                GetTransforms();

        // make sure that we have more than one transform in the list,
        // otherwise we can't draw lines between them
        if (transforms.Count < 2)
                        return;

        // draw our path
        // first, we grab the position of the very first waypoint
        // so that our line has a start point
        TEMPtrans = transforms[0];
```

```
        lastPos = TEMPtrans.position;
        // we point each waypoint at the next so that we can use this
        // rotation data to find out when the player is going the wrong way
        // or to position the player facing the correct direction after a
        // reset. so, first we need to hold a reference to the transform we
        // are going to point
        var pointT : Transform = TEMPtrans;

        // also, as this is the first point, we store it to use for closing
        // the path later
        firstPoint = lastPos;

        // set our line color to something we can see easily
        Gizmos.color = new Color(1, 0, 0, 1);

        // now we loop through all of the waypoints' drawing lines between
        // them
        for (var i : int = 1; i < transforms.Count; i++)
        {
                TEMPtrans = transforms[i];

                // grab the current waypoint position
                currentPos = TEMPtrans.position;

                // draw the line between the last waypoint and this one
                Gizmos.DrawLine(lastPos, currentPos);

                // point our last transform at the latest position
                pointT.LookAt(currentPos);

                // update our 'last' waypoint to become this one as we
                // move on to find the next...
                lastPos = currentPos;

                // update the pointing transform
                pointT=transforms[i];
        }

        // close the path
        Gizmos.DrawLine(currentPos, firstPoint);
}

@ContextMenu ("Update Waypoints.")
function GetTransforms()
{
        // we store all of the waypoints' transforms in an ArrayList,
        // which is initialized here (we always need to do this before we
        // can use ArrayLists)
        transforms=new ArrayList();

        // now we go through any transforms 'under' this transform, so all
        // of the child objects that act as our waypoints get put into our
        // ArrayList
        for(var t : Transform in transform)
        {
                // add this transform to our ArrayList
                transforms.Add(t);
        }
```

```
        totalTransforms=transforms.Count;
}

function GetWaypoint(index : int) : Transform
{
        // make sure that we have populated the transforms list. if not,
        // populate it
                if(transforms==null)
                        GetTransforms();

        // first, let's check to see if this index is higher than our
        // waypoint count. if so, we return null, which needs to be handled
        // on the other side'
        if(index>transforms.Count)
                return null;

        return transforms[index];
}

function GetTotal() : int
{
        return totalTransforms;
}
```

Before we look at this script in detail, let's look at how the waypoints are set up and stored. Open up the example project "iWhiskerKarts – Waypoints" and double click the Level_1 scene from the "scenes" folder of the project.

In the Scene View, click on the *y*-axis gizmo in the top right. This will move the camera up to an orthographic, top-down viewpoint. Zoom out from the track (use the scroll wheel to move) and you should see the AI path shown in red (Figure 6.2).

Figure 6.2. The waypoints go together to make up the AI path in the Scene window of the Unity editor.

In the Hierarchy window, there is a GameObject called Waypoints with an arrow to the left of it. Click on the arrow to show all of this GameObject's child objects. Each one of these is a waypoint on our path. It works like this:

- The parent object (that Waypoints GameObject) has our Waypoints.js script attached to it. All of the waypoints themselves are empty GameObjects, children to this game object.

- Our waypoint script goes through all of its children and stores them to use as waypoints in our game.

- During editing, the waypoint script draws a line between each of the waypoints as our visual representation of the path.

Delving into the script, the first thing we see is:

```
@ExecuteInEditMode
```

We are building a waypoint system, which will need to provide a visual representation of the path in the editor, so we need the script to run even when the game is not playing. Whenever we are in the editor, a script containing `@ExecuteInEditMode` will receive `Update`, `FixedUpdate`, and `OnGUI` function calls every frame. This means that we can do things such as draw our waypoints path in the editor without having to hit Play each time to see it.

Following on from a whole bunch of variable declarations (which will make a lot more sense as we go on through the function), we reach the `Start()` function. Here, a single call to `GetTransforms()` will happen when we run the game. Note that this function will not get called from the editor, and it is here so that our waypoints are set up when the game starts, not to set up waypoints during editing.

In `GetTransforms()`, we loop through all of the children of this object to find each waypoint:

```
function GetTransforms()
{
        // we store all of the waypoint transforms in an ArrayList,
        // which is initialized here (we always need to do this before we
        // can use ArrayLists)
        transforms=new ArrayList();

        // now we go through any transforms 'under' this transform, so all
        // of the child objects that act as our waypoints get put into our
        // ArrayList
        for(var t : Transform in transform)
        {
                // add this transform to our ArrayList
                transforms.Add(t);
        }

        totalTransforms=transforms.Count;
}
```

The transforms of those GameObjects that make up our waypoints are stored in an *ArrayList*, a fast and efficient way of storing objects of any type. An ArrayList doesn't care what kind of object you put into it (GameObject, transform, Vector, etc.), and it's only when you come to access it that you need to do anything specific. Before we can use an ArrayList, we need to initialize it like this:

```
transforms=new ArrayList();
```

Now we're all ready to start populating the array:

```
for(var t : Transform in transform)
{
        // add this transform to our ArrayList
        transforms.Add(t);
}
```

To find all of our child objects, we loop through each transform in `transform`. Within the loop, we simply use the `Add` method to add each one to our transform's ArrayList.

The last line in `GetWaypoints()` increments an integer called `totalTransforms`:

```
totalTransforms=transforms.Count;
```

It wouldn't make any sense to calculate the total number of waypoints in our ArrayList every time we needed to know how many there are, and the total number of waypoints never changes during game play. This means we can set this `totalTransforms` variable right at the start of the game and use or return that instead, saving a few CPU cycles in the process.

The next piece of our puzzle is how we go about drawing our lines, to show the path created by our waypoints, in the editor. This happens in a function called `OnDrawGizmos()`:

```
function OnDrawGizmos()
{
        // if we didn't populate our list of transforms, do that now
        if(transforms==null)
                GetTransforms();

        // make sure that we have more than one transform in the list,
        // otherwise we can't draw lines between them
        if (transforms.Count < 2)
                        return;

        // draw our path
        // first, we grab the position of the very first waypoint
        // so that our line has a start point
        TEMPtrans = transforms[0];
        var lastPos : Vector3 = TEMPtrans.position;

        // we point each waypoint at the next, so that we can use this
        // rotation data to find out when the player is going the wrong way
        // or to position the player facing the correct direction after a
```

```
    // reset. so, first we need to hold a reference to the transform we
    // are going to point
    var pointT : Transform = transforms[0];

    // also, as this is the first point, we store it to use for closing
    // the path later
    firstPoint = lastPos;

    // set our line color to something we can see easily
    Gizmos.color = new Color(1, 0, 0, 1);

    // now we loop through all of the waypoints' drawing lines between
    // them
    for (var i : int = 1; i < transforms.Count; i++)
    {
            TEMPtrans = transforms[i];
            if(TEMPtrans==null)
            {
                    GetTransforms();
                    return;
            }

            // grab the current waypoint position
            var currentPos : Vector3 = TEMPtrans.position;

            // draw the line between the last waypoint and this one
            Gizmos.DrawLine(lastPos, currentPos);

            // point our last transform at the latest position
            pointT.LookAt(currentPos);

            // update our 'last' waypoint to become this one as we
            // move on to find the next...
            lastPos = currentPos;

            // update the pointing transform
            pointT=transforms[i];
    }

    // close the path
    Gizmos.DrawLine(currentPos, firstPoint);
}
```

The function `OnDrawGizmos()` is called by the engine whenever it draws gizmo items (such as icons, helper lines, or shapes) in the Scene View or Game View. As we are going to be drawing the path created by our waypoints in the editor, this is the place to do it. Within `OnDrawGizmos()` we are granted access to a number of helpful utilities within the Unity engine's Gizmo class.

No, this has nothing to do with gremlins! Gizmos are Unity's way of providing visual aids to the Scene View. Via the Gizmos interface, there are several useful tools at our disposal such as line drawing, shape drawing (spheres and cubes), texture drawing, and icons.

- `DrawRay(from : Vector3, direction : Vector3)` mimics the functionality of Unity's ray-cast methods, which means it's a great way to visualize ray casting when you are unsure as to whether the length or direction of a ray is correct.

- `DrawLine(from : Vector3, to : Vector3)` draws a line. We will use this type of gizmo in our Waypoints_Controller.js script to draw the path created by our waypoints.

- `DrawWireSphere (center : Vector3, radius : float)` draws a wire-frame sphere. It's great for visualizing invisible sphere colliders!

- `DrawSphere(center : Vector3, radius : float)` draws a solid sphere with the specified center and radius measurements.

- `DrawWireCube(center : Vector3, size : Vector3)` draws a wireframe box with the specified center and size measurements. This is useful for invisible box collider editor visualization.

- `DrawCube(center : Vector3, size : Vector3)` draws a solid box with center and size measurements.

- `DrawIcon(position : Vector3, icon filename : String)` draws an icon, centered at the specified position. The icon should be a regular image file, such as a .png or .jpg image, placed into a specific folder in your project. You can place your icons into either a folder called "Gizmos" in the root of your project or in the "Unity.app/Contents/Resources" folder. Whether or not the icon will be scaled and displayed or hidden is determined by the settings within the Gizmos drop-down menu of the Scene View.

- `DrawGUITexture (screenrect : Rect, texture : Texture, mat : Material)` or `DrawGUITexture (screenrect : Rect, texture : Texture, leftborder : int, rightborder : int, topBorder : int, bottomBorder : int, mat : Material)` draws a 2D texture in screen coordinates.

Note that these `gizmo` functions are only available from within `OnDrawGizmos()` function and have no use anywhere else.

Now that we know a little about gizmos, the first thing we need to do before trying to draw the path or do anything with our ArrayList of waypoints, is to make sure that it has been set up.

```
if(transforms==null)
            GetTransforms();
```

A simple null check takes care of this. If the `GetWaypoints()` function has not yet been executed, our ArrayList object will not have been initialized, and it will return null whenever we try to access it. If we didn't check this first and the waypoints were not yet initialized, the error Unity would throw as we try to access them would be something called a *null reference exception*, which is the engine's way of telling us that we are trying to access an object that has a null value.

Our check looks to see if the transforms variable is null and, if it is, the `GetTrans forms()` function is called to populate the ArrayList. You may wonder why the Array-List might be null at this stage, as we made a call to `GetTransforms()` in our `Start()` function. The reason is that the `Start()` function will not be called by Unity until we hit the Play button. As we are going to be running this script in the editor, to draw our path in the editor, we need access to those transforms regardless of whether or not `Start` has been executed.

Our next check ensures that there is more than one item in our waypoints list:

```
if (transforms.Count < 2)
                    return;
```

We need to check this due to the fact that our line drawing, at the very least, will require a start point and an end point. If there are fewer than two items in our array (fewer than two waypoints), we need to drop out of this function before trying to do anything else.

```
TEMPtrans = transforms[0];
lastPos = TEMPtrans.position;

// we point each waypoint at the next, so that we can use this
// rotation data to find out when the player is going the wrong way
// or to position the player facing the correct direction after a
// reset. so, first we need to hold a reference to the transform we
// are going to point
pointT = TEMPtrans;

// also, as this is the first point, we store it to use for closing
// the path later
firstPoint = lastPos;
```

Generating temporary variables within functions (or *instancing*, as it is often called) is bad for Unity iOS. What happens is that each time your script runs through, those temporary variables gather up in memory until something called *garbage collection* occurs. Garbage collection is the process of clearing out unused sections of memory, freeing up space for reuse. The downside to garbage collection is that it can be quite CPU intensive and can cause your game to stall as it happens. The less garbage collection has to work, the better performance we will get from it, so the trick is to try to avoid any kind of action that might lead to extra collection. Instancing is one such thing we avoid, and in this case, the distance variable is a simple float placeholder, which gets used to calculating distance within one of the main parts of our waypoint-finding functions.

The `TEMPtrans` is a temporary holder for a transform, used during our main way-point functions. Wherever we need to store a transform for temporary use, we will use `TEMPtrans`.

We also need to keep a reference to the first waypoint in the list so that we can draw a line from the last waypoint `lastPos` to the first, to form a closed path. We only need the vector position of the first point, so the vector is all we store in the variable named `FirstPoint`.

```
// set our line color to something we can see easily
Gizmos.color = new Color(1, 0, 0, 1);
```

The `Gizmos.color` command sets the color of the next gizmo drawn by our script to whatever color we pass in. To pass a color, we need to make a Color object with the keyword "new." Color takes an RGB value, followed by an alpha value from 0 to 1.

```
// now we loop through all of the waypoints' drawing lines between them
    for (var i : int = 1; i < transforms.Count; i++)
    {
            TEMPtrans = transforms[i];

            // grab the current waypoint position
            var currentPos : Vector3 = TEMPtrans.position;

// draw the line between the last waypoint and this one
            Gizmos.DrawLine(lastPos, currentPos);

            // point our last transform at the latest position
            pointT.LookAt(currentPos);
```

This code loops through each object in the transform's ArrayList and makes a temporary reference of it with the `TEMPtrans` variable. Once we have that, we go ahead and grab its position vector and place that into `currentPos`, which is cached here into this variable so that we can access it multiple times without having to look it up each time.

Our line is drawn with `Gizmos.DrawLine`, and it takes a start point and an end point, both Vector3 3D vectors. In this case, we draw the line from the last position (the last waypoint) to the current position (the current waypoint we are looking at in our loop).

Next up, we take the last waypoint and point it at the current one with the `LookAt` command. This means that we will be able to rely on the rotation of the waypoint if we ever need to; for example, we may want to respawn the player. To make sure that the player is facing the right way, we can just use the rotation data from the current waypoint and our play is guaranteed to be going in the right direction each time.

Okay, so that's it for the drawing. Now we need to make the last position variable our current position so that we can use it when we want to draw the next line. We also update the pointing transform to the current waypoint so that we can point the right one as the loop progresses.

```
            // update our 'last' waypoint to become this one as we
            // move on to find the next...
            lastPos = currentPos;

            // update the pointing transform
            pointT=transforms[i];
    }

    // close the path
    Gizmos.DrawLine(currentPos, firstPoint);
```

Finally, once the loop has gone through everything in the transform's ArrayList, the path is closed by a line drawn from the current position right back to the first waypoint. That's everything we need to render the path in the editor.

As for a one-stop shop for everything to do with waypoints, we can use the Waypoints_Controller.js script. Making this script self-contained has a number of benefits—other scripts will need to access this script in order to gain access to the waypoints. We need to figure out what functions will be required to support the other scripts, such as AI or race-position checking, and get those in place before we're done with the waypoints. Those requirements are a method to return a waypoint from an index number and a method to return the total number of waypoints. Providing a method to access waypoints via index number is a simple exercise in returning the value of an entry from our transform's ArrayList in our upcoming function called `GetWaypoint`:

```
function GetTotal() : int
{
        return totalTransforms;
}
```

6.3.3 Lap Counting and Waypoint Tracking

Now that we have a waypoint system ready to go, we can use it to track the player's position around the track and, in turn, use that to figure out when the player completes a lap.

When the player reaches the last waypoint, we know that a lap has been completed. Since our last waypoint may not be exactly on the start/finish line, we have a separate trigger to tell us when the player passes it. As the player hits that finish line trigger, since we know that a lap has been completed (thanks to waypoint counting), we can increase our lap counter by one and start counting waypoints, ready for the next lap.

The great thing about using the waypoints to monitor lap progress is that players are guaranteed to have completed a lap when we increase the lap counter. One racing game I worked on reached the Beta phase before anyone noticed that you could stop at a certain point on the track, then reverse backward through the finish line and the game would increase the lap counter without a full lap having been completed. It was a great cheat, as you could complete just under half of a lap, reverse, then get the extra lap. In that time, the other players were just reaching the finish line and you could easily take the lead, then repeat the action and win the race. In our system, there is no way that any strange behavior like this could occur.

Open up the "iWhiskerKarts – Waypoints" example project, if you don't already have it open. Double click on the Level_1 scene from the "scenes" folder in the Project window. Now click on the Waypoints GameObject in the Hierarchy window and notice that our Waypoints_Controller.js script is attached to it.

There are several things that the Car_Controller.js script needs to do to be able to handle our waypoints.

- We need some way to track which waypoint our car is currently at. We should know what the waypoint's index number is, and there's no point looking up its transform every time we need to find out where it is, so we will need to set up a couple of variables to store the current waypoint's transform and position.

- We need a function to return the current waypoint so we can compare way-point index numbers between players later on when we are ready to check race positions.

- We need a function to return the distance to the current waypoint, again for comparisons when we need to check race positions.

- We need a system for lap counting and storing the current lap in an integer. This should also have an accompanying function to return the current lap for when we check race positions.

- We have a function called `UpdateWaypoints()` that is called at each update and checks to see if we are close enough to the current waypoint to merit mov-ing on to the next one.

The Waypoints GameObject is an empty GameObject that does nothing other than hold our Waypoints_Controller.js script. We will use Unity's `GameObject.Find ObjectOfType` function to find this script and talk to it from our Car_Controller.js script (more on that later). Now would be a good time to look at the numerous methods available to us for finding other GameObjects, objects, or scripts.

Finding GameObjects, objects, or scripts. As we saw in our ball-rolling game, tags may be used to identify particular objects or types of objects. The `GameObject.FindWith Tag` method will find an object with the specified tag. Alternatively, `GameObject. FindGameObjectsWithTag` will return a list of objects marked with the matching tag. The function `Object.Find`. `GameObject.Find` takes the name of a GameObject, in the form of a string, and finds that specific GameObject. For example, if you wanted to find the Waypoints GameObject you would simply say:

```
var myObject : GameObject = GameObject.Find("waypoints");
```

`GameObject.FindObjectOfType` returns the first active object of the specified type. Note that if the object has been disabled in the editor, or if you have called a com-mand to make it inactive such as `GameObject.SetActiveRecursively(false)`, the object will not be returned by this search. `FindObjectsOfType` has the exact same functionality as `GameObject.FindObjectOfType`, except that it will return all active objects of the specified type in a list.

`GameObject.GetComponent.GameObject.GetComponent` will return a compo-nent attached to a GameObject, such as a script, collider, or physics component. Unlike the `Find` functions, this will not search and only provides a method to access a compo-nent attached to the specified GameObject.

`GameObject.GetComponents.GameObject.GetComponentsInChildren` has the exact same functionality as the `GameObject.GetComponent` function, except that it will return all of the components of the specified type, in a list.

`GameObject.GetComponentInChildren`. `GameObject.GetComponents InChildren` has similar functionality as the `GameObject.GetComponent` function, except that it will return a component of the specified type either in the specified GameObject or attached to any child of the specified GameObject using a depth-first search (that is, a search that begins at the root GameObject and traverses through all child objects).

GameObject.GetComponentsInChildren. GameObject.GetComponentsIn Children has similar functionality as the GameObject.GetComponent function, except that it will return all of the components of the specified type either in the specified GameObject or attached to any child of the specified GameObject in a list.

Cautions. All of these search functions are great at what they do, but they also have the power to ruin your game completely. They're not so great performance-wise. If you were to use just one of them every frame—for example, in your Update() loop—you would use up so much CPU that you could potentially grind your game to a halt. The method recommended by Unity is to make a cached version early on (such as in your Start() function) and access that whenever you need it. This is exactly what we did with our Waypoints_Controller.js reference when we add it to the Start() function of the Car_Controller.js script.

Open up the Car_Controller.js script and note the following line of code:

```
public var waypointManager : Waypoints_Controller;
```

The waypointManager variable is declared as type Waypoints_Controller. What we are going to do is turn this variable into a reference to our waypoint control script. The waypointManager variable will contain everything we need to talk to our Waypoints_Controller.js script and our gateway to the waypoint system from the car controller. Further down, in the Start() function of this script you will find:

```
waypointManager = GameObject.FindObjectOfType(Waypoints_Controller);
```

Here we tell Unity to find a Waypoints_Controller object (our Waypoints_Controller.js script attached to another GameObject). Our waypointManager variable was declared as a Waypoints_Controller type object earlier on, so when the object gets returned from the FindObjectOfType function, waypointManager will be available for calls directly to all of the functions that Waypoints_Controller.js contains. Note that we won't need to look this up again from Car_Controller.js unless the scene is reloaded—the FindObjectOfType function is only called once for this.

As our waypointManager variable is now all set up, the next part of the Start() function makes a call to the GetTotal() function in our Waypoints_Controller.js script to find out how many waypoints there are:

```
totalWaypoints = waypointManager.GetTotal();
```

Again, it's not as though this value will ever change, so we are safe to cache this value into a variable so that we don't have to make the function call every time we need to know how many waypoints there are.

Within the Car_Controller.js script, take a quick look at the variable declarations for the waypoint system at the top:

```
// waypoints
public var waypointManager : Waypoints_Controller;
public var currentWaypointNum : int;
public var currentWayDist : float;
public var waypointDistance : int = 15; // <-- how close can we get to
                                        // waypoints?
private var totalWaypoints : int;
private var currentWaypointTransform : Transform;
```

First up, we have waypointManager, which will contain a reference to our waypoint manager script (Waypoints_Controller.js) attached to the Waypoints GameObject in the scene. We don't have to set up the reference in the editor because a line of code in the Start() function takes care of finding it. We'll get to that in a moment.

The waypointDistance variable contains the minimum distance that we can get to a waypoint before the waypoint system moves on to reference the next waypoint. We'll explore this in more detail once we reach the code that does this, but remember that waypointDistance takes care of this distance value. When you make your own levels, it may be that you either work at a different scale or that your game variables change, and you may need to adjust this to suit.

Scroll down to find the UpdateWaypoints() function, which is where all of the core waypoint operations happen:

```
function UpdateWaypoints()

{
        // because of the order that scripts run and are initialized, it
        // is possible for this function to be called before we have
        // actually finished running the waypoints initialization, which
        // means we need to drop out to avoid doing anything silly or
        // before it breaks the game.
        if(totalWaypoints==0)
        {
                Debug.Log("DROPPING OUT DUE TO LACK OF WAYPOINTS!!!");

// grab total waypoints
                totalWaypoints = waypointManager.GetTotal();
                return;
        }

        // quick check to make sure that we have a reference to the
        // waypointManager
        if(waypointManager==null)
                waypointManager = GameObject.FindObjectOfType
                                (Waypoints_Controller);

        // here, we deal with making sure that we always have a waypoint
        // set up, and if not, take the steps to find out what our current
        // waypoint should be
        if(currentWaypointTransform==null)
        {
```

```
        currentWaypointNum=0;
        currentWaypointTransform=waypointManager.GetWaypoint
                         (currentWaypointNum);
    }

    // now we need to check to see if we are close enough to the
    // current waypoint to move on to the next one

    myPosition = myTransform.position;
    myPosition.y=0;

    // get waypoint position and 'flatten' it
    nodePosition = currentWaypointTransform.position;
    nodePosition.y=0;

    // check distance from this car to the waypoint

    currentWayDist = Vector3.Distance(nodePosition,myTransform.
                 position);

    if (currentWayDist < waypointDistance) {
        // we are close to the current node, so let's move on to the
        // next one!
        currentWaypointNum++;

        // now check to see if we have been all the way around the
        // track and need to start again

        if(currentWaypointNum>=totalWaypoints){
            // completed a lap! set the lapDone flag to true,
            // which will be checked when we go over the first
            // waypoint (so that you can't almost complete a
            // race then go back around the other way to confuse
            // it)
            lapDone=true;

            // reset our current waypoint to the first one again
            currentWaypointNum=0;
        }
    }

    // grab our transform reference from the waypoint controller
    currentWaypointTransform=waypointManager.GetWaypoint
                     (currentWaypointNum);

    // position our debug box at the current waypoint so we can see it
    debugBox.transform.position=currentWaypointTransform.position;
}
```

It is possible for this function to be called before we have actually finished running the waypoints initialization, which means we need to drop out to avoid doing anything silly or before it breaks the game. To avoid any problems, we do two checks: one to make sure that `waypointManager` actually contains a reference to the Waypoints_Controller.js script and another to make sure that the variable `totalWaypoints` is greater than zero, therefore making sure that we have waypoints for our `waypointManager` object to use.

The events that can make this script fail make perfect sense, when you think about it. Our `Start()` function may have been executed before the waypoints script had been fully initialized, meaning that the initial setting of the `totalWaypoints` variable resulted in it being set to zero because the waypoints weren't ready to go. As far as the Waypoints_Controller.js script knew at that time, there were no waypoints, yet we were already asking for them from the `Start()` function of our Car_Controller.js script.

If there are no waypoints, we try to correct the problem by resetting the `totalWaypoints` variable to whatever comes back from `waypointManager.Get Total()`.

```
if(totalWaypoints==0)
    {
            Debug.Log("DROPPING OUT DUE TO LACK OF WAYPOINTS!!!");

// grab total waypoints
            totalWaypoints = waypointManager.GetTotal();
            return;
    }
```

This is something that I try to do with all of my scripts, and it can solve a lot of problems that may otherwise have taken a longer time to debug. Let me explain this phenomenon with a little example.

Imagine a game controller script that spawns cars. The game controller script, for one reason or another, gets initialized before other scripts. In its `initialization` function, the cars are spawned. Those cars find other objects in the scene and begin to make calls out to components attached to them. But there's a problem. Those other objects in the scene haven't initialized yet, and their scripts are not ready to receive function calls.

What happens next? The car script initialization fails, most likely throwing an error, but sometimes even failing silently. I have seen instances where the script has simply stopped running without warning or error, then further down the line things started going wrong with little or no sign that it was caused by the script stopping. Trying to track down bugs like this can be a nightmare, but with some foresight, most can be avoided by some simple checks in each function.

```
if(currentWaypointTransform==null)
    {
            currentWaypointNum=0;
            currentWaypointTransform=waypointManager.GetWaypoint(current
                                        WaypointNum);

    }
```

Our third and final safety check is one that should always occur when the game first starts, as it looks to see whether we have a waypoint to aim for or not. If the variable `currentWaypointTransform` is null, we know that our script hasn't found a waypoint yet and that it needs to be populated with the first waypoint. Doing it this way means that our first waypoint should always be close to the finish line, and it should always be the first waypoint that the players aim for. As a possible improvement (if you wanted to expand this so that the first waypoint could be anywhere), you could perhaps write some code to find the nearest waypoint and start from that, instead of always starting with whichever waypoint has an index of 0 in the transform's ArrayList of the Waypoints_ Controller.js script.

```
myPosition = myTransform.position;
        myPosition.y=0;

        // get waypoint position and 'flatten' it
        nodePosition = currentWaypointTransform.position;
        nodePosition.y=0;
```

Since our waypoints are used for steering (and not for flying), the y-axis (or height) is irrelevant. If we leave the y value in place when we try to work out the distance from our car to a waypoint, it's going to mess things up. We are only interested in the flat distance from our car to the waypoint, so what happens next is that we copy the positions of both the player (variables `myTransform` into `myPosition`) and the waypoint (variables `currentWaypointTransform` into `nodePosition`) and set their y values to 0.

```
currentWayDist = Vector3.Distance(nodePosition,myTransform.position);
```

The variable `currentWayDist` will contain the distance from our flattened waypoint position to our flattened player position. The distance is calculated using `Vector3.Distance`, which is a nifty built-in function for comparing two vectors and returning the difference. We simply pass in the two vectors and Unity does the rest. As a side note, you can also do this with 2D vectors by using `Vector2.Distance`.

```
if (currentWayDist < waypointDistance) {
        // we are close to the current node, so let's move on to the
        // next one!
        currentWaypointNum++;
```

When the player gets close enough to a waypoint (remember that `waypointDistance` variable, which tells us how close we can get?), the `currentWaypointNum` is increased by one. `currentWaypointNum` is an integer that tells us which waypoint the player is currently at.

```
        // now check to see if we have been all the way around the
        // track and need to start again
        if(currentWaypointNum>=totalWaypoints){
                // completed a lap! set the lapDone flag to true,
                // which will be checked when we go over the first
                // waypoint (so that you can't almost complete a
                // race then go back around the other way to confuse
                // it)
                lapDone=true;

                // reset our current waypoint to the first one again
                currentWaypointNum=0;
        }
```

After `currentWaypointNum` has been increased, we need to make sure that it isn't going to go past the end of the transform's ArrayList in our Waypoints_Controller.js script and break the code when we try to reference it. If our `currentWaypointNum` value has gone over the total number of waypoints in the level (held in the `totalWaypoints` variable), we also know that a lap has just been completed, so we can set a flag called `lapDone` to `true`.

At the end of this section of code, `currentWaypointNum` is reset to 0 and we start all over again with the waypoints.

```
        // grab our transform reference from the waypoint controller
currentWaypointTransform=waypointManager.GetWaypoint
                        (currentWaypointNum);
    }
```

We're done checking the distances, checking for lap completion, and checking for null values, and now we can go ahead and grab the transform of the current waypoint from the `waypointManager` object via `GetWaypoint()`. The `GetWaypoint()` function takes a single index number and returns a transform.

```
        // position our debug box at the current waypoint so we can see it
        // (uncomment if you're debugging!)
        debugBox.transform.position=currentWaypointTransform.position;
    }
```

I have taken the liberty of leaving in some debug code to help you visualize things as you test new levels or test out changes to the code. Here, we set the position of a `debug` object to the position of the current waypoint. Scroll up to the `Start()` function of the Car_Controller.js script and near the end we have:

```
debugBox = GameObject.CreatePrimitive(PrimitiveType.Cube);
        debugBox.collider.enabled=false;
```

In the above code, we generate a cube and disable its collider. By making the `debugBox` as a cube, we will see the current waypoint as a cube as we race around the track. Feel free to comment this out for more CPU cycles. I find having a visualization like this makes the debugging of waypoints much easier, so I left it in.

6.3.4 Wrong-Way Detection

Since we have those waypoints all set up, we should make good use of them and add in some direction checking. If our players stray from the path somehow or start going the wrong way around the track, we can detect this and tell them about it in just a single `CheckWrongWay()` function in our Car_Controller.js script. This function is located just below the `UpdateWaypoints` function:

```
function CheckWrongWay()
{
        if(currentWaypointTransform==null)
                return;
```

```
        relativeTarget = transform.InverseTransformPoint
                         (currentWaypointTransform.position);

        // grab the ideal 'straight on' angle
        targetAngle = Mathf.Atan2 (relativeTarget.x, relativeTarget.z);

        // Atan returns the angle in radians; convert to degrees
        targetAngle *= Mathf.Rad2Deg;

        if(targetAngle<-90 || targetAngle>90){
               goingWrongWay=true;
        } else {
               goingWrongWay=false;
        }

        if(oldWrongWay!=goingWrongWay)
        {
               // we will need to update the UI here
               Debug.Log("GOING THE WRONG WAY!");
        }

        oldWrongWay=goingWrongWay;
}
```

To find out if our player is facing the wrong way, we are going to do four things:

- Make sure that we have a waypoint to aim toward.

- Calculate the angle between the heading of our car versus the angle between our car and the next waypoint.

- If the player is at an angle of 90 degrees or more off-course from pointing straight at the next waypoint, we will assume that this is the wrong way.

- We store whether or not the player is going the wrong way so that we can check to see if it has changed on the next pass. If it has changed, we are going to tell the UI to show or hide the wrong way message. In this case, however, for simplicity's sake, we will simply dump a quick message out to the Console.

```
        if(currentWaypointTransform==null)
               return;
```

Checking for the waypoint is as simple as checking `currentWaypointTransform` to see if it's null. If it is null, we just drop out of the function.

```
relativeTarget = transform.InverseTransformPoint (currentWaypointTransform.
position);

        // grab the ideal 'straight on' angle
        targetAngle = Mathf.Atan2 (relativeTarget.x, relativeTarget.z);

        // Atan returns the angle in radians, convert to degrees
        targetAngle *= Mathf.Rad2Deg;
```

Step one is to find a vector-based expression of the angle between our car and the way-point. We do this by converting the position of the waypoint from world space to local space in relation to our own transform (as this script is attached to the car's transform). We now have a vector-based expression of what the difference is between our car and the waypoint based on our car's orientation. So now we go ahead and convert this into an angle using the `Atan2` function.

`Mathf.Atan2` provides us with the angle, expressed in radians, between the x-axis and a 2D vector starting at zero and terminating at (x,y). Once we have this in radians, we can convert it into degrees (something we can deal with more easily) with the `Mathf.Rad2Deg` function.

At this point, `targetAngle` tells us exactly at how much of an angle our car is from facing the current waypoint. Let's go ahead and check it:

```
if(targetAngle<-90 || targetAngle>90){
        goingWrongWay=true;
    } else {
        goingWrongWay=false;
    }
```

If our angle is less than −90 or greater than 90, it's quite likely that the player is going the wrong way on the track. Feel free to change this value if you find that it is either not sensitive enough to the wrong direction or is reporting the wrong direction too often because it is too sensitive. In this game, we check for a 90-degree angle; however, I have a commercial racing-game engine that uses 110 degrees. The type of racetrack will also affect this.

```
    if(oldWrongWay!=goingWrongWay)
    {
        // we will need to update the UI here
        Debug.Log("GOING THE WRONG WAY!");
    }

    oldWrongWay=goingWrongWay;
```

At the end of our `CheckWrongWay()` function, there is a condition to see whether or not the `goingWrongWay` flag has changed so that the next time we run this function, it doesn't keep displaying the message over and over. It only displays when `goingWrongWay` is no longer the same as `oldWrongWay`. If this is the case, we show the debug message in the Console. Note that in the full game example, we go ahead and tell the game controller script to show the wrong way message on the screen. Right now, we're just keeping it simple with a call to `Debug.Log` instead.

Finally, `oldWrongWay` is set to `goingWrongWay` so that we know what the last state of `goingWrongWay` was when we run the function again.

That's it! Wrong-way checking is all done. Now, it's time for the most complex part of the whole engine: the AI players!

6.3.5 Computer-Controlled (AI) Players

Open the "iWhiskerKarts – Complete" example project and open up the Car_Controller.js script. Since we built the initial Car_Controller.js script, it has changed quite a lot.

We've added waypoint detection, wrong-way detection, and, for the final version, there is (amongst other things we will cover later in this chapter) AI computer control.

This is an extremely basic implementation of a kart-style racer AI system. An AI player will follow a set path of waypoints around the track, slowing down when the angle between the direction the car is facing and the direction of the next waypoint becomes too high. We'll offset the position it aims for in an effort to avoid them all grouping together at the start, but that's about it for extra features. No fancy stuff here; just enough to give us a fun little race.

The original kart-racer physics were built to be controlled by a CheckInput() function, which provides input to the physics functions to turn the kart and accelerate or decelerate. By separating the input out into a separate function, we can easily modify things to take input from different sources just by calling an alternative function to CheckInput(). Our scripts don't care where the input comes from, so it can be anything we want it to be, just as long as it provides input to drive the physics.

In the case of our AI, we have an input function that finds out where the car is supposed to be pointing and provides input to steer it in the right direction (as though it were a user steering left or right). The core AI functions are UpdateAIInput() and SlowVelocity(), as shown below.

```
function updateAIInput()
{
        if(waypointTrack==0)
                waypointTrack=Random.Range(1,2);

        if((mySpeed>-5 && mySpeed<5) && !possiblyStuck){
                // we're going slow - are we stuck? possibly!
                stuckTimer=Time.time;
                possiblyStuck=true;
        }

        if(mySpeed>3 && possiblyStuck){
                // we have unstuck!
                possiblyStuck=false;
        }

        if(possiblyStuck && stuckTimer<Time.time-timeBeforeStuck){
                // looks like we're stuck, so let's force reverse gear for a
                // few seconds
                forceReverse=true;
                forceReverseTimer=Time.time;
        }

        if(possiblyStuck && stuckTimer<Time.time-timeBeforeStuck*5){
                // looks like we're stuck for a long time, so let's respawn
                // instead
                possiblyStuck=false;
                forceReverse=false;
                //FlipCar();
        }

        if(forceReverse && forceReverseTimer<Time.time-forceReverseTime){
                // we've done some time in reverse; let's get back to going
                // forward!
```

```
                forceReverse=false;
        }

// quick! check to make sure that our waypoints are set up, otherwise drop
// out now
        if(currentWaypointTransform==null)
                return;

roadWidth=3;

        if(oldWaypointNum!=currentWaypointNum){
                if(waypointTrack==1){
                        AIoffset=currentWaypointTransform.right*roadWidth;
        } else if(waypointTrack==2){
                        AIoffset=currentWaypointTransform.right*-roadWidth;
                }
        }
        oldWaypointNum =currentWaypointNum;

        nodePosition=currentWaypointTransform.position + AIoffset;

        // ----------------------------------------------------------------
        throttle = 1;

        // calculate the target position relative to the target of this
        // transform's coordinate system; e.g., a positive x value means
        // the target is to the right of the car; a positive z means the
        // target is in front of the car
        relativeTarget = transform.InverseTransformPoint (nodePosition);

        targetAngle = Mathf.Atan2 (relativeTarget.x, relativeTarget.z);

        // Atan returns the angle in radians; convert to degrees
        targetAngle *= Mathf.Rad2Deg;

        // the wheels should have a maximum rotation angle
        targetAngle = Mathf.Clamp (targetAngle, -120-targetAngle, 120);

        if(mySpeed>10)
        {
                // too fast? need to turn too much? slow down!
                if(Mathf.Abs (targetAngle) > 55){
                        // we are too fast
                        throttle=-1;
                        slowVelocity();

                } else if(Mathf.Abs (targetAngle) > 35){
                        // We are too fast
                        throttle=-1;
                        slowVelocity();

                } else if(Mathf.Abs (targetAngle) > 15){

                        // We are too fast
                        //slowVelocity();
                        //throttle=0;

                } else if(mySpeed>20 && Mathf.Abs (targetAngle) > 5){
```

```
                                // we are too fast
                                slowVelocity();
                        }
                }

                // ------------------------------------------------------------
                horizontal = targetAngle * 0.05;

                if(forceReverse){
                        // force reverse!
                        throttle=-1;
                }
        }

function slowVelocity ()
{
        myRigidbody.AddForce(-flatVelo * 0.8);
}
```

Rather than all of the AI players aiming for the waypoint directly (usually aiming for the center of the road), we apply a small offset to each one, which is the first thing we do in the updateAIInput() function:

```
function updateAIInput()
{
        if(waypointTrack==0)
                waypointTrack=Random.Range(1,2);
```

Not only does it look better to have your AI cars driving on sides of the road rather than the center, but it also serves a purpose in stopping your cars from clumping together into a big crash at the start of the race. When all of the AI cars are in the same area, if they all aim for the same waypoint, they are certain to cause a pileup. Offsetting avoids this.

We choose whether or not the offset should be left or right of the waypoint for each player by setting the waypointTrack integer to either a 1 or a 2. Random.Range, the method we need to use for generating random numbers within the specified range, decides this.

Every now and then, the AI cars will get stuck. It happens in every racing game, and it means that we need not be afraid of a little kart-to-kart collision! When our AI players get stuck, we can detect it like this:

- If the speed of the car is slow, we time how long it has been going slow.

- If the car has been going slow for a certain period of time, we can assume that the car is stuck.

- To try and address the problem, we set the car to reverse for a set amount of time. If the car is stuck in front of an obstacle, it is hoped that the period of time in reverse will correct the issue. Our car will still try to aim toward the current waypoint during this time.

- If we are still stuck after the reverse period, the car needs to be repositioned.

```
if((mySpeed>-5 && mySpeed<5) && !possiblyStuck){
        // we're going slow - are we stuck? possibly!
        stuckTimer=Time.time;
        possiblyStuck=true;
}

if(mySpeed>3 && possiblyStuck){
        // we have unstuck!
        possiblyStuck=false;
}

if(possiblyStuck && stuckTimer<Time.time-timeBeforeStuck){
        // looks like we're stuck, so let's force reverse gear for a
        // few seconds
        forceReverse=true;
        forceReverseTimer=Time.time;
}

if(possiblyStuck && stuckTimer<Time.time-timeBeforeStuck*5){
        // looks like we're stuck for a long time, so let's respawn
        // instead
        possiblyStuck=false;
        forceReverse=false;
        FlipCar();
}

if(forceReverse && forceReverseTimer<Time.time-forceReverseTime){
        // we've done some time in reverse, let's get back to going
        // forward!
        forceReverse=false;
}
```

The first part of our AI script deals with the problem of stuck players, in the code shown above.

Whenever our car goes over a certain speed, we know that the car is not stuck, so we can reset the possiblyStuck variable to false. If our speed (from the variable mySpeed) is less than 5 and greater than −5, we know that the kart is not going at the kinds of speeds we expect it to be at since mySpeed should hold a value higher than a 5. It may be stuck. To reflect this, we set a Boolean variable called possiblyStuck to true. We also begin timing how long possiblyStuck has been set by setting stuckTimer to the current system time (Time.time).

When possiblyStuck has been true for an amount of time, it probably means that the car is stuck and action needs to be taken to fix it. In the code above, forceReverse is set to true so that our car will back up and set forceReverseTimer to the current system time (Time.time) so that we can keep tabs on how long the car has been reversing.

```
if(possiblyStuck && stuckTimer<Time.time-timeBeforeStuck){
        // looks like we're stuck, so let's force reverse gear for a
        // few seconds
        forceReverse=true;
        forceReverseTimer=Time.time;
}

if(possiblyStuck && stuckTimer<Time.time-timeBeforeStuck*5){
```

```
            // looks like we're stuck for a long time, so let's respawn
            // instead
            possiblyStuck=false;
            forceReverse=false;
            FlipCar();
    }

    if(forceReverse && forceReverseTimer<Time.time-forceReverseTime){
            // we've done some time in reverse, let's get back to going
            // forward!
            forceReverse=false;
    }
```

If the car is still having trouble, even after reversing, we go ahead and reset our stuck detection variables and call the function called FlipCar(), which takes care of repositioning the player. The FlipCar() function can be found further down in the Car_Controller.js script:

```
function FlipCar ()
{
        // reset forces as a precaution
        myRigidbody.velocity=Vector3.zero;
        myRigidbody.angularVelocity=Vector3.zero;

        // grab the last waypoint
        if(currentWaypointNum>0)
        {
                TEMPtransform = waypointManager.GetWaypoint
                                (currentWaypointNum-1);
        } else {
                TEMPtransform = waypointManager.GetWaypoint(0);
        }

        // move and rotate our rigidbody to the position and rotation of
        // the waypoint
        myRigidbody.MovePosition(TEMPtransform.position);
        myRigidbody.MoveRotation(TEMPtransform.rotation);
}
```

The function FlipCar() simply grabs a reference to the last waypoint and sets the player's rigidbody position and rotation to that of the waypoint. We need to use the last waypoint rather than the current one, as the current waypoint is always in front of the player, and it would be wrong to teleport them forward for repositioning. If you ever implement a button to reposition the player, he or she could also cheat by tapping the reposition key all the way around the track!

We also check to see whether or not our currentWaypointNum is greater than 0. As we're trying to get the last waypoint, we use currentWaypointNum-1 to determine which waypoint to look at. (Of course, if the currentWaypointNum was 0, that would give us a negative index value and when we call upon GetWaypoint, the Waypoints_Controller.js script would break as it tried to access the transform's ArrayList at index −1.)

Moving back to the UpdateAIInput() function again, we quickly check that currentWaypointTransform contains a waypoint transform (as a safety measure), then go on to calculate the waypoint offset to the left or right:

```
// quick check to make sure that our waypoints are set up, otherwise drop
// out now
        if(currentWaypointTransform==null)
                return;

roadWidth=3;

        if(oldNodeNum!=currentWaypointNum){
                if(waypointTrack==1){
                        AIoffset=currentWaypointTransform.right*roadWidth;
        } else if(waypointTrack==2){
                        AIoffset=currentWaypointTransform.right*-roadWidth;
                }
        }

oldWaypointNum =currentWaypointNum;

nodePosition=currentWaypointTransform.position + AIoffset;
```

When the offset is calculated, the `roadWidth` provides the amount (in units) that we can go on either side of the waypoint. There are two tracks that our players may aim for; they're held in the `waypointTrack` variable set earlier in the script by a `Random.Range` call for either a 1 or a 2.

If we need to find a vector to represent the direction to the right of a transform, we can use `transform.right`. In the code above, when the `waypointTrack` variable is 1, we grab the right direction from the `currentWaypointTransform` object and multiply it by our `roadWidth` variable to give us a vector to use as an offset to the waypoint's position. When `waypointTrack` is 2, we multiply it by negative `roadWidth` instead, giving us an offset on the opposite side.

Note that we only calculate out the offset when the `currentWaypointNum` differs from `oldWaypointNum`, as there is no point in having to calculate it every single frame. We only calculate it when the current waypoint has changed.

The final position we will use for targeting the AI player is held in a Vector3 typed variable called `nodePosition`, which is set in code by taking the position of the current waypoint's transform (`currentWaypointTransform.position`) and adding the newly calculated `AIoffset` vector to it.

```
throttle = 1;
```

We can assume that the AI player has its foot down on the gas, making our throttle value default to 1. Further down in the script, we may adjust this, but if nothing stands in the way of it, our AI player will continue to have full throttle.

Next in the function, the angles are calculated, and we establish what the AI player needs to do in order to be heading toward the current waypoint:

```
        relativeTarget = transform.InverseTransformPoint (nodePosition);

        targetAngle = Mathf.Atan2 (relativeTarget.x, relativeTarget.z);
```

```
        // Atan returns the angle in radians; convert to degrees
        targetAngle *= Mathf.Rad2Deg;

        // the wheels should have a maximum rotation angle
        targetAngle = Mathf.Clamp (targetAngle, -120-targetAngle, 120);
```

The main part of this function is identical to the wrong-way detection we described in Section 6.2.4. The `relativeTarget` is worked out by converting the position of the waypoint into the coordinate space of the player. We use `Mathf.Atan2` to convert this vector into an angle and `Mathf.Rad2Deg` to convert the radians to degrees.

As we reach the final line in the above code, `targetAngle` contains the exact angle between our car and our waypoint. That final line takes care of restricting the target angle to a reasonable amount. If it is greater than 120 degrees (either −120 or +120), it will be restricted by the `Mathf.Clamp` function.

```
        tempAngle=Mathf.Abs(targetAngle);

if(mySpeed>10)
{
        // too fast? need to turn too much? slow down!
        if(tempAngle > 55){
                // we are too fast
                throttle=-1;
                slowVelocity();
        } else if(tempAngle > 35){
                // we are too fast
                throttle=-1;
                slowVelocity();
        } else if(tempAngle > 15){
                // we are too fast
                //slowVelocity();
                //throttle=0;
        } else if(mySpeed>20 && tempAngle > 5){
                // we are too fast
                slowVelocity();
        }
}
```

The next part of our AI code deals with trying to stop the car from crashing by slowing down on tight bends. I wouldn't say that this is the best solution; ideally, you would want to write something that would look ahead at the upcoming waypoints and anticipate them rather than react to them, but this works well enough for a simple kart racer like this.

As long as the kart is moving at a speed faster than 10, all we do here is check the angle we need to turn, then slow it down if it is too high. These numbers are not exactly scientific, however, and I've arrived at them through nothing but play testing and tweaking until I reached something that worked. It is highly likely that you will have to change these around some once you start building out your own games, so don't blindly trust them—they just act as a good starting point.

Earlier, we saw that the value of throttle is set to 1. If we are going too fast, in the most extreme cases, we reverse throttle to −1 to try and get the kart to slow down quicker. The function `slowVelocity()` also acts to slow down the kart by applying a force in the opposite direction of the `flatVelo` (our flat velocity) vector. When the angle is high, we call `slowVelocity` to slow things down quickly, which, in turn, should help to prevent our AI players from crashing at each corner.

```
horizontal = targetAngle * 0.05;

if(forceReverse){
        // force reverse!
        throttle=-1;
}
```

The next part of the `UpdateAIInput()` script provides a value for turning (held in the variable named `horizontal`) by taking a fraction of the target angle (`targetAngle * 0.05`).

Finally, if this AI-controlled kart is supposed to be reversing, `forceReverse` will be set to `true`, in which case, we need to force throttle to the value of −1 so that our kart will go backward.

With the core functions now in place, we can modify the `Update()` function to include calls to update AI. In the final version of the Car_Controller.js script, the function looks like this:

```
function Update()
{
        // update gets called automatically by the engine. this is where
        // we do all of our major updates

        if(!lockedInPlace)
        {
                // if we are locked in place (such as at the start line
                // waiting) then we update the physics, but not any input.
                // we also constrain the rigidbody on its x and z so that
                // gravity can drop it but it won't slide around if we are a
                // user-controlled car, update input
                if(doUserInput)
                {
                        checkInput();

                } else if (doAIInput) {
                        // if we are an AI-controlled car, update the AI
                        updateAIInput();
                } else {
                        // no one is controlling this, so reset the input
                        // vars
                        throttle=0;
                        horizontal=0;
                }
        }

        // update our car physics
        updatePhysics();
}
```

When we create a computer-controlled car, we set the Boolean variable doAIInput to true, which is we use to divert specific calls toward their equivalent AI-based calls. As you can see in the final Update() function, the function call used to get the user's input, CheckInput(), is replaced by a call to updateAIInput() whenever doAIInput is true.

The only other place in that final Car_Controller.js script where we use doAIInput to act differently is in LateUpdate():

```
if(!doAIInput)
        CheckWrongWay();
```

Normally, we check to see if the player is moving in the wrong direction (a call to our CheckWrongWay() function), but now we check for doAIInput, and if this is an AI car, the call is not made to check direction. The reason for this is simple: wrong-way checking's main purpose is displaying a message to users to tell them where to go. Obviously, we don't need to display that message if this is an AI car.

The doAIInput variable is set from a function called setAIInput, which gets called by the Game_Controller.js script during initialization.

```
function setAIInput(state : boolean)
{
        // should we allow user input on this car?
        doAIInput = state;
}
```

The game controller spawns all of our cars in the final version and is responsible for setting up their properties (such as whether or not they are AI controlled). Before we look at the game controller script in detail, there is another piece of the puzzle that needs to be understood first. That is, how we deal with figuring out race positions—who is winning the race?

6.3.6 Race-Position Detection

We use the waypoint system described earlier in Section 6.2.2, combined with the lap counter, to find out which player is in which position during a race. With the waypoint system, we know exactly where each player is on the track. To figure out who is winning, we need just three pieces of information:

- what each kart's current lap number is,

- the index number of each kart's current waypoint, and

- the distance between each kart and its current waypoint.

When we attempt to find out the race position of one of the karts, we begin by making the assumption that the kart is in first place; as we go through and compare information from the waypoint system, we decrease the race position.

Our Game_Controller.js script contains the code to work out all of the race positions within the function named updatePositions().

```
function updatePositions()
{
        // start with the assumption that the player is in last place and
        // work up
        myPos=numberOfRacers;

// the player we are concerned with, position-wise, is our focused player
        car1=focusPlayerScript;

        // now we step through each racer and check their positions to
        // determine whether or not our focused player is in front of them
        // or not
        for(var b : int=0;b<numberOfRacers;b++){
                // assume that we are behind this player
                isAhead=false;
                // grab a temporary reference to the 'other' player we want
                // to check against
                car2=playerList[b];

                if(car1.id!=car2.id){ // <-- make sure we're not trying to
                                      // compare same objects!

                        // is the focused player a lap ahead?
                        if(car1.getCurrentLap()>car2.getCurrentLap())
                                isAhead=true;

                        // is the focused player on the same lap, but at a
                        // higher waypoint number?
                        if(car1.getCurrentLap()==car2.getCurrentLap() &&
                           car1.getCurrentWaypointNum()>car2.getCurrent
                           WaypointNum())
                                isAhead=true;

                        // is the focused player on the same lap, same
                        // waypoint, but closer to it?
                        if(car1.getCurrentLap()==car2.getCurrentLap() &&
                           car1.getCurrentWaypointNum()==car2.get
                           CurrentWaypointNum() && car1.getCurrent
                           WaypointDist() < car2.getCurrentWaypointDist())
                                isAhead=true;

                        // has the player completed a lap and is getting
                        // ready to move onto the next one?
                        if(car1.getCurrentLap()==car2.getCurrentLap() &&
                           car1.getCurrentWaypointNum()==car2.get
                           CurrentWaypointNum() && (car1.isLapDone()==true &&
                           car2.isLapDone()==false))
                                isAhead=true;

                        if(car1.getCurrentLap()==car2.getCurrentLap() &&
                           (car1.isLapDone()==true && !car2.isLapDone()))
                                isAhead=true;

                        if(isAhead)
                        {
                                myPos--;
                        }
```

```
            }
        }

        // if we're the local car (and not AI), update onscreen position
        focusPlayerRacePosition=myPos;
        updateRacePositionText();
}.
```

The `updatePositions()` function begins by setting `myPos` to the total number of karts, putting the non-AI player in last place. (`myPos` is an integer that will hold the player's position.)

```
        myPos=numberOfRacers;

// the player we are concerned with, position-wise, is our focused player
        car1=focusPlayerScript;
```

During the game, our game controller script focuses on one player—a single player that has its position and current lap number displayed on screen during the game. A reference to the Car_Controller.js script component attached to this focused car is held in the variable named `focusPlayerScript` so that we can access its functions easily. The `updatePositions()` function only calculates the position of the player referenced by `focusPlayerScript`, as all other player positions are irrelevant.

```
// now we step through each racer and check their positions to determine
// whether or not our focused player is in front of them or not
        for(var b : int=0;b<numberOfRacers;b++){
                // assume that we are behind this player
                isAhead=false;
                // grab a temporary reference to the 'other' player we want
                // to check against
                car2=playerList[b];
```

In this piece of code, you can see that we start out with a loop from 0 to the `numberOf Players`. The index number (`i`) from the loop is used with an ArrayList called `playerList` to get a reference to each player's controller script.

We will get to this in Section 6.2.7, but the game controller script (Game_Controller.js) is the one that creates the player karts at the start of each race. As it does so, a reference to each Car_Controller.js script belonging to each kart is put into the ArrayList called `playerList`. The `playerList` ArrayList lives in that game controller script, so we can use it to talk to the karts when we are doing things like checking race positions.

In the code above, the variable `car2` holds the reference (copied from the `player List` ArrayList) to the car we want to look at.

```
if(focusPlayerScript.id!=car2.id){ // <-- make sure we're not trying to
compare same objects!
```

When cars are first created, they are given a unique ID number by the game controller script. In the code above, we use the ID number to make sure that we are not trying to compare the same cars. The `playerList` ArrayList will contain a reference to our focused player script, too, which is the one we are going to be using to compare against the other cars to determine which position it is in. If we didn't have this ID check, we would end up comparing the focused car to itself, leading almost certainly to unreliable results in our race position.

The next part of our `updatePositions()` script are the comparisons that will determine whether the focused car (`focusPlayerScript`) is in front of or behind the car we are looking at through the loop (`car2`).

- Has the focused car completed more laps than the comparison car? If so, it is ahead.

  ```
  if(focusPlayerScript.getCurrentLap()>car2.getCurrentLap())
                        isAhead=true;
  ```

- Is the current lap numbers of both cars the same? Is the focused car's current waypoint index number higher than the comparison car? If so, it is ahead.

  ```
  if(focusPlayerScript.getCurrentLap()==car2.getCurrentLap() &&
  focusPlayerScript.getCurrentWaypointNum()>car2.getCurrent
  WaypointNum())
                        isAhead=true;
  ```

- Are both cars on the same lap, with the same current waypoint? If so, we compare both car's distances to the current waypoint to find out if our focused car is closer. If so, it is ahead.

  ```
  if(focusPlayerScript.getCurrentLap()==car2.getCurrentLap() &&
  focusPlayerScript.getCurrentWaypointNum()==car2.getCurrent
  WaypointNum() && focusPlayerScript.getCurrentWaypointDist() < car2.
  getCurrentWaypointDist())
                        isAhead=true;
  ```

- If both cars are on the same lap and their waypoints are the same, but the focused car is the only one that has completed a lap, it is ahead.

  ```
  if(focusPlayerScript.getCurrentLap()==car2.getCurrentLap() && fo-
  cusPlayerScript.getCurrentWaypointNum()==car2.getCurrent
  WaypointNum() && (focusPlayerScript.isLapDone()==true && car2.
  isLapDone()==false))
                        isAhead=true;
  ```

- Are both cars on the same current lap, but only the focused player has completed a lap? If so, then it is ahead.

  ```
  if(focusPlayerScript.getCurrentLap()==car2.getCurrentLap() &&
  (focusPlayerScript.isLapDone()==true && !car2.isLapDone()))
                        isAhead=true;
  ```

The last part of the position-checking loop checks to see if the `isAhead` Boolean flag has been set to `true` by our checks.

```
if(isAhead)
        {
                myPos--;
        }
```

If this is the case, we decrease the `myPos` variable, in effect moving our race position closer to first place. By the time the loop has completed, the `myPos` variable will be somewhere between `numberOfPlayers` (last place) and 1 (first place).

```
focusPlayerRacePosition=myPos;
updateRacePositionText()
```

Once the loop has finished running, we know the race position of the focused player. We finish up the function by telling our focused car which position it is in and call on a function within Game_Controller.js to update the UI race position display. The UI will be discussed in Section 6.2.10, so don't worry about how that works just yet.

6.3.7 Setting Up the Race and Creating the Cars from Game_Controller.js

The game controller script is always central to every game I make. It takes care of almost all of the game-related things, such as keeping track of who is winning the race or telling the cars when the race ends. So far, we have looked at how the individual components of our game are built (which is, in fact, how I put it together).

When I started developing the kart racer, the first thing I did was to build the basic kart physics, then I set up the environments followed by the waypoint system and then AI, UI, and fancy things like pedal graphics and a wrong-way indicator. I like to work in as much of a componentized way as possible, trying to ensure that each piece of the puzzle could function on its own or without another. Most game developers start out working this way, but as deadlines loom and the pressure to complete is on, some find themselves beginning to take a few shortcuts. Try to avoid this, but don't be surprised if it happens to you. It's so frequent that the industry has a term for it: *spaghetti code*. I've seen spaghetti code in everything from indie projects to AAA game engines.

Open the example project file (if it isn't already) "iWhiskerKarts – Complete" and find the "Prefabs" folder in the Project window. There is only one prefab in there: the Player_car prefab. Open up the Level_1 scene from the "Project/Scenes" folder; notice that there are no cars in the scene.

In the kart-racing game, earlier versions had the car already in the scene. You can see this in either the "iWhiskerKarts – Only Kart physics" example project or in the "iWhiskerKarts – Waypoints" files. Having the car already in the scene was a quick and easy way of testing the car physics without having to write the rest of the game, but now we're at the stage where the game controller script needs to start taking control of things, so the player kart is the first thing to be deleted from the scene. Deleted, that is, once we made a prefab out of it.

Creating a prefab is easy. Unity 3.4 allows you to simply drag your item into the Project window and the prefab is automatically built and ready to use. In the game controller script (Game_Controller.js), we will see both how it creates the cars for our game from the Player_car prefab and how each one is set up.

The game controller script also deals with starting and stopping the race, drawing some parts of the UI (the position and lap counters), keeping tabs on how many laps have been completed by the user-controlled player (the focused player), and keeping the race position updated onscreen. Once the cars are created, they are held in place (by default). Once the "3, 2, 1, Go!" countdown has finished, the game controller script tells all of the cars to release and start racing.

```
function Start()
{
        Init();
}
```

The Game_Controller.js script starts out with a call with `Init()`. The `Init()` function is where all of the main setup happens before a race.

```
function Init()
{
        // initialize a list to hold our players
        playerList=new ArrayList();
```

The `playerList` ArrayList will hold references to the Car_Controller.js scripts attached to each car.

The user's kart is created separately from the AI karts, since we need to treat it a little differently. For a start, our user's kart is going to need to become the focus of the game and will be controlled by the keyboard rather than by our AI control scripts. This is why we begin the game controller `Init()` function by creating our user's kart before anything else.

```
        // create local player
        localPlayer = GameObject.Instantiate(carPrefab,startPoints[0].
                        transform.position,startPoints[0].transform.rotation);
```

Using `GameObject.Instantiate` is a method for *instantiating* (creating instances of) objects in a scene. By passing in a GameObject, component, or script object, the `Instantiate` command will make a clone of the original and place it into the scene at the specified position and rotation. In this script, the Car prefab (which is set in the editor to the prefab within the "Assets/Prefabs" folder) is created and placed at the first start point stored in the `startPoints` array. A reference to this new cloned version will be returned into the `localPlayer` variable, making it easily accessible to this script after instantiation.

The `startPoints` array is set in the editor to several empty GameObjects, which are placed near the start line (Figure 6.3). These points are used to position all of the karts at the start of the race. These GameObjects are also oriented so that their rotations may be used to point the karts in the right direction at the start of the race. Note that their z-axes point toward the start line.

```
        localPlayer.transform.name="USER";
```

Figure 6.3. The start points are empty GameObjects in the scene.

Notice that we used `gameObject.Instantiate` to create our player, which means that `localPlayer` must be declared as a GameObject. At this stage, however, we need to get to the transform so that we can change its name to USER. Having a clear name for the transform will make it easy if we run into any trouble, since we will easily be able to look it up in the Scene window and check its state, if needed. The line above takes care of this, and whenever you see the player's GameObject in the scene, it will appear as USER.

```
// we need the camera and lap counter to belong to this player, so
// we set the focusPlayer to this localPlayer
focusPlayer = localPlayer;
```

As mentioned in Section 6.2.7, the game controller script has a player object that it focuses on, meaning that this player will be the one for which we display the race position of in the UI and the one that will be followed around by the camera, etc. Here, we set the variable `focusPlayer` to be our user's player.

```
thePlayerScript = localPlayer.GetComponent("Car_Controller");

// tell this player about this game controller, so that it can talk
// back here when it needs to (sending messages such as completing
// the race, etc.)
thePlayerScript.gameControl = this;
```

Next, we use `GetComponent` to find the Car_Controller.js script attached to our user's kart in `localPlayer`. `thePlayerScript` will be used next to set up some required properties, starting with telling it about the game controller script. At some point, the player will need to call functions on the game controller script (for example, telling the game controller that it completed a lap), so we tell `thePlayerScript` about the game controller by setting its publicly declared variable `gameControl` to `this`. In this context, `this` represents the script object—in this case, it represents our Game_Controller.js script attached to the Game Controller GameObject in the scene. Once `thePlayerScript` has its `gameControl` variable set up, we can call back to the game controller functions easily—example calls might be `gameControl.finishedLap()` or `gameControl.quitGame()`.

```
// assign this player the ID of 0
thePlayerScript.id=0;

// set player control
thePlayerScript.setUserInput(true);
```

The user's player is always assigned the ID of 0.

The function `setUserInput()` of Car_Controller.js is called with its parameter set to `true` by the above code. Since this is the user, not a computer-controlled AI kart, we tell its car control script to accept input from the user with this simple function call:

```
// save a reference to this script in our playerList ArrayList
playerList.Add(thePlayerScript);

// as this is the user, we want to focus on this for UI, etc.
focusPlayerScript = thePlayerScript;
```

The code above takes care of adding our user's player to the `playerList` ArrayList. It will be accessed later on when we need to compare race positions; it will also tell all the karts when they are allowed to move (when the countdown has finished and the race starts). Note that `playerList` contains references to each player's car controller script, not to its GameObject or transform. The car controller script contains everything we need, and by having a reference directly to it, there is little overhead in finding the script whenever we want to call functions directly on it.

Again, `focusPlayerScript` contains a reference to our user's car controller script so that we can get to it quickly.

```
cameraScript.SetTarget(focusPlayer.transform);
```

Remember when we instantiated the player, we stored a reference to its GameObject in `focusPlayer`? Well, we're using that reference here to get to its transform, and then we pass that to the camera script. The camera script will control the camera, but it needs a target to aim at and to follow around: `SetTarget` tells the camera script what it is we would like it to follow. When the scene is first loaded, the camera has the camera script attached to it, but no assigned target. We can't set its target until the karts have been instantiated by this script, so we need to do it here.

```
// do initial lap counter display
updateLapCounter(1);
```

Here, we simply tell the lap counter to display the number 1, since we know that it's the first lap. We will cover the UI in Section 6.2.10, so for now, let's just leave it at that and get to the meat of this function where the AI players are created:

```
// make AI players
for(var i : int = 1; i<numberOfRacers; i++)
{
        localPlayer = GameObject.Instantiate(carPrefab,startPoints
                    [i].transform.position,startPoints[i].
                    transform.rotation);
```

First, we loop through all of the required players. Note that our index starts at 1 this time. This is because we already have a Player 0—the user's player we created above. We're going to use the index number from the loop as the ID numbers for each AI player, as well as a counter to make sure we create the right number of players.

As per the code we used to instantiate the user player, `GameObject.Instantiate` is put to work above to create the AI player. So that we can set up some parameters on this player, the reference to the GameObject returned by the `Instantiate` call is stored in the variable named `localPlayer`.

```
// grab a reference to the focused player's car controller
// script, so that we can do things like access its speed
// variable
thePlayerScript = localPlayer.GetComponent
                ("Car_Controller");

// tell this player about this game controller so that it
// can talk back here when it needs to (sending messages
// such as completing the race, etc.)
thePlayerScript.gameControl = this;

// assign an ID
thePlayerScript.id=i;

// set player control
thePlayerScript.setAIInput(true);

// save a reference to this script in our playerList
// ArrayList
playerList.Add(thePlayerScript);
```

Just as we did earlier with the user's player, here we grab a reference to this AI player's Car_Controller.js script using the `GetComponent` function. That goes into the variable called `thePlayerScript` and is then used to tell it about this instance of the Game_ Controller.js script so that it can talk back to it later.

We then use the index from our loop to provide the player with an ID number and use `thePlayerScript` to call `setAIInput`, which will tell the player that it should accept input from the AI functions rather than the user. The `playerList` ArrayList receives a new object, since we add the reference in `thePlayerScript` to it:

```
// finally, alter the car speeds for each car. this number
// will need tweaking if you change the number of cars, or
```

```
// perhaps even the power
thePlayerScript.setPower( thePlayerScript.power -
( ( thePlayerScript.power * 0.1 ) * i ) );

if(i==1)
{
        // if this is the first AI player, we are going to
        // give it a little boost to make the game more
        // challenging
        thePlayerScript.setPower( thePlayerScript.power +
        ( thePlayerScript.power * 0.3 ));
}
```
}

It's not the most interesting race if everyone goes at exactly the same speed. For one, it means that players who are new to the game will easily fall behind and lose. For another, it often means that the AI players will clump together all the way around the track, lap after lap. It is much more interesting for users if each player has different kinds of attributes, and you will see this in commercial racing games, particularly kart racing, where you will have more aggressive players, faster players, or perhaps players who avoid obstacles better. Our AI isn't that complex, but we can make it a little more enticing for a wider range of players by offering opponents that are not all the same speed. Here in the function, we alter the power of each AI car to give a more interesting race, having a fast opponent, and then three progressively slower ones.

The values we use to send to the setPower() function are not scientific. Again, they come from play testing and tweaking in an attempt to find an algorithm that makes a fun game. Feel free to remove it, play around with the numbers, or come up with something better!

```
// start the game in 4 seconds from now
Invoke("StartRace",4);

// update positions throughout the race, but we don't need to do this every
// frame. just do it every half a second instead
        InvokeRepeating("updatePositions",0.5,0.5);
```

The Invoke command is a fantastic command with all kinds of different uses. All it does is call a function within the same script as was executed, but in a set amount of time. The code above simply calls the StartRace() function in four seconds from when the Invoke command is executed, which is the amount of time it will take for our little "3, 2, 1, Go!" countdown to complete. Its syntax looks like this:

```
Invoke(function name as a string, time before the function will be called)
```

The InvokeRepeating command is a derivative of the Invoke command, offering automatic calling of a function every x seconds. You use it like this:

```
InvokeRepeating(function name as a string, time before the function will be
called for the first time, time to wait between every call after the first)
```

The `InvokeRepeating` command will continue to occur as long as the script is active and in the scene, or until the command `CancelInvoke()` is used to stop it. Use `CancelInvoke` like this:

```
CancelInvoke(which function is being invoked)
```

Note that `CancelInvoke` may also be used to cancel upcoming function calls that have been set by either `Invoke` or `InvokeRepeating`. One example of where this might be useful would be an action that demanded that a user hold down a button for a certain amount of time. When the button was first pressed, you could use `Invoke` to schedule a function call in a set number of seconds. If the button is released within the set number of seconds, you could use `CancelInvoke` to stop the scheduled function call from happening.

```
    // hide our count in numbers
    hideCount();

    // schedule count in messages
    Invoke("showCount3",1);
    Invoke("showCount2",2);
    Invoke("showCount1",3);
    Invoke("hideCount",4);

    // hide final position text
    finalPositionText.gameObject.active=false;
```

Since we are going to talk about the UI in Section 6.2.10, we will come back to most of the above code; however, you can see how I used multiple `Invoke` calls to show and hide UI elements.

```
    doneFinalMessage=false;

    // start by hiding our 'wrong way' message
    UpdateWrongWay(false);
}
```

Above, we set a quick Boolean variable, called `doneFinalMessage`, which is used to make sure that we only call to show the final game message once.

A function to `UpdateWrongWay()` sets the state of whether or not the player is going in the wrong direction to its default value of `false`. In Section 6.2.4, we discussed how the waypoint system is used to track the direction of the player. In the final version of the kart-racing game, the detection code calls out to the `UpdateWrongWay()` function whenever the state of `WrongWay` changes.

Another function of interest in the Game_Controller.js script is the `StartRace()` function. Earlier in the `Start()` function, we used `Invoke` to call this function in 4 seconds time:

```
function StartRace()
{
    // tell all of the players to release their locks
```

```
for(var i : int = 0; i<playerList.Count; i++)
{
        thePlayerScript = playerList[i];
        thePlayerScript.SetLock(false);
}
}
```

The `StartRace()` function loops through all of the objects in the `playerList` ArrayList, which, you may remember, is where we store references to each player's car controller script. Each object is copied into the `thePlayerScript` variable, and we call `SetLock()` on each one, releasing the lock on each player so that the race can begin and the racers can move.

```
function LapComplete(aScript : Car_Controller, theLaps : int)
{
        if(aScript.getCurrentLap()>=totalLaps && aScript.isFinished==false)
        {
                finalPosition++;
        }
}
```

In Section 6.2.3, we looked at how the waypoint system is used by Car_Controller.js to count laps: when the player reaches the last waypoint, a flag is set to say that the lap is done (`lapDone`), then, as the player hits the start/finish line trigger, it counts as a completed lap. When this happens, the car controller script will call out to the game controller with this line:

```
gameControl.LapComplete(this, lapsComplete);
```

Above, the car controller script calls the `LapComplete()` function, passing in a reference to itself (`this`) and the number of laps that player has completed so far. The `LapComplete` function does a quick check to make sure that this player has not already finished the race, then it increases a counter called `finalPosition`. `finalPosition` is used to keep tabs on how many players cross the finish line. It's a quick and easy way of assigning final positions to players, since it will be increased only as they cross the finish line.

The next part of the script deals specifically with the user's car:

```
if(aScript.id==focusPlayerScript.id && doneFinalMessage==false)
        {
                // this is the player we want to focus on, so update the lap
                // counter but remember that the value coming in is the
                // number of laps completed by the player, not the current
                // lap, so we add one to it
                updateLapCounter(theLaps+1);

                if(theLaps==totalLaps)
                {
                        // race is finished! Tell this car to stop now
                        aScript.setUserInput(false);
                        aScript.setAIInput(true);
```

Note that, again, we are using the ID numbers. Here, we check to see if the player that just finished a lap is the player we are focused on (`focusPlayerScript`). If it is, we proceed to update the onscreen lap counter, then check to see whether or not we should finish the race for all players. The `updateLapCounter` function is a simple function of Game_Controller.js to update the onscreen lap counter UI. (We will cover this in full in Section 6.2.10.)

If this player is the focused player and its completed laps (currently held in the variable called `theLaps`) matches the value of `totalLaps`, we return a call to the object or script that called this function and tell it to stop accepting user input and to only accept AI input. This is, essentially, turning off the user input and having the computer control the car from there on. Having all of the cars continue to drive around after the race is done is common to the genre and has a nicer effect than just stopping the cars or fading out at the end of the race.

6.3.8 The Car Camera Script

Until the final version of our kart game example projects, the camera was simply parented to the player. In our final version, the camera gets its own script that makes it orbit nicely around the player—something we're more used to seeing in this type of game. Your camera is a hugely important part of the whole game and it is something often neglected by developers new to the genre.

How the camera moves around the player's car and its distance and rotation from the player will affect the way that your game feels to the user. For this example, we will put together a simple third-person camera script, but you should try to look at some commercially available racing games and take some notes on how the camera is used. Some racing games have the camera tight to the player's car, with slow orbital movement around it. This helps to lessen the sense of rotation and focus more on the direction that the player is travelling when the car turns (often making the car feel more controllable) than a slower orbiting camera. Slower orbiting cameras tend to focus the action more on the car than the direction it is heading (resulting in a sense of less control).

The settings on your camera can be used to enhance the type of experience you are hoping to deliver through your game. Never underestimate how much difference it makes and be sure to allow some time in your development schedule to experiment with several different parameters to find the best settings.

The camera code is based on the SmoothFollow.js script provided by Unity as part of the Standard Assets camera scripts.

```
@script AddComponentMenu ("Car Camera")
```

We haven't touched on `@script` so far, but it is such an important feature of Unity that it deserves a little time. `@script` tells the compiler that we are about to set an attribute. As well as `AddComponentMenu`, there are several options available to make the most out of scripting in Unity:

- `@script AddComponentMenu` will add a new entry to Unity's Component drop-down menu. This is great for creating reusable scripts or sharing them with other people. Once this command is in your script, you will be able to click on the Component menu and your script will appear in the list.

- `@script ContextMenu` (Figure 6.4) is accessible via the small button in the Inspector window. You can add commands to this menu that will call functions in your scripts:

  - `@ContextMenu ("Say Hello!")`

  - `function SayHello () {`

  - `Debug.Log ("Hello!");`
    `}`

  This would add a new option to the menu reading "Say Hello!," which when pressed would write "Hello!" to the Debug Console. You could, of course, change the function name or the contents of the function to anything you like. This is useful for scripts that may need to be manually updated through the editor or as a scene-editing tool after a script has affected something permanently.

- `@script ExecuteInEditMode` was covered in Section 6.2.2. When `Execute InEditMode` is assigned, the script will run in the editor as well as when the game is playing.

- `@script HideInInspector` stops a public variable from appearing in the editor. (As you probably know by now, when you declare a public variable, it will normally appear as an editable field in the editor's Inspector window.)

Figure 6.4. The Context menu of the Inspector window in the Unity editor.

- `@script NonSerialized` works if you don't need variables to appear in the editor and you have no need for them to be serialized (though it takes only a moment to serialize during declaration).

- `@script RPC` is specific to networking, and it means that the function may be called through the networking system. (Unless you are building multiplayer games using Unity's built-in networking system, you can ignore this one for now.)

- `@script RequireComponent` is useful when a script relies on another component, such as a physics component like rigidbody or perhaps a box collider. You can use the `RequireComponent` attribute to make sure that one gets added to the GameObject that has the script attached to it.

- `@script Serializable` allows you to embed a class with subproperties in the Inspector. It will be displayed in the same way that a Vector3 is. Write a simple class that contains the variables you would like to have available to set in the editor and place the `@script Serializable` call just before it. By serializing public variables, their values will be shown in the editor, available for editing via the Inspector window when the GameObject containing the script is selected. Values entered from the editor (via the Inspector window) will override those values provided as defaults by your script. Keep an eye on this, as it can sometimes cause confusion when changing public variable values.

Our camera script uses `@script AddComponentMenu` to add a car camera to the menu. In the Unity editor, click on Component and see it for yourself! It will be grayed out unless you have a GameObject selected that it can be applied to.

```
public function SetTarget (t : Transform) {
    target = t;
}
```

After the variable declarations in our camera script, the `SetTarget` function is up first. There's nothing complex about this at all; it takes a transform as a parameter and stores a reference to it in the variable named `target`. Perhaps unsurprisingly, `target` is the object that our camera will look at and follow around as the game is played, which means it is called by our game controller when the user's car is created.

```
function Start () {
    currentDistance = distance;
    myCam=Camera.main;
    myTransform=transform;
}
```

The `Start()` function sets up a few variables we will need in the main update loop of the script. The `currentDistance` variable is used as a temporary holder for the distance between the car and the camera during the main loop.

The `myCam` variable holds a reference to the main camera in the scene, which is the camera we will use to follow the player around. In this game, we only use a single camera (although there is nothing stopping you from adding more if you feel the need).

The `myTransform` variable is set to the transform of the GameObject that has the Car_Camera.js script attached to it. By caching a link to the transform, we don't have to look it up each time we need to reference it—a tiny performance boost that may make a difference in the long run.

```
function LateUpdate () {
    if (target) {
            // Calculate the current rotation angles
            wantedRotationAngle = target.eulerAngles.y;
            currentRotationAngle = myTransform.eulerAngles.y;
```

All of the camera calculations are made in the `LateUpdate()` function, which is called automatically by the engine after physics updates have completed. The reason it lives here is that we don't want to move the camera until after physics have been updated. If the camera moved prior to the physics update, the camera would be out of sync with the movements. We want everything to have finished updating before trying to follow them.

```
            // Damp the rotation around the y-axis
            currentRotationAngle = Mathf.LerpAngle
                            (currentRotationAngle,
                            wantedRotationAngle,
                            rotationDamping * Time.deltaTime);

            // Convert the angle into a rotation
            currentRotation = Quaternion.Euler (0,
                            currentRotationAngle, 0);
```

This function starts by taking the current rotation and working out a damped version of it with the `Mathf.LerpAngle` function. We use this damped angle for our camera rotation so that it will orbit around the player smoothly, rather than just being locked at a certain point in space behind the player. The resulting angle, as calculated by `LerpAngle`, will be somewhere between the current angle and the target angle.

`LerpAngle` interpolates between two numbers over a chosen time. (In this case, the two numbers are `currentRotationAngle` and `wantedRotationAngle`, with the time being `Time.deltaTime`.) Using `Mathf.LerpAngle` is a great way to interpolate between two angles, as it will wrap around 360 degrees correctly when required. For example, try to imagine that the current angle is 350 degrees and the angle we are aiming to get to is 10 degrees. We wouldn't want the rotation to go all the way around clockwise to reach its target (travelling all the way around from 350 down to 10); the best behavior would be to go from 350 up to 360, then to 10 degrees to reach the target rotation. `Mathf.LerpAngle` ensures that this happens correctly, which is why we use it here for the camera rotation.

Once we have a rotation angle, we convert it into a Euler angle. This happens because it is easier to set an Euler than to deal with quaternion angles (which, as any mathematician will tell you, were invented by scientists to drive game developers insane).

```
            targetPos = target.position + targetOffset;
            direction = currentRotation * (-Vector3.forward);
```

We set about copying the target transform's position to a variable named `targetPos` and adding on the `targetOffset` (a Vector3 set in the editor) to it. The `targetPos`

Figure 6.5. Before: The view looking straight at the player car.

variable represents the target position for the camera, which, rather than appearing at the same position of the car, will now have the offset applied to it to move it up. The `direction` variable will tell us which direction is backward from the car so that we can use it to move the camera back from the car.

```
myTransform.rotation = currentRotation;
myTransform.position = targetPos +
                       direction *
                       currentDistance;

myTransform.Rotate(20,0,0);
    }
}
```

The last part of the camera code sets the camera rotation to our `currentRotation` variable and positions the camera at the target position (`targetPos`), adding on the direction vector (`direction`) multiplied by `currentDistance`.

Figure 6.6. After: The view rotated up from the player car.

Finally, we rotate the camera on its *x*-axis a little so that the car is in the bottom third of the screen rather than the middle. This is a more desirable and conventional angle for the camera to sit in a kart-racing game (see Figures 6.5 and 6.6).

6.4 Choosing Random Textures for the Cars

Our car contains an array for holding textures, called `carTextures`. Open up the "iWhiskerKarts – Complete" project example. Now find the Car_Controller.js script within the "Scripts" folder and open it up. If you look near the top of the script, you will see the declaration for our `textures` array:

```
public var carTextures : Texture2D[];
```

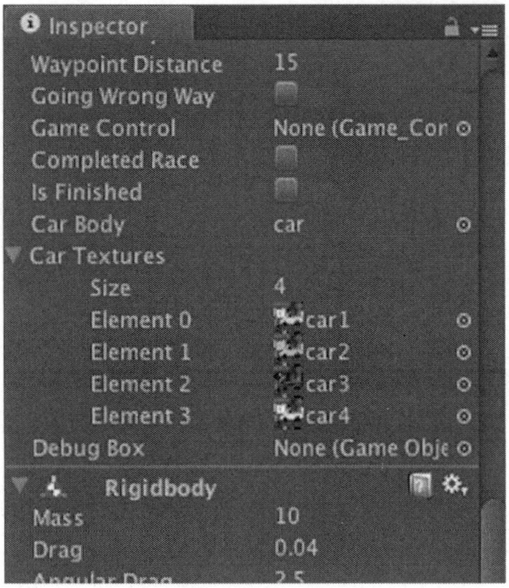

In the Project window of the Unity editor, find the Prefabs window and expand it. Inside that folder is the main car prefab named "player_car." Click on this to highlight it and take a look in the Inspector window. You may need to scroll down a little within the Inspector window, but you should be able to find the `carTextures` array and expand it to reveal its contents (if it is not already expanded). See Figure 6.7.

Figure 6.7. The car textures populating an array in the Inspector window of the Unity editor.

Each one of those textures was dragged and dropped from the Project window (more specifically from the "3DAssets/Textures/Car & Driver" folder of our project) to the Inspector one by one. We can access them through code easily by referring to the `carTextures` array in the usual way; for example, `carTextures[indexNumberOfTextureToUse]`.

Perhaps in your own kart games, you will provide the option for players to choose their textures for their cars. In this game, however, everything is random. It all happens through a single line of code in a function called `setCarTexture()`.

```
function setCarTexture ()
{
        carBody.renderer.material.mainTexture=carTextures[Random.
                                Range(0,carTextures.Length)];

}
```

The above code simply picks a random number between zero and the total number of textures in the array (`carTextures.Length`). Note that it references the car body model via the `carBody` variable, which is the mesh we want to change the material on.

A renderer contains at least one material. It is important to note that this is an instance of the material, not the original material you set up within the Unity editor.

The instance of the material is unique to that renderer, which means that changing its texture will only change the texture on that one renderer, not all of them. (To change the original material, you would need to use `renderer.sharedMaterial`, although this is not a recommended practice and Unity recommends that you stick to changing only individual materials.)

Once the function is in place to set our car to a random texture, all that is left to do is make a call to the function upon initialization. This now happens in the `Start()` function of the Car_Controller.js script, the final line of the function being:

```
setCarTexture();
```

6.5 Drawing the In-Game User Interface

The UI (shown in Figure 6.8) is a mix of GUIText objects and some graphics drawn from the `OnGUI` function within the Game_Controller.js script. In the level scenes, all of the GameObjects and components for UI can be found as children of the UI empty GameObject in the scene:

- `count_1`
- `count_2`
- `count_3`
- `lap`
- `position`
- `race_Complete`
- `wrong_way`

Figure 6.8. The game HUD (Heads Up Display) in the *iWhiskerKarts* game.

In all honesty, this is not the way that I would deal with UI on a commercial project. Time constraints and simplicity's sake have led to using this GUIText-based UI, but I would normally use many more images and most likely some kind of bitmap font for text display.

Each UI item represents an extra `draw` call for the engine to deal with, so it's not exactly the most efficient method either. By using a graphic-based system, it is possible to reduce the `draw` calls significantly. The easiest way to accomplish this would be to use one of the third-party libraries available from the Unity Asset Store, and, if you are going to go ahead with your own kart racer and you will be demanding more complex UI, that's exactly the route I would recommend until you are confident enough to build your own sprite management system.

Race position display. The race position indicator is a GUIText object. All that happens is that the car controller script calls on the game controller to update it, and the game controller simply resets the text of the GUIText object to reflect the current position:

```
function updateRacePositionText()
{
        posText.text="Pos "+focusPlayerRacePosition.ToString()+" of
                    "+numberOfRacers;
}
```

Race start counting in. There are three GUIText GameObjects used to display the count-down (which is displayed just before the race starts):

- `Count_1`,

- `Count_2`, and

- `Count_3`.

Open up the Game_Controller.js script in the "iWhiskerKarts – Complete" example project and look at the `Start()` function. Near the bottom of that function is where we deal with the countdown. I am still quite surprised by how simple this is to implement.

```
// start the game in 3 seconds from now
        Invoke("StartRace",4);
```

When the game controller script has finished creating the players and setting every-thing up for the race, the actual race doesn't start right away. It starts four seconds from the execution of the `Start()` function, as set up by the `Invoke("StartRace.,4);` statement.

```
// update positions throughout the race, but we don't need to do this every
// frame, so just do it every half a second instead
        InvokeRepeating("updatePositions",0.5,0.5);

        // hide our count in numbers
        hideCount();
```

The `InvokeRepeating` statement makes repeat calls like this an absolute breeze to do. We don't need to check and update the race position display every single update or frame, so we schedule the repeating `Invoke` call to update the race positions every half second instead.

The `hideCount()` function is called next, which hides all of the GUIText objects. (We'll look at the actual `hide` and `show` functions a little later in this section.)

```
// schedule count in messages
Invoke("showCount3",1);
Invoke("showCount2",2);
Invoke("showCount1",3);
Invoke("hideCount",4);
```

Yes, dealing with the countdown is really that simple! We just schedule calls to each function at one-second intervals until we reach the fourth second, at which point we make another call to `hideCount()` to hide everything as the race will be starting (remember that the call to `StartRace()` was scheduled to happen at four seconds).

```
// hide final position text
finalPositionText.gameObject.active=false;
doneFinalMessage=false;

// start by hiding our wrong-way message
UpdateWrongWay(false);
}
```

The other messages in our UI are incidental and only need to be active (displayed) when required. Here, we hide both the final position message and the wrong-way message. Later in the function, as the race completes, we will be setting the text of the final position message object (`finalPositionText`). We only need to do this once, so we have a simple Boolean flag called `doneFinalMessage` to make sure that happens.

Although Boolean variables will return false by default, I like to set them to false in initialization functions anyway. One reason for this is that we may, in the future, end up reusing the initialization functions to reset the game state (although in this particular game we don't), so it's good practice to keep things tidy in case we need them later.

If you're wondering how those `show` and `hide` functions work, it's really simple. Here are all of the functions we use for the countdown:

```
function showCount1()
{
        count1.active=true;
        count2.active=false;
        count3.active=false;
}
function showCount2()
{
        count1.active=false;
        count2.active=true;
        count3.active=false;
}
function showCount3()
```

```
{
        count1.active=false;
        count2.active=false;
        count3.active=true;
}
function hideCount()
{
        count1.active=false;
        count2.active=false;
        count3.active=false;
}
```

Setting a GameObject's active property to `false` both hides it from the scene and stops the regular `update` calls to any components attached to it. If other scripts call functions on those inactive scripts, the functions will still run, but automatically updated functions such as `Update`, `FixedUpdate`, or `LateUpdate` will not be called by the system.

Wrong-way indicator. The wrong-way indicator takes the form of a simple GUIText object. The game controller takes care of showing or hiding it whenever it detects that the angle of the player to its next waypoint is too far in either direction to be the right way (as seen in Section 6.2.4; see Figure 6.9).

The last time we looked at the wrong-way detection in the Car_Controller.js script, we left it having a simple `Debug.Log` message when the wrong way was detected, but in the final version, you will see this in its place (just under halfway down through the script):

```
if(oldWrongWay!=goingWrongWay)
        {
                // we need to update the UI
                gameControl.UpdateWrongWay(goingWrongWay);
        }
```

Figure 6.9. A wrong-way text object in the kart-racing game UI.

As you can see, when the state of whether or not we are going the wrong way changes, we make a call to the game controller's `UpdateWrongWay()` function to tell it what the current state is. Our game controller takes care of the display within that function, like this:

```
public function UpdateWrongWay(isWrongWay : boolean)
{
        if(isWrongWay)
        {
                wrongWaySign.SetActiveRecursively(true);
        } else {
                wrongWaySign.SetActiveRecursively(false);
        }
}
```

`SetActiveRecursively` is used to make GameObjects inactive or active, which may or may not have child objects under them. When you use `SetActiveRecursively`, it will make the specified object and all its child objects inactive (meaning they're no longer visible or running scripts).

Since we are referring to a GameObject, rather than a particular type of object like a text object or a graphic, the GameObject could take any form you like. If you wanted to use a GUITexture, you could. Or if it was a script that used `OnGUI` (not advisable because it will slow performance), you could. Or if you were using a separate third-party library to display 2D images, you could, and our code would stay the same. The type of object doesn't matter when we use `SetActiveRecursively`; it will just make the GameObject and its children inactive regardless.

Final race result message. At the end of the race, our users will want to find out which position they came in at. That's why we put up a huge text message to tell them if they finished in first, second, or third position. Anything after that just gets a "Race finished" message, instead.

That final result message is a single GUIText object that gets its text set at the end of the race by the game controller script. Each time the `LapCompleted()` function is called, it checks to see if the race has finished. (We discussed this in Section 6.2.3 when we dealt with player lap counting.) If you open up that script to take a look at it, scroll down to the section that deals with the final race result message:

```
if(theLaps==totalLaps)
                {
                        // race is finished! tell this car to stop now
                        aScript.setUserInput(false);
                        aScript.setAIInput(true);

                        if(finalPosition==1)
                                finalPositionText.text="FINISHED 1st";
                        if(finalPosition==2)
                                finalPositionText.text="FINISHED 2nd";
                        if(finalPosition==3)
                                finalPositionText.text="FINISHED 3rd";
                        if(finalPosition>=4)
                                finalPositionText.text="FINISHED";
```

```
                                     finalPositionText.gameObject.active=true;
                                     doneFinalMessage=true;

                                     Invoke("finishRace",10);
                            }
                   }
          }
```

In this code, we look to see if this player has finished the race by comparing `theLaps` to `totalLaps`. If this is true and the player has completed the right number of laps, it's time to display that final message and bring the race to a close. This couldn't be simpler, as we just check the `finalPosition` and set the text appropriately:

```
          if(finalPosition==1)
                   finalPositionText.text="FINISHED 1st";
```

Since `finalPositionText` is a GUIText object, to make it active and visible onscreen we need to quickly access its GameObject and set the active property:

```
          finalPositionText.gameObject.active=true;
```

Pedals. In the final version of our karts game, we have two pedals (one on either side of the screen) to show players where to press to accelerate and brake. The images are .png format, stored in the "2DAssets" folder of the project. They don't animate or do anything fancy, but they do provide users with a clue as to where to put their thumbs to make the karts go and stop. The two public variables, `acceleratePedalGraphic` and `brakePedalGraphic`, are set in the editor to reference our pedal images.

Using `OnGUI` is not recommended at all for Unity iOS due to how processor-intensive it is. That said, we only need to display two images, and our game is hardly pushing the limits of the device right now, so I would say that as long as we don't see a huge impact on the frame rate, it's okay to use.

Note that you should test your projects on older devices before making this conclusion! Just because it doesn't affect things on the iPad 2 doesn't mean that a second-generation iPhone won't crumble under the pressure. Of course, regardless of how you draw your UI, you should test on as many different devices and types of devices as possible!

```
public var acceleratePedalGraphic : Texture2D;
public var brakePedalGraphic : Texture2D;

function OnGUI()
{
          // okay, so this breaks the golden rule of iOS Unity dev, but using
          // OnGUI means that we can easily resize the GUI to fit different
          // resolutions. we are only using it for two UI elements, so the
          // performance impact (hopefully) won't grind the game to a
          // complete halt

          // first, enter the matrix to resize the GUI
          GUI.matrix = Matrix4x4.TRS (Vector3.zero, Quaternion.identity,
```

```
            new Vector3(Screen.width / 480f, Screen.height /
            320f, 1));
GUI.DrawTexture(Rect(25,240,32,64),brakePedalGraphic);
GUI.DrawTexture(Rect(430,240,32,64),acceleratePedalGraphic);
}
```

Our code starts out by setting up `GUI.matrix`. This is a 4 × 4 transformation matrix that, in the case of GUI, can be used to automatically resize everything drawn within the `OnGUI()` function to suit whatever screen resolution or aspect ratio is required. I am not even going to attempt to explain 4 × 4 transformation matrices—if you need to know that, please buy a math textbook. All we need to know is that we put in the desired width and height and the UI will automatically be proportionally scaled based on the correct proportion at that resolution. For example, non-retina iPhone resolution (in landscape view) is 480 × 320 pixels. Figures 6.10 and 6.11 show the iPhone landscape versus the iPhone portrait views and how it affects the scaling of the UI.

Again, if the game were scaled to any other resolution, the UI would appear in the same place proportionally, although the width and height of the elements would also be stretched proportionally, resulting in sometimes ugly results. On the other hand, if the aspect ratio doesn't change too much, it's a nice, quick way to deal with multiple resolutions!

Figure 6.10. The HUD stretched by an incorrect aspect ratio.

```
GUI.DrawTexture(Rect(25,240,32,64),brakePedalGraphic);
```

Drawing the texture is straightforward, with a call to `GUI.DrawTexture`. Here, we pass in a `Rect` object to define the rectangle we are going to draw (with *x* and *y* positions and height) and the 2D texture we want to draw (stored in the `brakePedalGraphic` variable).

Figure 6.11. The HUD at normal proportions, as it should look.

6.6 Sound Effects

The sound effects in our example project are very basic. We simply have an engine sound and a car crashing sound stored in a folder named "Audio."

The car engine audio is a single looped sample; its pitch is adjusted by Car_Controller.js. The crash sound is a single sample played by Crash_Sound_Controller.js when a collision happens; the sample script is capable of using multiple sounds and picking a random one.

To see how the sound is handled, open up the "iWhiskerKarts – Complete" example game project in Unity. Open a new scene (an empty scene via the menu File–>New Scene). In the Project window, find the "Prefabs" folder and drag the player_car prefab into the Scene View window to add it to the scene.

Audio in Unity is very straightforward but extremely powerful. Each scene needs one (and no more than one) *audio listener*, which is usually attached to the main camera so that the audio heard through the speakers matches up with the picture onscreen. An audio listener picks up the audio from audio source components, which are attached to objects in the 3D space. The listener or source system means that there is no extra work in creating great spatial audio, as the listener acts like an ear that, as the camera moves around the scene, will "hear" sources just as though they were in the real world.

Expand the player_car prefab in the Hierarchy window so that we can get to its child objects. In the Inspector, scroll down to see the AudioSource section. Notice that the audio clip is set to our engine sound file and that the "Play On Awake" and "Loop" checkboxes are checked so that the sound will play automatically and keep on playing through the game. Hearing a sound stuck at the same pitch all the way through the game wouldn't be much fun at all, so we change its pitch in the Car_Controller.js script. Find this script in the Project window and double click on it to open it in the editor.

Everything we need is contained in a single function, updateEngineSound(). Find this function.

```
function updateEngineSound()
{
        audio.pitch=0.5f+mySpeed*0.05f;
}
```

Changing the pitch of the attached audio component really is as simple as it looks. Since the audio source is attached to the same GameObject as the Car_Controller script, we can access it with audio. The updateEngineSound() function simply takes the speed of the car and applies some arbitrary multiplication to it to reach a value suitable for pitch shifting. As the car goes faster, the pitch is shifted up (and vice versa). We start at a pitch of 0.5 so that the engine sound idles at a reasonable pitch when the car is not moving (and, therefore, the value of mySpeed would be zero).

Our game world would feel very empty if there were no sound when we ram into the walls at full speed or collide with the opposition on the track. Unity makes it easy to know when a collision happens and to react to it. Find and double click the Crash_Sound_Controller.js script, from the "Scripts" folder in the Project window:

```
public var threshold = 10;
public var impacts : AudioClip[];
```

```
public var audioSourceGO : AudioSource;

private var whichCue : int;

function OnCollisionEnter (col : Collision) {
        // when our car has a collision, this function will be triggered.
        // here, we check the magnitude of the collision to see if it is
        // higher than our threshold, in which case we play one of the
        // crash sounds from our AudioClip array, impacts
        if (col.relativeVelocity.magnitude > threshold) {
        // pick random sound to play from our sound array
                whichCue=Random.Range(0, impacts.length);
                // tell our audio source to play a one-shot sound of our
                // chosen random sound
                audioSourceGO.PlayOneShot(impacts[whichCue]);
    }
}
```

The Crash_Sound_Controller.js script is applied to the car. Whenever a collision occurs, Unity automatically calls OnCollisionEnter() and passes in some information about the collision through the Collision class (information that we stored in the col variable in the script above). As a collision is reported to our function, col contains the following information:

- relativeVelocity—the relative linear velocity of the collision,

- rigidbody—the rigidbody hit by the object with this script attached to it,

- collider—the collider on the other object hit,

- transform—the transform of the object hit,

- gameObject—the GameObject of the object hit, and

- contacts—the contact points of the collision.

In our Crash_Sound_Controller.js script, we simply compare the relative Velocity to a number held in the threshold variable to decide whether or not to make the crash sound:

```
if (col.relativeVelocity.magnitude > threshold) {
```

The threshold variable can be tweaked higher to only react to crashes that occur at higher speeds, or lowered to catch slower crashes. If the condition is met, we choose a random sound to play from those sounds held in the impacts array (all of the sounds in the array have been dragged and dropped into the Inspector one by one):

```
whichCue=Random.Range(0, impacts.length);
```

The PlayOneShot function is used here, which is perfect for little incidental sounds like this. By using PlayOneShot, this script tells the audio source which sound to play so that we can play one of however many sounds are referenced in our audio clip array impacts. To keep things tidy, we use a dedicated audio source attached to the car rather than the one attached to the player_car GameObject. Another good reason for using a separate audio source is that we can modify its audio parameters (such as volume) without affecting the engine sounds.

The audio source we use is named "Crash_Sound_Source," and you can find it in the player_car prefab, parented to the root player_car object. This is just an empty GameObject with the *AudioSource component* attached to it. The GameObject is referenced in our Crash_Sound_Controller.js script by the variable `audioSourceGO`, and all we do to play the impact sound is call `PlayOneShot` on it:

```
audioSourceGO.PlayOneShot(impacts[whichCue]);
```

6.7 Making the Game Even Better

I am not going to pretend that this game is perfect or that it is ready to go on sale on the iTunes Store. Although it is a great framework and a starting point for racing games, there are a few extra things that it could do with before I would be ready to put it out for sale.

Of course, the sky is the limit, and there is nothing stopping anyone from swapping out the simple car physics for fully realistic ones or changing the game from a kart racer to a tuned car challenge. To close up this chapter, I offer you a list of suggested features that most commercial kart racers offer that our game currently does not:

- *Tire screeching sounds.* Hearing the car sliding around corners would make a big difference to the game experience. One way to handle it might be to have a screeching audio sound that loops and plays in the background all of the time. When the car slides, you set the volume of the looping screeching audio to an amount reflecting how much the car is sliding (such as a fraction of the `slideSpeed` variable). If you really wanted to get realistic, you could also set the pitch of the screeching sample based on how much the car is sliding.

- *Better UI.* Our UI is quite bland, using only text to display information. It would be much nicer to add fancy graphics such as a speedometer or a funky lap counter. If you don't fancy coding your own UI rendering system, you might want to consider a third-party solution to render nice bitmap fonts and graphics.

- *Stuck detection.* If an AI player crashes, a simple timing system should establish whether or not the player is stuck. If it is stuck, first we would try to have the car move in reverse to become free, continuing forward within a set time to continue the race. If this first attempt to free the AI player fails, we would reposition the player on the track, facing the right direction.

- *Lap timing.* A simple timer would make a great addition to the game, timing each lap and giving a total time to display at the end of the race.

- *Customization.* Letting your users customize their ride will go a long way to increase replayability and user satisfaction. Even if you are just swapping textures to have different colored cars, your users will appreciate it.

- *Level unlocking and achievements.* Everybody likes unlocking stuff and gaining achievements, so why not add some to your racing game?

- *Mini map.* Racers love maps. For an example of a really well put together mini map, check out the BootCamp demo included with Unity that will work with either Unity or Unity Pro (although you may have to do a little extra work to get it functioning on iOS). A mini map will require some advanced code in order for it to work correctly and you may also want to take a look on the Unity Asset Store for a ready-made solution, before setting out on your own.

- *Position checking for all players.* If you wanted to keep tabs on all player positions during the race, the `updatePosition()` function of the Game_Controller.js script could be easily modified to loop through all of the cars rather than just the player referenced by `focusPlayerScript`.

CHAPTER 7

Debugging and Script Optimization

7.1 Introduction to the Debugger

Games are very complex machines containing incredible amounts of logic, mathematics, art, and sounds—it goes without saying that bugs are inevitable. There are so many things that can go wrong, such as programming logic failures, collision mesh problems, graphic import problems, audio compression, and so on. All projects, even those carefully planned down to the tiniest detail with 1500-page design documents and development by professional teams, will experience bugs and go through a debugging phase.

Debugging is never easy and there may even be unsolvable problems that require creative workarounds to change or reduce the side effects of a particular bug. Today, there are an increasing number of games that ship with bugs, then release patches soon after, fixing all of the major issues that probably should have been fixed before the game launches. Debugging is a necessary and essential part of all software development, and the more tools you can get to help during the debug phase, the better.

7.2 Strategies for Wiping Out Bugs

Prior to Unity 3, there was no full debugger built into the engine, and the only debugging tools were those provided by Unity's Debug class. The process of finding and eliminating script bugs was difficult, as there was no way to stop and step through scripts line by line to find out what was happening. In Unity 3, developers were treated to a custom version of MonoDevelop with a new, built-in debugger as part of the Unity download package (Figure 7.1).

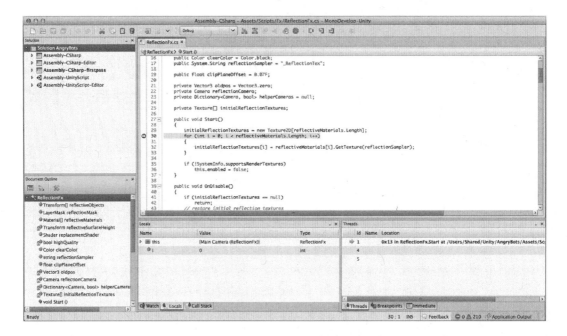

Figure 7.1. The Unity Debugger window.

Before the debugger, the most effective method for debugging was to use a Console log, whereby developers send messages and log them to a file. To track down a bug, you could add commands to the scripts to send unique messages to the Console; then, as soon as the error occurred, a developer could read through the Console to find out at which point the last message was sent. Through trial and error, messaging out to the Console makes it possible to narrow things down until you find the offending lines of code. Using the Console in this method of narrowing down is common for finding bugs. It is a convenient and fast way to track values and script activity and usually a good place to start when trying to find out where your script is going wrong. When Console debugging fails, however, then it's time to bring in the big guns: the Unity Debugger.

The Unity Debugger has been conveniently built into the version of MonoDevelop that ships as part of the Unity download. The Debugger allows you to place what are known as *breakpoints* into your scripts—essentially flags that you place on a particular line in one or more of your scripts to tell the game to stop running at a certain point so that you can examine the variables or follow the flow of your code step by step. By stopping at points where you suspect the bug might be happening, the Debugger is there to help you to track down and, in turn, eliminate those pesky bugs in the programming.

There are a few more tools that Unity provides through its Debug class, and we will look at those in Chapter 7.

7.3 Console Debugging

One important tool in the arsenal of debug weapons is the Console (Figure 7.2), which is a place to write log messages to use in diagnosing problems. It also contains messages,

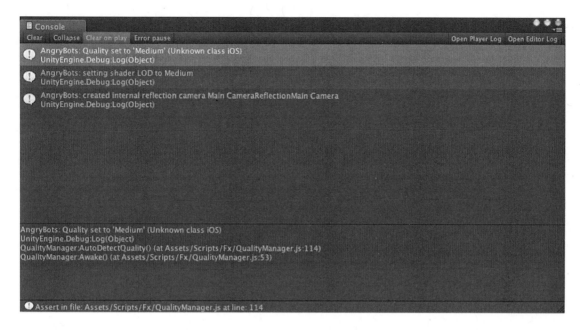

Figure 7.2. The Console window of the Unity editor.

warnings, or custom debug messages. In the Unity editor, the Console window is accessible either through the menu Window–>Console or by pressing CTRL + SHIFT + C (CMD + SHIFT + C on a Mac).

There are three different methods you can use to write to the Console, `Debug.Log()`, `Debug.LogWarning`, or `Debug.LogError()`:

- `Debug.Log` writes a regular message to the Console.

- `Debug.LogWarning` writes a message to the Console that will be flagged as a warning. When you view the Console, any messages written with `LogWarning` will have a little exclamation mark next to them. This function is useful for messages that are not important enough to stop the game completely.

- `Debug.LogError` logs an error in a similar way to how the Unity engine writes errors. Upon viewing the Console, `LogError`-made errors will show up in red.

You can use these log functions to send out Console messages including values of variables, object names, or system values (such as time or joystick input levels).

When you first write complex scripts (or scripts that you think may take a little revising to get right), include some debug lines as a part of their development. When you run the script for the first time, take a look at the Console to ensure that everything is flowing as expected.

Keep your debug messages relatively detailed or, at least, detailed enough that you will be able to find them or make sense of them later on. I like to follow the format below, which helps me to know exactly where things are happening:

```
Debug.Log("<script name>/<function name>/<what is happening>");
```

For example:

```
Debug.Log("gameControl/Start/Calling Init()");
```

A common error you may experience is called a *null exception*. This is when a variable has a null value and a script tries to access it as though it contains an object or script reference. Beware when you are writing to the Console that you don't try to write null variables, as it will raise an error and stop the game. Null references can sometimes be difficult to track, but you can reduce risk by checking for them whenever you try to access objects; use something like this:

```
if(<object>==null){
        Debug.Log("<object> was null.");
} else {
        <do whatever you need to do>
}
```

When you are experiencing a bug with no error reporting back from the engine, or perhaps a null exception error, the objective is first to discover where the crash is happening so that you can look at why. Place regular Console debug messages in any scripts you think might be causing the problem, making sure to keep them unique so that they are easily identifiable.

If you are trying to trace values that are often the same, add a *time stamp* to your debug messages to keep them unique; for example:

```
Debug.Log("Something happened at "+Time.theTime);
```

Try to avoid statements with multiple objects, such as this:

```
theName = monster.monsterGameObject.transform.position;
```

These types of chained object statements can sometimes fail silently, meaning that it may not report any kind of an error and will sometimes just stop running or ignore the line of code and continue even though it is broken. This can lead to strange crashes or null exceptions, so it is safer to use something more like the example below, which also makes it easier to log any null exceptions to the Console:

```
                theMonsterRef = monster;
                if(theMonsterRef!=null){
theMonsterGO = monster.monsterGameObject;
                        if(theMonsterGO!=null){
theMonsterTransform = theMonsterGO.transform;
                                thePosition = theMonsterTransform.position;
```

```
} else {
        Debug.Log("theMonsterGO was null");
}
} else {
        Debug.Log("Monster was null.");
}
```

7.3.1 Managing the Unity Console Data

When you are logging a lot of content to the Console, it can sometimes be a little over-whelming to sort through and get the information you need. The Console window has several helpful functions to help you use it more effectively.

Along the top of the Console window, there are several buttons (Figure 7.2):

- *Clear.* To clear the Console completely and wipe out all messages, this is the button to press. Its content will still have been written out to a physical log file, but the Console window will be cleared out.

- *Collapse.* Sometimes, you may end up pushing many of the same messages to the Console. For example, if you were dumping the value of a variable to find out when it changes, you could easily send out hundreds or thousands of the same value. Searching through that would be a tedious task and the collapse function is here to help! If multiple messages with the same content are written to the Console, when the Collapse toggle button is selected, only one of the messages will be shown. This makes it much easier to deal with duplicate messages.

- *Clear on Play.* When the Clear on Play toggle button is selected, all previous log entries will be cleared when the Play button is pressed. If the Clear on Play button is not depressed, messages will stack up between plays until you choose to clear them out.

- *Error Pause.* If Error Pause is selected, `Debug.LogError` messages will pause the engine. This is useful for tracking important events.

- *Open Player Log.* This opens the player log. This is a log file containing all of the messages written to the Console either by the system or by debug messages.

- *Open Editor Log.* The editor log is a text file written by the editor and containing editor messages. Most of its content can be ignored, but it will also contain some information about loading and unloading objects from memory. If you are having problems within the editor, this may be a good place to check.

7.3.2 Basic Console-Based Debugging with Xcode and Your iOS Device

When your game runs from Xcode and the device is plugged in via USB, its default state is to relay debug information back to Xcode's Console (Figure 7.3). Messages from the Unity engine (those seen in the editor log, such as initialization messages and warnings) and any debug messages from your game will appear.

Figure 7.3. The Console window in Xcode.

The principle for Console debugging in Xcode is the same as it was for debugging within Unity, in that your objective is to lay out `Debug.Log` messages in enough places in the code to be able to identify where a failure might be occurring. By writing out variable values, time stamps, or notifications of the names of functions being executed, you should eventually be able to narrow down the location of where a problem is happening.

Under some circumstances, there may well be errors that show up on the iOS device that may not be apparent in the editor. These types of issues are the worst to track down, as you need to compile a new build every time you try out a new solution or add new debug messages. When something like this happens, it is easy to jump to the conclusion that if an error happens on the device but not in the editor, it must be caused by some kind of bug in Unity itself. This is not necessarily true; often these kinds of issues may be a result of a change in the operating environment's changing variables such as frame rate, input systems (accelerometers, touchscreen, etc., versus using the Unity Remote in the editor), or a number of other factors like restricted memory or slower graphics processing.

If you hit something like this, remember that debugging is a process in game development and it is a normal process that may sometimes require a lot of patience. It takes time. Make a cup of tea and settle in—sometimes, you just can't rush it.

7.3.3 How to Use the Debugger

Unity uses the *MonoDevelop IDE* for debugging, which is provided free of charge with the Unity download. It doubles as your script editor and debugging solution, providing the functionality to edit, stop, and execute C#, JavaScript, or Boo code line by line or to watch as it is executed and see its effect on variables in real time. Sadly, however, the debugger doesn't have a magic Fix All Bugs button, and there is actually an amount of work involved in tracking down and eliminating issues.

The debugger is an advanced feature and there is a great guide to using it in the official Unity documentation, so let's go through the very basics to give you a taste for it; if you need more info, I would highly recommend taking a read through Unity's own guide.

Sync the project. To use the debugger, your project needs to be synced with the MonoDevelop project. This will already have happened if you have used MonoDevelop before, but if this is the first time using it with your project, you need to go through and sync up via the menu Assets−>Sync MonoDevelop Project.

Set your breakpoints. When you use the debugger, you need to tell it where to stop running and to start debugging. A debugger will not tell you where the bugs are happening, and you will need to know, at least roughly, which scripts could be causing problems. By adding breakpoints at key points in the script, you can analyze the variables within it and step through the code execution line by line.

To add a breakpoint, open the script in MonoDevelop (if it is not already open). Add a breakpoint by clicking to the far left of the Script window (see Figure 7.4). A red bullet point should appear, and a red background will highlight the line of code next to it. When the engine executes the highlighted line of code, playback will stop and you will be able to check variables' values at that time.

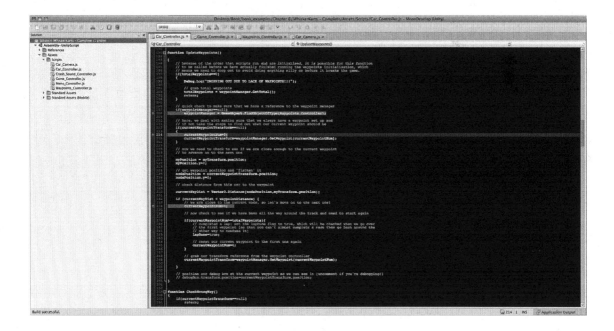

Figure 7.4. Breakpoints in the MonoDevelop IDE.

Attach the debugger. For MonoDevelop to be able to talk to your game, it needs to be connected to it. There are two ways to debug. One is to debug in the editor, and the other is to debug a player. To debug in the editor, you need to tell MonoDevelop to launch Unity for you (assuming that you do not have Unity open already); to debug the player, attach the debugger to an already running instance of Unity or to an instance of a player, such as a web player in a browser. The only difference between debugging through the Unity IDE and debugging through a player is in the way that you attach the debugger to the game.

To debug a game running in Unity, click the Attach to Process button at the top of the MonoDevelop IDE. When the Attach To Process window appears, an item named "Unity editor" should be one of the options under Process. Click on it to highlight Unity editor, then click the Attach button.

To debug a player, start the player running, then click on the Attach to Process button at the top of the MonoDevelop IDE. When the Attach to Process window appears, one of the options under Process should be your player. Click on it to highlight the player and click the Attach button.

Squash bugs! Once the debugger is successfully attached to the game process, you will be able to play the game up until the point where those breakpoints you added earlier are hit by the runtime engine. At that point, everything will freeze and the expected behavior is that MonoDevelop will automatically appear onscreen. If this is not the case, you will know when it is time to go back to MonoDevelop when the Game window freezes. Do *not* close the game! Keep it open as you bring up the MonoDevelop IDE.

MonoDevelop should automatically open up in its Debug View. If not, use the menu View–>Debug. Figure 7.5 shows the Debug window.

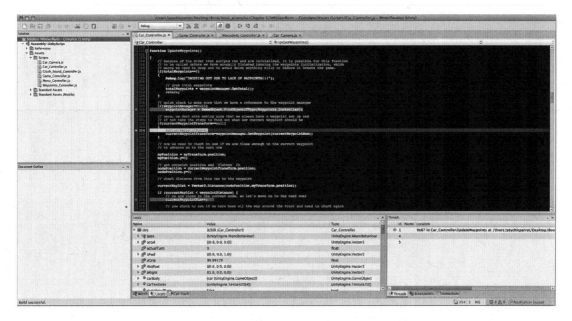

Figure 7.5. The Debug View in the MonoDevelop IDE.

Figure 7.6. The Debugger window buttons in the MonoDevelop IDE.

In the main Script window, the line at which the breakpoint occurred will be highlighted. Below the Script window, on the left side is the Variable window. This is where you can view all of the local variables and check their values at the time the breakpoint was hit. There are three tabs on this window: Watch, Locals, and Call Stack.

Under the Locals tab, the Variable window will display the script instance named "this." Expand it to show all of the variables belonging to the script instance and their values.

Under the Watch tab, you can tell the debugger to watch specific variables. Once you have added variables to the watch list, you can step over, into, and out of your scripts and see them change as the code is executed.

The Call Stack tab will help you to establish from where in the class the current function has been called. For example, the UpdateWaypoints() function in our racing game's Car_Controller.js script is called by the LateUpdate() function, so the Call Stack will show both UpdateWaypoints and LateUpdate in the list.

How you go about chasing the bugs from here depends on how your script is set up and how you like to work. Essentially, debugging is all about watching the variables to find out where their values are going wrong and watching the way in which the scripts are executed to make sure that your conditional statements (if, else, etc.) are doing what they should. The main tools in your arsenal are the Variable Watcher, the Call Stack, and the three buttons to move execution of the code forward (Figure 7.6).

The little icon that looks like gears (on the left of Figure 7.7) is the Debug or Continue button, depending on whether or not you are currently debugging. If you are not debugging, the Debug button will start the debugging process. Note that if you do not have Unity open, clicking on the Debug button will open a new instance of Unity for you and attach the debugger; if you have Unity open but you have not attached the debugger to it, clicking on the Debug button will open another instance of Unity. Running two instances of Unity at the same time is not advisable,

Figure 7.7. The three debugger buttons.

as you can run into all kinds of problems with overwriting files, etc. If you find that you have two copies of Unity open, close the debugger and both copies of Unity, then start the debug setup process again to be safe.

Once you have finished debugging, you can click the Continue button to go back to executing the code. The game will then run until another breakpoint is hit (or the function containing the current breakpoint is called again, and, therefore, the current breakpoint is hit again). If you do not want the script to hit the same breakpoint again, you can remove it from the Script window before pressing the Continue button.

To the right of the Continue button is the red Stop button. This will stop all debugging. Unity will return to regular playback without the debugger attached and you can continue to play through the game normally.

Alongside the Stop button are three Step buttons. When you are trying to track down a bug or watch variables, you may not always want to execute the code line by line; in some situations you may need to skip to the end of a loop, for example. The three Step buttons tell the debugger to deal with execution differently. From left to right, their functionality goes like this:

- *Step Over* executes the current line of code and stops again at the next line. If the next line is a function call or a loop, the debugger will move over it (hence the name, Step *Over*) and stop on the next line of code after the function call or loop. The game engine will execute the skipped code, but the debugger will ignore it until either another breakpoint is hit (which could be within the function call or loop) or the next line of code after the end of the loop or function call is reached.

- *Step Into* executes the current line of code and stops again at the next line. This button is different than Step Over in the way it continues execution after the current line of code; if the next line of code is a loop or a function call, the debugger will continue onto the specified function or loop and stop on its first line of code.

- *Step Out* will step out of the current function or loop and up one level, if it is nested. If the debugger is in the function that had the original breakpoint in it, the script will be executed to the end or until the next breakpoint is hit. The game engine will still execute the skipped code, but the debugger will ignore it until the next breakpoint.

7.3.4 Using the MonoDevelop Debugger with an iOS Device

To be able to use the MonoDevelop debugger with Unity iOS games, you need to carry out some extra steps. The following is an excerpt from the Unity documentation[1] on the subject:

- Attach your iDevice to your Wi-Fi network (the same requirement as for remote profiling).

- Hit Build and Run in the Unity editor.

- When the application builds, installs, and launches via Xcode, click Stop in Xcode.

- Manually find and launch your application on your iDevice. (Note: if the application is launched via Xcode, you will not be able to resume after reaching a breakpoint.)

- When the app is running on the device, switch to MonoDevelop and click on the Attach icon in the debugging toolbar. Select your device from the avail-

---

[1] http://unity3d.com/support/documentation/Manual/Debugger.html

able instances list. (If there are several instances shown, then select the bottom one.)

Once the debugger is attached to the process, you should be free to use it in exactly the same manner as debugging with the Unity editor (as explained in Section 7.3.3).

7.4 Retrieving PlayerPrefs and Application-Specific Files from an iOS Device

If you are saving data using `PlayerPrefs` or file writing to `Application.dataPath` or `Application.PersistantDataPath`, you may need to check their output and make sure that the game is writing the correct data.

The easiest method to check the output is to run the game in the editor and check the files it saves locally. From the editor, `Application.dataPath` or `Application.PersistantDataPath` will write to `<path to project folder>/Assets`. `Player Prefs` will write to a different location, depending on whether you are using Windows or a Mac. Here is what the Unity documentation says about it:

> On Mac OS X PlayerPrefs are stored in ~/Library/Preferences folder, in a file named unity.[company name].[product name].plist, where company and product names are the names set up in Project Settings. The same .plist file is used for both Projects run in the Editor and standalone players.

> On Windows standalone players, PlayerPrefs are stored in the registry under HKCU\Software\[company name]\[product name] key, where company and product names are the names set up in Project Settings.

That's great for the editor, but what if you need to get the preferences or data files from the iOS device itself? To do that, you will need to be on your development-ready Mac system:

- Open up Xcode, and once it is fully loaded, click on the menu Window–>Organizer (Figure 7.8).

- Highlight your device from the list on the left.

- Underneath your device are several headings. Select Applications.

- A list of installed applications (the ones you have built and installed) will appear on the right. Select your app.

- Underneath the selected app is the Data Files in Sandbox window. Select Library and click the Download button below it. When prompted, save the file somewhere easy to remember.

Navigate to the saved files and notice that it has saved in some kind of format that is not accessible (a .xcappdata format file). If you cannot see the .xcappdata file extension on this file, make sure that the finder is set to show all filenames. To do this, open the finder and go to the menu Finder–>Preferences, then click on the Advanced tab and check the box next to "Show All Filename Extensions."

Figure 7.8. The Organizer window in Xcode.

To change the file to a readable format, click on the filename and remove the whole file extension (all of the .xcappdata part). Once you have changed the file extension, the file's icon will change to a folder and you can go ahead and open it just like a regular folder.

Opening the folder, you should see an AppDataInfo.plist file and an "AppData" folder. Click on the "AppData" folder to open it. Within AppData, there are several folders. The one you want to open is the "library" folder.

Inside the "library" folder, you should find the "preferences" folder, which contains the .plist file—your game's preference file. By default, these .plist files will open up in Xcode and you can go through and analyze the output from `PlayerPrefs` to your device. This is a one-way system, however, and you can't write preferences back to the device without specialized software to browse and write files directly to the device.

7.5 Script Optimization

There are a few tricks that every Unity iOS developer should know about when it comes to optimization. Several apparently small changes can turn out to make a big difference to the speed at which your game runs, and in this section, we will look at some of the most dramatic. While some of the optimizations may not appear to have an immediate effect when applied to less CPU-intensive projects, in the long run, your projects will run smoother and potentially faster if you adhere to them.

7.5.1 Avoid Instancing to Prevent Stalls with Garbage Collection

Allocating a new chunk of memory every time a script is run is a sure-fire method to making an iOS game run badly. Consider this line of code:

```
Vector3 newPosition = new Vector3(0,0,0);
```

Every time this line of code is run, a chunk of memory gets allocated to store the value of `newPosition`. When garbage collection happens (the process of clearing out unused memory), if there are a lot of things to clear out, there will be a stall or glitch as the clearing out process happens. iOS, with its limited memory and processing power, makes this a lot more prevalent, and your game will literally pulse horribly if garbage collection begins to struggle.

The second part of the above line of code also makes a fatal mistake in creating a new vector object and assigning it a value of 0,0,0. The more efficient method is to use `Vector3.zero`, which doesn't require a new instance to be used every time.

7.5.2 Avoid String Comparisons

Comparing strings is expensive. A few comparisons here and there may not appear to have much of an impact, but there is a whole bunch going on behind the scenes that will eventually negatively affect your performance, so just avoid them wherever possible.

It can take a little imagination to solve problems without string comparisons, but it is possible. Using enums or representing strings with numbers are two ways to get around it.

7.5.3 Use Layers Rather than Tags for Trigger Checking

If you are checking a collision to find out which objects collided the easiest, a solution may look something like this:

```
If(hit.gameObject.tag=="enemy")
        doDeath();
```

A much more efficient way of doing it would be to use layers to identify object types instead:

```
If(hit.gameObject.layer==12) // layer 12 is reserved for enemies
        doDeath();
```

This can get a little confusing when you reach higher numbers of different objects and you have to identify each one by a number, but if you keep your code nicely commented to state what each layer is, you should be okay. A little code commenting goes a long way!

7.5.4 Avoid Using Calls to OnGUI during Game Play

Unity's built-in GUI functions are not at all optimized for mobile use and, as a result of this, using them is not advised. At the time of writing, Unity's GUI system is far from ideal. It is a code-based system, which is great for getting things going quickly, but not very good at all for anything other than basic UI. On top of that, the built-in GUI system that Unity offers will grind iOS games to a halt with anything more than a few elements. (This goes a long way in explaining the success of third-party GUI libraries!)

For the best results, you should either write your own quad-based UI system, try to use GUIText objects and GUITexture objects (via the GameObject–>Create Other –>GUI Text or GUI Texture menu), or consider a third-party solution.

7.5.5 Lowering the Physics (Fixed) Time Steps to Improve Frame Rate

Physics are calculated independently of your games frame rate. To ensure that the simulation runs correctly (and is stable), the engine needs to update physics calculations at fixed intervals. By running x number of times per second, we can be sure that the physics simulation will be the same across all devices, regardless of what is happening with the frame rate.

The more times the physics engine updates, however, the harder the processor has to work to update the game. More steps lead to a more accurate physics simulation, but more load on the CPU. Fewer steps lead to increased performance, but with a greater chance of unstable physics simulation. That said, there are times when you can get away with fewer updates without any diverse effects, releasing some CPU cycles and boosting performance.

To change physics timing properties, in the editor open the menu Edit–>Project Settings–>Time (Figure 7.9). The Inspector window will show the available timing variables and you should be able to click on them and change their values. We need to look at the `Fixed Timestep` value. Its default number is 0.02, but I have seen games that didn't rely on physics running perfectly fine at 0.1 with interpolation.

As an experiment, try lowering the physics steps in your project (noting the original value, just in case you have to go back) and see what happens. If the movement starts to become jerky, you may be able to solve this by turning on interpolation on your rigid-bodies, meaning that the physics are smoothed out between updates. If you are running the physics engine with lower steps, interpolating the movement of the rigidbodies should give you a smooth result to a point.

Experiment with this value and see if you can free up some CPU.

Figure 7.9. The Time window in the Unity editor.

7.6 An Introduction to the Profiler (Pro-Only Feature)

7.6.1 What Is the Profiler?

The profiler is an advanced tool for finding out all kinds of important information about your system resources during playback. It can be used to profile CPU, rendering, memory, audio, and physics so that you can find ways to optimize toward a better-performing game.

Open the final example racing project in the Unity editor and press the Play button. As the game runs, go through the menu Window−>Profiler to open the Profiler window (Figure 7.10). After a short period of time, the Profiler begins to fill up with performance data as it is recorded.

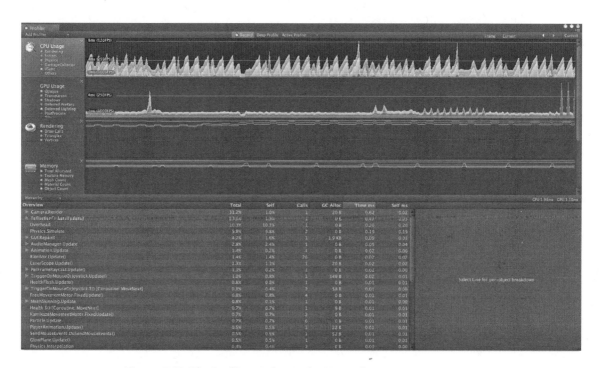

Figure 7.10. The Profiler window in the Unity editor.

7.6.2 What Do the Squiggles Tell Me?

The profiler takes the form of a timeline, showing the performance data recorded from the time it was launched to the present moment. The vertical white line shows where on the timeline the currently displayed data has come from, and you can move this to focus on data from any recorded time by clicking wherever you would like.

As seen in Figure 7.10, to the left of the timeline are the profilers, each one representing the types of information being recorded during profiling. You can reorganize them (by dragging them around), delete them, or add new profilers from the Add

Profiler drop-down menu in the top left of the Profiler window. There are a number of profilers available:

- *CPU Usage* shows how time is spent in the game and which tasks (or at the very least, which type of tasks) are taking up the CPU during playback.

- *Rendering* will record data related to rendering, such as the number of draw calls, triangles, VRAM usage, etc.

- *Memory* records total allocated memory, texture memory, and object count (the total number of objects created in memory).

- *Audio* captures the number of audio sources playing in the scene at that time (playing sources), the number of paused audio sources (paused sources), the number of audio channels being used, and the amount of memory being used by audio.

- *Physics* records the number of active rigidbodies and the number of contacts between rigidbodies.

The buttons across the top of the Profiler window are as follows:

- *Record* toggles on or off performance data recording.

- *Deep Profile* profiles your code down to every function call. When deep profiling is on, only the overall classes will be recorded. Deep profiling will impact performance significantly, as it will be recording every function call across every script. In some cases, where complex scripting is employed, it may not even be possible to use deep profiling at all.

- *View SyncTime* gives you more information on wait times. If your game runs at a fixed frame rate or vsync is enabled, there may be an amount of time where the engine waits between frames. By default, this number is hidden, but you can turn it on or off using this button.

- *Active Profiler* can be used to profile both the Unity editor and external players (such as a web players or iOS players). This drop-down lists available players and allows you to choose one for profiling.

7.6.3 Using the Profilers

First, the bad news: the profiler does not automatically make your game work better and run at a higher number of frames per second. The good news is that the profiler will help to find out which parts of your game are using up the most resources so that you can target them for optimization.

As the profiler begins to capture information, it should quickly become apparent which processes are using the most resources and, if you arrive at the profiler looking for reasons as to why your game might be underperforming, it is usually quite straightforward to find bottlenecks. Be sure that your profiler captures performance data from the parts of your game you are specifically interested in finding out about by playing the game as it records. Once the profiler has been recording data for a while, you can begin to work through the data. Look toward the areas that have the highest time percentages (look to the Totals column) in the profiler's Hierarchy window. Those are the ones you need to examine for potential optimization—but if your game is performing well on its target machines, only a minimal number of passes should be necessary through the profiler and you should be careful not to get too wrapped up in trying to fix problems that simply are not there just because the profiler shows several items with high percentages. There will always be some items that will end up higher than you would like, and there are usually trade-offs involved. The trick is, as you attempt to fix performance in one area, don't ruin performance in another.

As per the mantra elsewhere in this book, keeping the draw calls as low as possible will go a long way in iOS game performance. Avoid transparencies where possible and try to keep the triangle and vertex counts to acceptable levels. If you are still seeing performance issues, they should become apparent quickly in one of the profilers. Of particular interest should be the time spent in your own functions. Also, when doing a deep profile, look to see how much time is spent drawing GUI if you decide to use Unity's built-in GUI system.

7.6.4 Profiling Live on the iOS Device

One of the most amazing features of the profiler is its ability to run live on the iOS device and display the recorded information in the Unity editor.

To enable profiling on your iOS device, start by connecting it to your Mac development machine via USB cable. Connect the iOS device to the same Wi-Fi network as your Mac development machine. Wi-Fi is used to carry profiling data from the device to the Unity editor. In the Unity editor, open the Build Settings window (via the menu File–>Build Settings) and check the "Autoconnect Profiler" checkbox.

Click Build and Run to build the game. When Xcode appears (assuming that the build was successful), make sure that the target scheme is set to the name of your device (the scheme is in the top left of the window) and click the Play button to begin playback.

Once the app has copied over onto the device, return to the Unity editor on your development Mac and open up the Profiler window (menu Window–>Profiler). The profiler should begin recording data immediately, and you can proceed with profiling in the same manner you would if it were profiling in editor playback. If the Profiler does not connect to the device automatically, you should use the Active Profiler drop-down menu to select your device from the list.

CHAPTER 8

///

Optimizing for File Size and Performance

8.1 Texture Import Settings

Making your game work on the iOS device is one thing, but making it work well and look good can sometimes be one of the most challenging things about iOS development. In this chapter, you will learn about some of the tricks that will help your iOS game to be more efficient and perform better on the device.

At the time of writing, the Unity engine itself uses up around 60 MB of memory (often referred to as its *memory footprint*) on an iOS device. On an iPad 3 with its 1 GB of RAM, this is no problem, but on an iPhone 3G, that's nearly half of your memory budget eaten up. This leaves you with just 68 MB for music, sound, 3D models, textures, and other game assets. If you are aiming to support older iOS devices such as the iPhone 3G or iPod Touch third generation, you are more than likely going to have to compress things—from audio to textures.

Building a 2D game makes the task of image compression a lot more difficult, as there will often be a high number of different textures for sprites and backgrounds. Naturally, you are going to want to try and keep the quality as high as possible, but if your solution is to use uncompressed images, you could be looking at filling up the memory quicker than you can say "this development stuff is hard work."

When your game is suffering from memory problems, it's usually quite easy to tell. Often, it will just silently crash. When your game silently and mysteriously disappears with no explanation, the first place to look is at how much memory it is using, because the most likely explanation is that it's just too much for the device.

Back in Section 3.2, we looked at the build settings area and learned that there are a few methods that Unity provides to improve performance and reduce physical file size. We will look at these again in a little more detail, and by the end of the chapter, you should have the knowledge to make your game more of a streamlined, memory-efficient experience without losing too much in the way of quality.

8.2 Why Compression Is Important

Getting your image compression settings just right takes time, and you should be sure to account for this whenever you are timetabling a game project. The polish and optimization stage of development is key in producing great games. If you've just spent six months building your dream, making it look great, and tweaking the feel of everything until you think your game is ready, the last thing you want to do is rush it out the door without optimizing things.

There are several reasons that optimization and compression are so important to the success of your game:

- Your game should perform as well as it can on as many devices as possible, including devices that may be a few years out of date.

- You should try to make your game download as quickly as possible once buyers have purchased it.

- Your game must take up as little space on the user's devices as possible. When the device gets full, larger games might be the first to go.

- You need your game to avoid maxing out the memory of current generation iOS devices, as it may result in Apple rejecting it during review. At the time of writing, the current gen is made up of the iPad 3 with its 1 GB of RAM, the iPhone 4S with 512 MB, and the iPod Touch (fourth generation) with just 256 MB.

Without optimizing and compressing, you may be failing in one of these areas. Let's try to hit as many of them as we can. A happy customer can be your most powerful sales force, as well as the first customer of your next game.

Developing on fast, high-end systems usually means that you develop games for fast, high-end systems. When I work on browser-based games, I use a computer that is at least a few years old. When I am working on iOS games, I try to test frequently on the oldest device that I can find. (Up until its recent demise, my lowest common denominator test machine used to be a first-generation iPod.) It means that development gets a little harder as you try to allow for both ends of the performance spectrum, but your market substantially increases if you retain lower-end machines. It makes sense to try to cater to them by optimizing wherever you can.

8.3 Quality versus Quantity: What's Available and What's It About?

When it comes to optimizing your textures, there is almost always a compromise required. You cannot compress images without degradation in quality, but if you want your 20-MB texture to come down to 2 MB, that's just what you are going to have to deal with. The trick is to try and build your game so that optimization is possible without being too noticeable, using tricks such as reducing the amount of alpha transparency in textures so that you can use a nonalpha compression system, or using texture atlases to put everything onto a single texture rather than several separate ones.

Select your texture in the Project window to bring up the texture settings in the Inspector window as shown in Figure 8.1. As you plan and build out assets for your game (both 3D textures and UI textures), you should keep optimization in mind. Wherever you can reuse a texture, wherever you can share a texture, or wherever you can use a solid texture rather than an alpha transparency, you should.

In Unity iOS, there are a number of image compression settings available to you (although you may only end up using three or four of the main ones). We will get to that in a moment, but for now, let's take a look at the presets and options that Unity offers for textures.

Preset texture settings are organized into several types. What Unity has done is provide those texture types to help you to easily get the right settings for the right applications. With a texture highlighted in the Project window, the first drop-down in the texture importer (within the Inspector window) is Texture Type. Texture types are:

- Texture. This is intended for use with a texture applied to a mesh. There are a limited number of modifiable properties under this texture type.

- Normal map. Under this setup, Unity will automatically turn off all color channels so that the assigned texture becomes suitable for real-time normal mapping.

- GUI. Using the GUI type will set up your texture to be as crisp as possible and perfect for display through an orthographic camera for GUIs or HUDs.

- Reflection. This method of reflection is often called *cube mapping*. It is used with a specific shader to simulate reflective surfaces, such as chrome.

Figure 8.1. The image importer in the Inspector window of the Unity editor.

- Cookie. Use this if your texture is going to be a Cookie for your lights.

- Lightmap. This offers parameters specifically relevant to textures used for lightmapping.

- Advanced. Under this setting, you will have access to all of the available parameters that the Unity texture importer has to offer.

Note that some texture types only provide access to particular properties of the texture importer in an effort to remain authentic to the overall theme's parameters. For example, the `texture` texture type only allows you to change the `Alpha`, `Max size`, and `Format` values, whereas the `advanced` type allows you to change a lot more. The Format drop-down, within the `texture` texture type, has only three options, whereas the `advanced` type has no less than 15.

The compression format you choose from the Format drop-down of the texture importer will have a huge impact on the size of your image and how much RAM it will use once it gets to the iOS device. There are a number of different compression options available, but before we get to those, let's take a quick look at how images are dealt with in Unity and what potential gotchas there may be.

The physical size of textures makes a huge difference to their uncompressed size because data is stored about every pixel that goes to make up an image. Mipmapping also increases texture sizes by around 33%, as it creates different versions of your texture to be used at different distances from the camera. The *color depth* determines how much color data we need to store for each pixel, which means that if you can use smaller textures with a lower color depth (16 bit rather than 32 bit), you can substantially lower the image size.

Compression	Memory consumption (bits per pixel)
RGB 16 bit	2 bpp
RGB 32 bit	4 bpp
RGBA 16 bit	2 bpp
RGBA 32 bit	4 bpp
PVRTC	2 bpp
Alpha PVRTC	4 bpp

Total texture size = width × height × bpp.

Note that the size of an image saved on a disk (the file size as reported by the finder or Windows Explorer) can differ wildly due to the amount of memory that the same image takes up once it is imported into the Unity engine. For example, if you have an 18-KB .png texture, that very same texture could turn into a 1-MB (or more) image once it is in Unity. The reason for this is that textures are only in a compressed state when they are on disk. As they are loaded into memory, they are stored in an uncompressed state, resulting in a dramatically larger memory footprint than the compressed originals.

When it comes to compression settings, it will really depend on the actual application and type of image you are using. For GUI and menus, I try to avoid using compression at all because of the artifacts it causes. For in-game graphics, the more compressed graphics I can get away with, the better, but there are times when you need to use an uncompressed format to avoid degradation in the image quality. In those cases, you should always try to use 16-bit compression settings and see if it is good enough before committing to 32-bit settings. Obviously, 16-bit images are half the size of 32-bit images, so the savings can be considerable and the definition much better than a compressed format.

8.3.1 Draw Calls and Their Importance

It is no secret that large textures can eat up your available memory pretty quickly, especially on mobile platforms where memory is limited. For that reason, we need to try every trick we can to preserve memory without compromising too much in quality. One effective method is to try to use as few textures as possible. By doing so, you will not only save memory but also reduce *draw calls*, resulting in a more optimized game experience.

The most important method that the 3D modeler should employ to help keep draw calls under control is to reduce the number of materials in a scene and to share materials across different meshes where possible. Try to avoid using multiple textures for a single mesh; instead, share the same image for all parts. Every material on a single mesh counts for a new draw call, so if you have four materials on a single mesh, it is the equivalent of drawing four meshes.

By sharing materials, the CPU can also communicate with the rendering hardware or software more efficiently because it doesn't have to send out material information for every item in the environment. In Unity, this process is referred to as *batching* and it comes in two flavors: static (available only to Unity Pro users) and dynamic. Batching costs in the vertex count, but the overhead is usually a lot less than that of several separate meshes generating several separate draw calls. We'll talk about this more in Section 8.6.

8.3.2 Textures and the Importance of Texture Atlases

It is no secret that large textures can eat up your available memory pretty quickly, especially on mobile platforms where memory is limited. For that reason, we need to try every trick we can to preserve memory without compromising too much in quality. One effective method is to try to use as low a number of textures as possible. By doing so, you will not only save memory but also reduce draw calls, resulting in a more optimized game experience.

Building 3D environments using texture atlases is not a new concept, and game artists have been using them for a long time. It takes a little more thought than simply putting textures onto objects as you go, but in the long run, the extra work on texturing could make or break the performance of the final game.

To reiterate the point made earlier in Section 8.3.1, each material is a new draw call, so if you have a single mesh that requires four separate textures, it is as though you are drawing the same object four times. Use a single texture atlas, and the information to draw everything on that mesh only needs to be sent once—a single draw call (Figure 8.2).

For 3D games, you will most likely just use a tool like Gimp[1] to put together your atlases; however, if you need more than just a few images on an atlas, you may want to use some custom software. To help you build complex texture atlases, there are several software solutions available, both paid and free.

One of the most commonly used atlas generators is TexturePacker.[2] Texture-Packer takes a sequence of images and puts them all onto one single, large texture atlas. This is ideal for 2D games, where you might have a number of frame-by-frame

---

[1] http://www.gimp.org/
[2] http://www.texturepacker.com

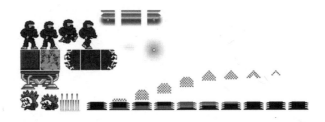

Figure 8.2. An example of a texture atlas.

animations or situations where your graphics have been exported as lots of separate pieces (Figure 8.3).

8.3.3 Fill Rate and Its Impact on Performance

Processor speeds are getting better and devices are no doubt getting faster at rendering more complex scenes, but we must still take into account the impact of transparencies on performance and how fill rate impacts the amount of CPU we need to use up during the draw process.

When the iPad first came onto the scene, one of the challenges developers were faced with was getting games to render at double the size. The miniscule 128-MB RAM coupled with a processor containing a fraction of the power of a $200 laptop meant that games that were rendering just fine at 320 × 480 resolution began to struggle at 1024 × 768. Drawing transparent images was always expensive (iOS processor-wise), but when faced with rendering them at such a large scale, it was enough to grind otherwise sound environments down to a crawl.

The retina display means that newer iPhones and iPods actually render double the amount of pixels than their predecessors. The 320 × 480 is now 640 × 960 for the same-sized screen, which looks great, but means more work for the renderer. The iPad3 screen resolution is 2048 × 1536. Avoid using too many transparent textures, particularly large-sized transparent textures such as vignettes, frames around the screen, or any large elements that demand transparency.

Figure 8.3. TexturePacker is software to take multiple images and convert them into a single atlas image.

Due to the nature of compression, images made up of solid blocks of color compress much better than images with lots of different colors in them. Antialiased edges rarely compress as well as solid edges and you may find that antialiased-edged transparent images often need to be stored in 16- or 32-bit uncompressed formats to retain any level of quality. Work with your artist or designer to experiment early on with different styles and settings to reach the best result with the minimum impact on memory usage.

8.4 Scale and Why It's Important

One important point to consider, regardless of the 3D program you choose, is your modeling scale. Getting the correct scale is vitally important in building a realistic physics simulation. One way to imagine this is to picture a ball dropping from the sky. In the real world, a ball will fall in the way you expect a ball to fall—at the rate of real-world gravity. Now make the ball one hundred times bigger and try to play tennis with giant tennis rackets. The way the ball moves and the way that the rackets swing are no longer what you would see at Wimbledon, and the effect might resemble playing tennis on the moon. Now scale everything back down and apply exactly the same physics to those smaller objects and they'll move as they should.

8.5 Why Audio Can Make or Break Your Game

The soundtrack to your game can make or break it. Its game play is, of course, vitally important, but the overall experience is what people are going to be talking about after the "game over" screen. There are many great games that have been let down by a lack of consistency between their elements. As an obvious example, try to imagine a cute bouncing tiger game with a survival horror soundtrack. Without that consistency between the game play and the audio, users will find the game worlds harder to immerse themselves into.

Decompression of lots of sound effects can hog up the CPU, and streaming long audio files can cause jumps and stalls in your frame rate. Choosing the right audio format can help, although Unity doesn't really offer you much in the way of choice on that.

When preparing audio for use in a Unity iOS game, you should import uncompressed WAV files. That way, you start with a clean source and you can use the compression settings within Unity where required.

8.5.1 Sound Effects and Compression

For small sound effects, such as laser blasts or explosions, it is recommended that you do not use compressed audio files. Decompression is a mathematical process that requires calculation, and therefore CPU. If you are doing this every time the player shoots in a shoot 'em up, the effect won't take long to show up.

Although perhaps not an exhaustive list of techniques for dealing with sound effects in Unity, here are a few common approaches.

1. Use the `Audio.PlayOneShot` function to play multiple sounds from the same audio source. This is great for player sounds such as jumping, dying, etc., where it will be unlikely for several sounds to play at the same time.

2. To use `PlayOneShot`, a GameObject that has a script attached to it must have an AudioSource component (from the Component–>Audio–>AudioSource menu). Whenever you need to play a sound from the script, you call

    ```
    audio.PlayOneShot(anAudioClip);
    ```

3. In the case of missiles or objects that are generated on the fly (such as explosions), we can attach audio sources to them and begin playback of the sound effect automatically at the point of instantiation.

4. Instantiate audio GameObjects wherever the audio is required. That is, we instantiate empty GameObjects containing only an audio source and some kind of autodestructor to delete themselves after playback.

Using the `GameObject.Instantiate` function to generate objects at runtime during an iOS game is not recommended due to the performance overhead. Instead, I use option 1, which is using multiple audio sources and the `Audio.PlayOneShot` to make sounds. I normally have a GameObject in my scene for music and any additional audio emitters attached to the actual objects they are representing. If an object needs to make more than one sound, I add another emitter to the object.

8.5.2 Streaming Music

It is accepted that most games have background music. On a device such as the iPhone, this represents several problems: storage of a long audio track drives up your file size (and initial download size), large audio tracks are going to use up a chunk of your precious memory space, and it takes up CPU to decompress audio as it plays, which can be detrimental to your frame rate.

Recommended practice is to try to stick to smaller audio clips, which may be looped to create seemingly longer music. It may even be possible to sequence audio clips randomly, so as to provide an interesting and dynamic soundtrack to your game (I've done something like this on several projects), or perhaps go so far as to change the loop based on what is happening in the game itself.

If you absolutely *must* use long audio clips, try to compress them as much as possible and use the "streaming from disk" option in the import settings in Unity. Without streaming, your game will try to load the entire music file into memory before playing it, resulting in a huge stall as it loads everything in at the start of the scene, along with an unnecessary usage of memory.

8.5.3 What Settings Are There, and What Are Best to Use?

Unity supports a wide range of audio formats, such as .aif, .wav, .mp3, and .ogg, but with Unity iOS, the best option is to import all of your sounds as uncompressed .wav files and set them up so that the engine will take care of compressing or not compressing them. By using raw .wav files, you will gain the flexibility to experiment with different compression settings in the editor to find the best fit for your project. In Unity, you can choose how the device will play individual audio files, what their compression rates are, and how they will behave in the game environment.

To bring up the properties of an audio file, click on the file in the Project window of the Unity editor and the Inspector window will show the audio importer component and all of its options (Figure 8.4).

Audio format. This drop-down determines how the audio file is delivered to the iOS device. Unity iOS offers two options here: compressed (MPEG) or native (WAV).

When the compressed format is selected, although there are several alternative formats available to iOS developers, the Unity engine will compress your audio as .mp3 format files. This format uses significantly less RAM and disk space than the uncompressed alternative, the downside being that it takes more CPU work to decompress the file. This setting is ideal for music and longer sounds (background audio loops, etc.).

Native (WAV) format is uncompressed, which means better quality audio and no decompression process required. The device's CPU works considerably less to play the sound file than it will with a compressed file, however, the downside is that native files will use up a lot more RAM and disk space. This setting is best for short sounds, or sounds that will be played a lot during your game.

3D sound. This setting determines whether or not playback of this sound should be represented in a 3D space (as if it were being emitted from an object within the environment). When a sound is set to 2D, it will sound as though it is close by and emitted from the speaker with no spatial coordination.

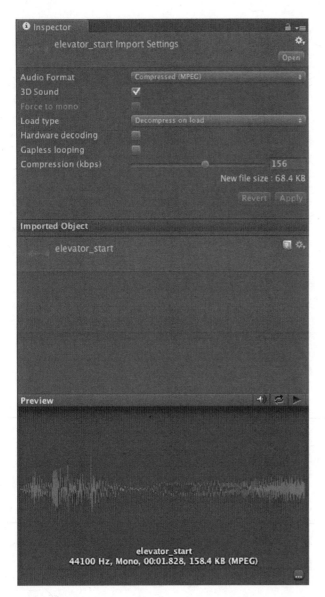

Figure 8.4. The audio importer within the Inspector window of the Unity editor.

Force to mono. When this option is enabled, the audio file will be mixed down to a single-channel mono sample.

Load type. Unity iOS is capable of loading audio files in three different ways. Whichever one you choose will affect performance, and you should be sure to go through each sound file in a project.

- *Decompress on load.* This setting decompresses compressed audio files at runtime. It is useful for avoiding the performance overhead of decompressing on the fly, but it has the huge disadvantage of using up to 10 times more memory than when keeping them compressed. Certainly, this setting should be avoided for larger audio files (if not avoided completely) if you find you are pushing the RAM limits of the device.

- *Compressed in memory.* This setting keeps audio samples compressed in memory, which results in a small performance overhead during decompression when the sound is played. Unity recommends only using this setting for larger audio files to avoid a performance hit.

- *Stream from disc.* Selecting this option means that your audio file is streamed as it is played, taking up a much smaller amount of memory than if it were loaded into RAM. Unity advises the use of only 1 or 2 streams at any one time to avoid performance issues. This is ideally suited for use with a main music track or for a long background audio sound.

Hardware decoding. On iOS devices, Apple provides a hardware decoder for audio playback, which means much less work for the CPU during decompression.

Gapless looping. This option prepares the audio file to provide a loop with no interruptions. A typical use for this might be a short audio sample that will loop to provide background music; without this gapless looping option checked, there may be a stall (or gap) in playback between the end of the sample and the start of it being replayed.

Compression. This slider sets the amount of compression applied to a compressed audio file (so, it is only effective when the audio format is set to compressed). Finding the right amount of compression is as much an art as it is guesswork. The target is, of course, to try and set this to an amount that is a small enough not to use up too much memory at a quality that is not too detracting from the overall quality of the experience.

8.6 Draw Call Batching

iOS in particular is susceptible to performance issues because of the nature of mobile devices and the limitations it presents in terms of both RAM and CPU power. Optimizing scripts, keeping down the poly count, and avoiding excessive `draw` calls are the best ways to improve performance, but you can squeeze out some extra FPS with something known as *draw call batching.*

When Unity draws objects, the engine issues a draw call (a piece of information representing the object and its properties) to the graphics rendering system. Each of these calls puts a strain on the CPU, and too many draw calls will cause performance issues, grinding your frame rate down to a crawl. To reduce the strain on the CPU, Unity combines several objects into a single draw call. This process is called batching, and the Pro version of Unity offers two types: static and dynamic.

Draw call batching is much better for performance than combining everything within the 3D modeling package, as the engine can figure out which objects need to be drawn and cull them appropriately. When exporting environment models suitable for use in Unity, it is better to break them up into smaller pieces than export a single combined model, although you need to make sure that there are not so many pieces as to cause more overhead in drawing each one. Rather than simply splitting a scene into hundreds of pieces, you should consider separating the scene into areas with incidental objects such as barrels, crates, or smaller pieces of scenery grouped into smaller areas for better culling.

It can be a difficult task to find the right balance between model sizes, the number of models in the scene, and the way they are grouped together. It often takes some back and forth between the engine and the modeling package before reaching the best result. It takes patience; understand that this is all part of the process of making a better game.

8.6.1 Dynamic Batch Rendering

This is an automatic type of batching that will group objects sharing the same material into a single draw call. Unity takes care of everything with this type of batching; it is fully automatic, although you will still need to make sure that your objects are split up (not just a single combined mesh) in order for this to prove effective during culling. It is also important to remember that objects need to share materials. If you use multiple materials on a single mesh, each material will add an extra draw call when it is rendered, so be aware of that if you intend to use more than one on an object.

There is a vertex limit on models that the engine will batch, as there is an overhead per vertex. The cap is set at 300 vertices, and models with more than that will be rendered in the regular way. If you are unsure as to how many vertices a model uses, you can use the Stats button in the Game window to check the verts reading in the Stats window. The count in the Stats window will be a total for the scene, which could be used to work out the difference between the number of vertices in the scene with the object and without.

8.6.2 Static Batch Rendering (Pro Feature)

Unity Pro offers static batch rendering. Static batching has several advantages over dynamic batching, including using less CPU and having no vertex limit on what can be combined.

Objects to be batched should be stationary: no moving, rotating, or scaling at runtime. By setting the Static property of stationary models (Figure 8.5), any that share materials will be combined together to reduce draw calls. Unfortunately, there is a tradeoff to this wonderful performance-enhancing technology: it requires extra memory to store copies of each object as they are combined.

Again, the trick is to avoid batching too much (and using up too much memory as a side effect) while finding a way to batch enough to increase performance to a reasonable level. The Unity documentation uses the example of a dense forest; marking trees as static would have a serious memory impact.

8.6.3 Static Batch Rendering for Runtime-Generated GameObjects (Pro Feature)

It is not immediately obvious how to set up static batching for dynamic objects (such as scenes generated with instantiated objects or procedurally-generated environments), but it is possible via the `StaticBatchingUtility` class.

```
StaticBatchingUtility.Combine(transform.gameObject);
```

Instead of checking each item's Static flag, each one of your created models should be added through code, via the `StaticBatchingUtility.Combine` function (shown above).

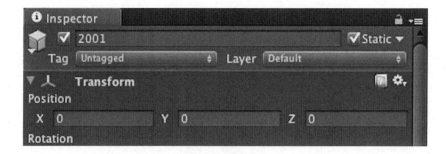

Figure 8.5. The Static flag needs to be checked for objects that will be batched together.

8.7 Occlusion Culling (Pro Feature)

We could all use a performance boost! Unity Pro offers something known as *occlusion culling*. This is a line-of-sight–based system that means the renderer will only draw when it needs to, freeing up precious CPU cycles and helping to keep up the frame rate.

8.7.1 How Does Occlusion Culling Work?

Rendering starts with farther objects being drawn first, then closer objects drawn atop them, then closer objects still atop them, and so on until the view is complete. As the objects are layered one in front of the other, we may end up with a whole host of objects that are actually hidden behind other objects, which do not necessarily need to be drawn.

At runtime, occlusion culling works by disabling the renderers for unseen objects. It uses precalculated data, which is put together in the Unity editor using a virtual camera, to build up information about the visibility of objects in a scene. This data comprises cells that go together to form a binary tree. Two trees are used at runtime, one for static objects (view cells) and one for moving objects (target cells).

As the data required for occlusion culling is precalculated, everything must be set up in the editor beforehand. Your environment and the objects within it should be broken into appropriately sized pieces, and all of the objects to be affected by the culling should be set to Static in the Inspector window.

Once the scene is set up with static objects, you need to go ahead and build occlusion data. Unity will split up the scene into *cells* (small areas), which will be used to calculate the visibility of the other cells and any objects within them. As you can imagine, these cells need to store a significant amount of data, and when you multiply that amount of data by the number of cells in a scene, it may come as no surprise that it takes quite a while for the engine to calculate it. Thankfully, you only need to do this in the editor, and once you have a setup that you are happy with, there is no need to regenerate it unless you make significant changes to the scene.

As occlusion data is substantial in size, it is important to try and get a balanced cell size. Having too many cells in the scene will eat up your RAM; too few will mean that there is no point in culling in the first place. Finding a balance can be time consuming, but it is usually an effort that will pay off in the form of improved performance at the end of it.

Unity does not break up meshes or cull separate pieces of mesh; it simply decides whether or not the renderers attached to the objects should be enabled. To be able to cull a scene correctly, the engine requires level geometry to be split into separate objects. As with the cell sizing, the actual amount of splitting may require a little experimentation. A modeler should try to take occlusion into account when designing levels, as well as aim to break scene objects into reasonably-sized pieces. Having too many separated pieces in a scene will have an adverse effect on performance; a sensible method of grouping should be employed. For example, with realistically-scaled rooms of a house, there would be little benefit in going any smaller than grouping objects on a per-room basis.

The code and logistics behind the occlusion culling system is complex and the system may at first seem a little intimidating, but Unity actually makes it really easy to do. Here is a summary of what it takes for a Unity developer to make occlusion culling happen:

- You are going to check the Static box on your stationary objects and then draw a big rectangle around them.

- Once you've done that, you will tell Unity to calculate the data.

- After a long wait, you'll try the scene to see whether or not the culling worked correctly. If not, tweak a value and repeat until it works properly.

That's it. No complex skills required—just checking boxes and drawing a rectangle. If you are anything like me, that may come as a welcome relief.

8.7.2 Step 1: Static Meshes

To set up occlusion culling, start by setting all of your stationary objects in the scene to Static. The easiest way to do this is to select all of the stationary objects and click on the Static drop-down menu in the Inspector window. From the list, check "Occlusion Static" and select "Yes, change children" when the Confirmation window appears. Again, select the Static drop-down menu, but the second time, check "Occludee Static" and confirm that you want this to apply to all children.

8.7.3 Step 2: Check Occlusion Areas and Add More if Required

Open the Occlusion Culling window, which is available through the menu Windows –>Occlusion Culling. By default, the Occlusion window will appear tabbed in on top of the Inspector window. The Scene View will change to show occlusion cells automatically generated by the engine based on all of the objects that you marked as static in the scene.

It is very important that anywhere the camera might go is within the occlusion area (as shown in Figure 8.6). If your camera remains within the occlusion area, during rendering, Unity will use the occlusion data to decide what to draw. If the camera is ever allowed to move outside of the occlusion area, Unity will render everything and no culling will occur.

If the generated occlusion area does not cover everything that you need to include, or if it does not include the entire play area, you can add your own custom occlusion areas. To do this, in the Occlusion window, click the Object button to show object parameters and highlight occlusion areas in the scene filter area. Next to the Create New option is a button labeled Occlusion Area. Click this to add a new GameObject to the scene; it will be named "Occlusion Area." This new area will be automatically selected and the Occlusion window will extend to show a checkbox labeled "Is View Volume." When this checkbox is checked, the occlusion area will define where the camera can be and will occlude static objects.

Occlusion areas have three parameters:

- *Is View Volume.* When this checkbox is checked, the occlusion area will define where the camera can be and will occlude static objects.

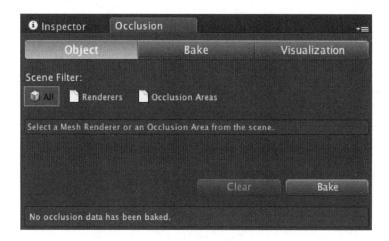

Figure 8.6. An occlusion area in the Scene window of the Unity editor.

- *Is Target Volume.* Moving objects will not be occluded unless this checkbox is checked. By default, this is set to true.

- *Target Resolution.* If you are culling moving objects (you have "Is Target Volume" checked), the resolution you describe here will directly affect the size of the cells used for culling moving objects in the occlusion area.

8.7.4 Step 3: Setup Occlusion Properties to Bake

In the Occlusion window, click the Bake button to show the technique, cell size, clip plane, and memory settings (Figure 8.7).

Technique. The Occlusion system currently offers three types of occlusion culling baking:

- *PVS only.* This method is quickest to calculate, but moving objects will not be culled. It is recommended for games with few moving objects and characters. Portals cannot be opened or closed at runtime, as culling is based on precalculated data.

- *PVS and dynamic objects.* Dynamic objects will be culled using portal culling, and static objects will be culled with precomputed visibility. Portals cannot be opened or closed at runtime, as culling is based on precalculated data.

- *Automatic portal generation.* This is the most CPU-intensive method. A portal culling method is used for both dynamic and static objects, and portals may be opened and closed at runtime.

For more information on occlusion portals, please consult the Unity documentation.

View cell size. This shows the size of the cells that make up the occlusion areas. Smaller values are more accurate, but use more memory.

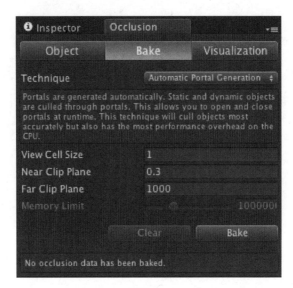

Figure 8.7. Bake settings of the Occlusion window in the Unity editor.

Near clip plane. This should be set to the nearest clip plane used by any of the cameras used in the scene during the game. It will be used to calculate visibility at close range.

Far clip plane. This value should be set to the farthest clip plane used by any of the cameras in the scene. It will be used to calculate visibility at a distance.

Memory limit. This sets a limit for the amount of memory available for portal culling. This setting is only available when Technique is set to either PVS only or PVS and dynamic objects.

8.7.5 Step 4: Bake!

Ensure that the editor is not running the game in play mode, double check the occlusion settings, then, in the Occlusion window, click on the Bake button at the bottom right to get baking. As Unity generates the data, you will be unable to play the game, change scenes, change occlusion settings, or close the editor. You can still minimize Unity and do other things on the system, although the CPU will be working quite hard to process the data quickly, so you may experience some slowdown across the board.

A progress bar and status message will report on the process in the bottom right of the Editor window.

8.7.6 Step 5: Did It Work?

When the Occlusion window is open (Window–>Occlusion Culling), the Scene View will have a small Occlusion Culling window of its own in the bottom right (as shown in Figure 8.8). Items can be toggled on or off in the display, and there are two modes to

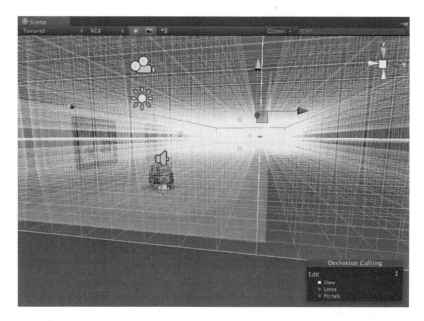

Figure 8.8. The Scene View with occlusion culling cell visualization.

affect the window.

- *Visualize.* This mode allows you to see the effects of occlusion culling on the scene. For example, if you move the main camera around within the scene, you should be able to see the occlusion system hiding and showing objects. You can also watch the effects of culling within the scene as the game is playing.

- *Edit.* When edit mode is set, a visualization of the occlusion areas and their cells will be shown with anchors to make sizing the areas easier.

There are two ways to test your occlusion culling data. The easiest is to play the game and make sure that nothing odd is happening with the hiding and showing of objects in the scene.

A more advanced method of testing your occlusion data is to use the visualize setting of the Scene View's Occlusion Culling window and move the main camera around the scene and into all of the areas that the game camera will go during game play. The Scene View will help to demonstrate which objects are being culled and why they are being culled, with a greater visibility of scene objects than an in-game camera might provide.

If you see any issues with culling, such as the entire scene disappearing or large objects disappearing at the wrong times, you will need to go back and edit either the occlusion areas or the settings in the Occlusion window. Once changes have been made, you will need to bake the occlusion data again.

If you find for any reason that you no longer need occlusion data, use the Clear button in the Occlusion window.

///

CHAPTER 9

Publishing to the iTunes Store

When your game is ready for a release and you are happy that you have a solid, bug-free build, the next step is to upload your files to Apple for review. To do this, we go through something known as iTunes Connect, which serves as our gateway to the iTunes Store itself. We begin this chapter by looking at what you will need to prepare before you can submit, then we will look at the actual iTunes Connect interface and the processes involved in getting everything up there.

9.1 The Approval Process

Your game may be finished and ready for the world, but there's still one final hurdle to jump. Apple needs to review and approve your app before it goes onto the iTunes Store. The Apple review process is usually relatively straightforward, where your application is checked and validated by Apple's top quality inspection squirrels to ensure that it conforms to their terms and conditions. The process usually takes a minimum of one week, though the timing will vary depending on many different factors such as the time of year (the holidays sometimes get busy), the type of app, the size of the app, any external assets, etc. But most of the apps I have worked on have been approved within two weeks. The review includes checks to make sure that your game doesn't crash (or burn) and that you are playing nice when it comes to user information and security. If you are doing anything naughty with the user's information, they will find it and they will reject the app. Most rejections will be returned along with helpful descriptions of the issue(s) and information about resubmitting, if it is allowed.

Apps get rejected all the time, and it is easy to take it personally after all of your hard work. Don't feel bad if this happens to you, though. If your game gets rejected, it can be a disappointing end to a long wait, but you have to see it as a QA review rather than an exercise in trying to get it past an evil gatekeeper. Your game will come out better for it and you won't annoy anyone by accidentally exposing their personal details to a torrent site or crashing their iPhone, so stay positive and try your best to keep those fickle reviewers happy.

9.1.1 What Are They Looking For?

Each review is an individual process, and there are too many variables to speculate on what an individual reviewer might be focusing on (variables such as the type of app, its feature set, external website links, your business model, what the reviewing squirrel mascot had for lunch that day, etc.). There are a few things that Apple tells us clearly in their documentation, so we can, at the very least, try to cover those and make sure nothing obvious is going to hold up the process.

The approval process begins with developer action, from creating an app through to preparing it for upload and uploading it. Once the app is within the Apple system, you will be informed if there is a problem with either a missing screenshot or an invalid binary. If your binary is incorrect, this is usually reported as soon as your upload completes.

As long as everything is okay so far, your app will then enter the "waiting for review" state. There is no set time for this state, and from here it could take hours, days, or perhaps even weeks. Apple is very good at keeping on top of things, and as far as my personal experience goes, the usual time in waiting for review is rarely more than a few days.

It is at this stage that the app could be rejected, if it has problems that are immediately exposed through Apple's review process. Hopefully, though, your app moves on into the "in review" state, and the next message you get back will determine whether or not you made it through.

At this stage, don't worry if you get rejected. It can be a sad day when the rejection email arrives, and it may be a little disheartening, but Apple usually provide a good description of the problem or problems that lead to the rejection, and the best thing that you can do is to pick yourself up and make the necessary fixes. There is no limit to the number of times you can resubmit, although the process will be a faster one if you can do your best to fully test your app and squash any obvious bugs early on.

From the "in review" state, progress comes in the form of your app either moving to a "processing for iTunes store" or a "ready for sale" state. When you submit your app, you can choose to release as soon as the review process completes, or choose to have the release wait until you log back in and manually launch. Whichever route you chose will determine what should happen after review. There is, however, another way that things can go here—a kind of app limbo state, if your contracts are not in order. Be sure to fill in, sign, and return all of the necessary documentation before you try to sell anything in the iTunes Store; if anything isn't ready, it will hold back the release of your game.

9.2 What You Need to Submit to Apple

On the desktop of my Mac lives a folder named "Apple deliverables." It is where I put everything before I upload a new game or application to the iTunes Store. I keep this folder separate to the actual source or build folders. When I create a distribution-ready build to send to the iTunes Store, I copy that over in to my deliverables folder and then I go through it, item by item, to make sure that I have included everything.

Creating icons of various sizes (depending on the devices you are supporting), writing the descriptions, adding tags, and getting everything onto the Apple site is a satisfying experience, but one that always seems to take longer than anticipated.

To get things started, here is a checklist of items that you will need to have ready when you send your final build to Apple for review:

- your build, published under an iTunes Store distribution profile,

- a 512 × 512 image,

- game icon(s),

- a full description and game instructions,

- search keywords,

- rating details, and

- screenshots.

In this section of the book, we will look at each item from the checklist in detail, and I will be providing some helpful tips on making each one work well for your game. These items can make a huge difference to your sales, downloads, and how people perceive your game. Remember that first impressions count for a lot and the items on the checklist are the first thing that your potential customers will look at when they decide whether or not to spend money on your product.

9.2.1 App File with Distribution Profile

To build an application for the iTunes Store, we must build it with an App Store Distribution Profile. When you build with this type of profile, it cannot be tested on a device and it has no use outside of the submission process. There is no way to gauge the success of the App Store distribution build, although it may be rejected during the upload and verify process by the basic automatic checks carried out by Xcode (we will get to the Xcode upload process in full, later on in this chapter).

At this point, it is important to note that if your banking and tax details are not set up with Apple, you will not be able to generate an App Store provisioning profile. If you are unsure of how to take care of this, see Section 9.4.1, and specifically, its Contracts, Tax, and Banking section.

9.2.2 A 512 × 512 image

Your 512 × 512 image will be used on the iTunes Store as the leading graphic on your game's own page. This normally takes the form of your game's icon blown up to 512 × 512, but there is no law stating that this must be the case, and you could use a different image here. When you produce your image, make sure that it does not have any rough edges or artifacts from the image compression process. Use an uncompressed .png file and keep in mind that potential customers may be affected by how this image looks when they are shopping for new games. Keep it clean and simple, but most of all, try to get across what type of game it is representing and the atmosphere of your game.

9.2.3 Game Icons

As per the 512 × 512 image, your icon should quickly and clearly identify what kind of game you are selling. Users are going to be trawling through literally hundreds of icons when browsing the iTunes Store, looking for something to fill whatever gap they would like to fill.

9.2.4 Full Description

The description will tell the world what your game is and how to play it. For tips on writing a good description, see Section 9.7.

9.2.5 Search Keywords

When people search the iTunes Store, they may be looking for specific types of games or games of a particular style. By providing search keywords relevant to your game and its content, potential buyers should be able to find it easier.

You are allowed to enter data that uses no more than 100 bytes. Each keyword should be separated by commas. Make sure that you choose your keywords wisely, because they cannot be changed after they are submitted unless you make an update to the app itself (the binary).

9.2.6 Rating Details

As you fill in the necessary review submission fields, there is a short survey on the types of content that your app contains (cartoon or fantasy violence, realistic violence, profanity or crude humor, etc.). From this, your game will be awarded a rating: 4+, 9+, 12+, or 17+.

9.2.7 Screenshots

You can upload iPhone, iPod touch, and iPad screenshots. It is a requirement that you provide screenshots for all platforms. For example, if your game is for iPad and iPhone, you must upload screenshots from both iPad and iPhone. Failure to do so will result in your app being rejected by Apple during the review process.

iPhone and iPad screenshots are required to be 960 × 640, 960 × 600, 640 × 960, or 640 × 920; at least 72 dpi; and in RGB color. iPad screenshots need to be 1024 × 768, 1024 × 748, 768 × 1024, or 768 × 1004; at least 72 dpi; and in RGB color.

9.3 An Introduction to iTunes Connect

Upon arriving at the iTunes Connect website, after logging in, you will be taken to the main page (Figure 9.1). Here, there are several options:

- *Sales and Trends.* See all daily and weekly sales data here.

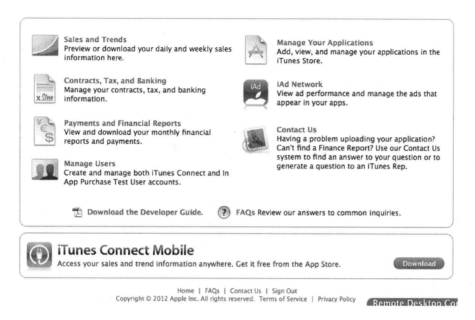

Figure 9.1. The iTunes Connect main page.

- *Contracts, Tax, and Banking.* Before you are able to sell applications on the store, there is some paperwork to do. Required forms and the status of submitted forms can be found in this section.

- *Payments and Financial Reports.* Once your app begins to sell, the iTunes Connect system will begin to collect sales data. Access everything to do with your sales and finance here.

- *Manage Users.* Although only the initial iTunes Connect user account (the Team Agent) has access to legal permissions, you can assign access to iTunes Connect admin for multiple users or set up test accounts for testing in-app purchases (not covered in this book). Note that the actual options available here will depend on the type of developer subscription belonging to the initial account.

- *Manage your Applications.* This is where you will create, upload, and manage applications for the iTunes Store.

- *iAd Network.* An additional revenue scheme provided by Apple is the iAd Network, which places advertisements into your game and provides an amount of money each time a user follows the ad.

- *Contact Us.* My personal experience of the Apple support team is that they are amazing! They will do their best to help, whether it is a technical, contractual, or financial problem. If you are struggling with something, follow this link and drop them a message.

9.4 How to Upload Your Game to Apple for Review

Are you sure that your build is stable, reliable, and ready to go? Congratulations! Let's get your game on its way for review.

In this section, we're going to go through the entire process of getting your game up onto the iTunes Store. This includes setting up a certificate and a profile for App Store distribution and your App Store page details, building your game in a special way suitable to go off to Apple, and finally, validating and uploading the build through Xcode.

Create a Distribution Certificate. The first step is to create and download a Distribution Certificate. Note that this is a Distribution Certificate, not a distribution provisioning profile. The certificate allows you to generate distribution provisioning profiles, and you will need to have both installed on your development machine to be able to build for the iTunes Store. The Distribution Certificate only needs to be generated once and it may be used for this and all of your future distribution provisioning profiles.

Enabling automatic device provisioning (Figure 9.2) is the easiest way to manage all of your certificates. If automatic device provisioning is enabled in Xcode, your Distribution Certificate will be generated automatically. Xcode will create a request, submit it for approval, and download and install the certificate on your development Mac. You can view, download, or revoke the Distribution Certificate in the iOS Provisioning Portal.

- Open Xcode, then open the Organizer window (Window–>Organizer).

- Click Devices at the top of the window, then select Provisioning Profiles in the Library section, to the left.

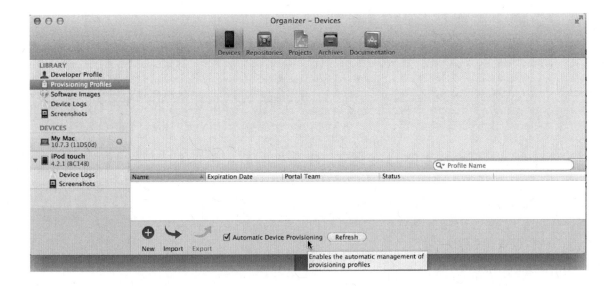

Figure 9.2. The XCode organizer, Provisioning Profiles, and the Automatic Device Provisioning checkbox.

- Select the Automatic Device Provisioning option at the bottom and click Refresh.

- If prompted, enter the Apple ID and password you used to register for the iOS Developer Program.

- A message stating that no iOS Distribution Certificate can be found will appear. Click the Submit Request button, and Xcode will generate the certificate for you automatically. If this message does not appear, click on the Developer Profile link on the left (under Library) and then back to the Provisioning Profiles screen. It may take a little while for Xcode to log in to your account and check the details, so be patient. If it makes you feel any better, you can try clicking the Refresh button if the message still fails to appear after a minute or two. It should appear without any input from you

It is quite possible to setup certificates manually via the Provisioning Portal of the Apple Developer Center, but I don't see why anyone would want to do that when Xcode can take care of it for you. If you really want to set up a Distribution Certificate manually, consult the Apple documentation.

Create a distribution provisioning profile. Log in to the Apple Developer Center and click on the iOS Provisioning Portal link on the right of the website.

Click the link to Certificates on the left of the site, followed by the Provisioning tab. Click on the New Profile button to get to the Create iOS Distribution Provisioning

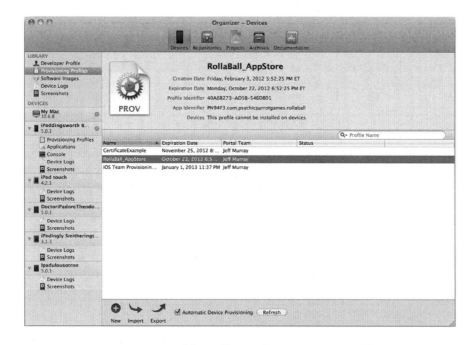

Figure 9.3. Successful installation of a provisioning profile.

Profile screen (Figure 9.3). Here, there are several compulsory fields to fill in. Those are:

- *Distribution method.* Select the radio button next to the App Store button.

- *Profile name.* Name the profile appropriately and in a descriptive enough way so that you will be able to recognize it later.

- *Distribution Certificate.* The name of your iOS Distribution Certificate should automatically appear here. If not, select the correct certificate from the list.

- *App ID.* This should be the same App ID (the Bundle ID) as the Unity game build (set in the Player settings). The Bundle ID in Unity and this App ID must be the same for the build to work.

Click on the Submit button to create the profile. The new profile should now appear in the list of distribution provisioning profiles, although its status will be "in process." Wait a short while before refreshing the page and the status should jump to "active." Once the new profile is in an Active state, click on the Download button. Either select it to open it immediately or save the file somewhere convenient.

After the download completes, find the downloaded file and double click it to open it in Xcode. Xcode should show the Organizer window in the provisioning profiles section. If everything has gone smoothly, the profile should appear in the list with no issues. Note that near the top there will be a message stating, "This profile cannot be installed on devices"—don't worry, this is the correct behavior. The App Store profile will only be used to make a build suitable for submission to Apple. As this is a special profile for the App store only, there is no need to install this to a device, and if you try it will fail. The App Store distribution profiles do not allow for you to make runable builds.

9.4.1 Setting Up Your Game on iTunes Connect

Before you can upload your binary to iTunes Connect, you need to add an app to the iTunes Connect system. To do this, open the iTunes Connect site in your browser and click on the blue Add New App button.

If you have more than one developer subscription (such as a subscription to the Mac OS Developer Program), you will be given the choice of the type of app you want to create. Click on iOS, if prompted. Next, you will be prompted for information about your app on the app information page (Figure 9.4).

App information page.

- *App name.* This is the name of your app *as it will appear on the App Store.* This name can be up to 255 characters, although when it is displayed on the store, it could be truncated, so try to keep your name relatively short.

- *SKU number.* This is a unique number used to identify your app. There are no guidelines as to what you should put here and it is up to you to devise a system. The only stipulation is that the number has two digits or more. Unless you have your own system, let me suggest perhaps the easiest system: start at 01 and increment the SKU number every time you make a new app.

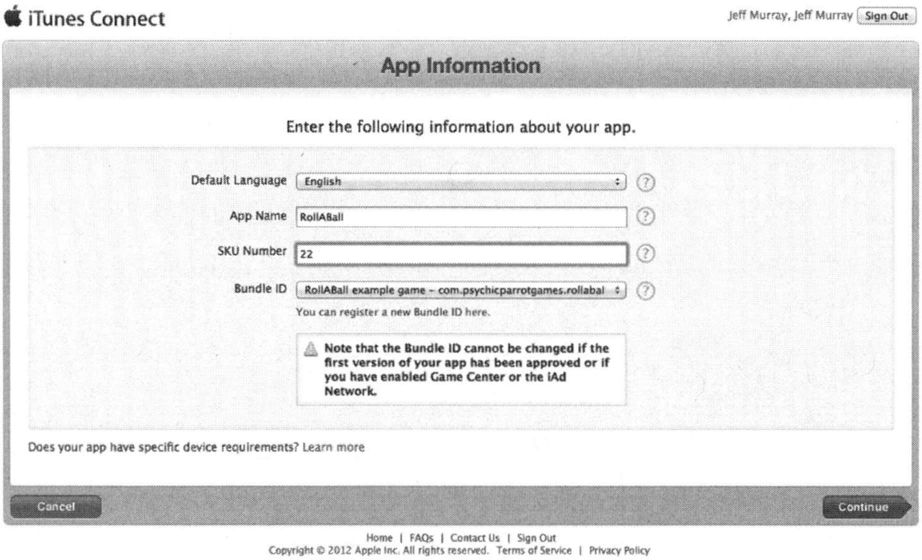

Figure 9.4. iTunes Connect app information page.

- *Bundle ID.* The bundle ID is an identifier used by iOS and Mac OS X to recognize any future updates to your app. The Bundle ID drop-down is populated by the app ID's details from the Developer Portal, and you should select the same bundle ID (the same app ID) that you have been using for development. Refer back to Chapter 2 for a refresh on setting up app IDs.

If you have been using a wildcarded bundle ID, or you haven't yet made an app ID for this specific app, you should click on the link that reads "You can register a new Bundle ID here" and make one. You will have to re-enter the new bundle ID into the player settings in Unity, however, and rebuild the binary file. (The bundle ID in Unity was covered back in Chapter 3.) If you go ahead and create a new bundle ID, you will need to refresh the app information page before it will show up in the list.

Note that if you do try to select a bundle ID that is wildcarded (one with "*" in it), you will be prompted to add a suffix. To make a build for the App Store, wildcards may not be used and the ID you put into the player settings in Unity must exactly match the one here.

Once you are finished with the App Information page, click Continue to move on to the next screen, where you will tell Apple about the launch date and pricing information (Figure 9.5).

Set the launch date and pricing information.

- *Availability date.* This is a proposed date for your game to become live on the iTunes Store. If you use the current date, the game will go live as soon as it has gone through the review process and been approved by Apple.

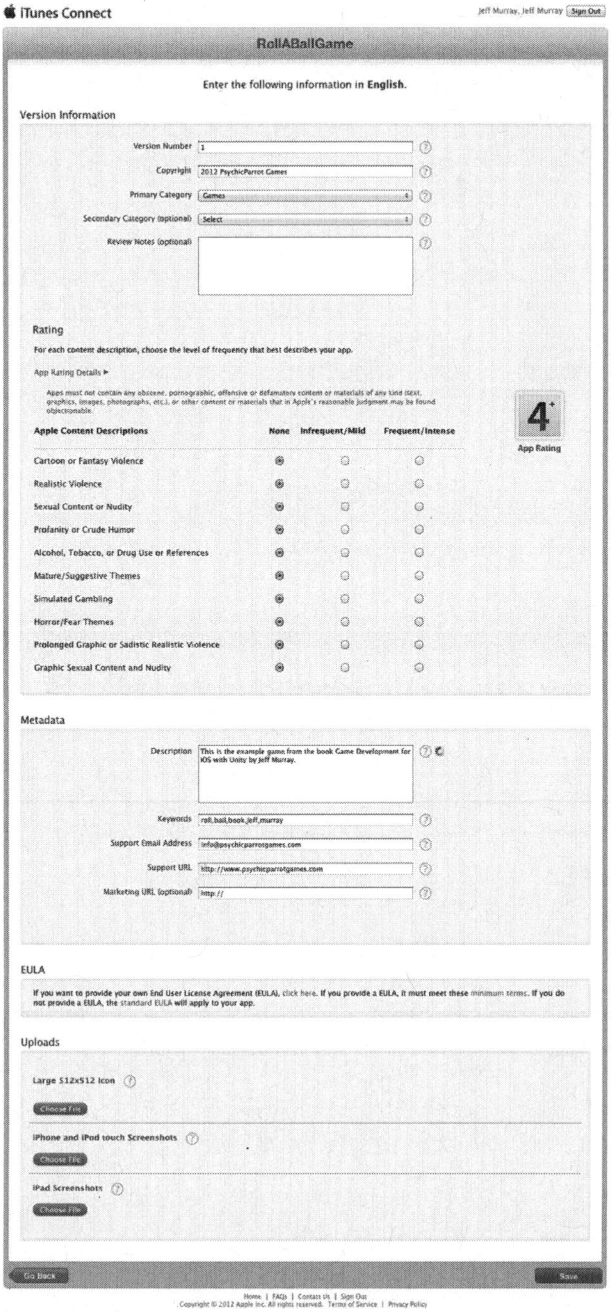

Figure 9.5. iTunes Connect entering launch, pricing, and store information.

- *Price tier.* If your game is free, select "free" from the drop-down. Otherwise, click on the link to view the available price tiers and what they mean; then, once you have chosen the one you want, select it from the drop-down menu. To be able to put a paid app onto the iTunes Store, you must have a paid commercial agreement in place. You can set up agreements in the Contracts, Tax, and Banking section of the iTunes Connect website.

Click the Specific Stores link if you would like to specify which regions of the world your app will be available in.

Entering the version number, description and uploading the icon and screenshots.

- *Version number.* Start at 1.0 and go up. There are several different schools of thought on how version numbers should be incremented. One straightforward and accepted method is to increment the dot number (e.g., 1.1, 1.2, 1.3, 1.4, etc.) whenever you do minor updates or fixes, and increment the major number every time you update something big.

- *Copyright message.* This should be your name or the name of your company and the current year. The usual format is something along the lines of <name> <date>; for example, "PsychicParrot Games 2012."

- *Primary and secondary categories.* Choose the categories that are most relevant to your game.

- *Review notes.* Normally, this should be left blank, although if you have anything that may affect the outcome of the review you should put it here (for example, if you were unsure as to whether or not a particular feature of your game is actually allowed by Apple's guidelines).

- *Rating.* You must be 100% honest when filling out the rating survey about your content! When your game goes through the review process, the reviewer will have access to all of the game graphics, audio, and other assets. If anything in the rating section is incorrect, your app will be rejected. If the app is approved and a complaint is made against it, there is a very good chance that Apple will take it down permanently.

- *Metadata.* You can enter the description, keywords, support email address (the address that your customers will use to contact you with technical problems), a support URL (a website for customers to visit who are looking for support), and an optional marketing URL to a promotional website.

- *EULA.* If you have specific license requirements that are not covered by the standard Apple licensing agreement, you can set up a custom EULA here. You should seek professional legal advice before submitting any custom agreements, and there are some minimum terms you need to include. (On this page of the site, there is a link to those minimum terms.)

- *Uploads.* Icons and screenshots should be uploaded here. See the checklist in Section 9.2 for exact image specifications. Remember to upload screenshots for *all* platforms. For example, if your game is for iPad and iPhone, then you will be required to upload screenshots from both iPad and iPhone. Failure to do so will result in your app being rejected by Apple.

After filling in all the details and uploading everything for the app description, your app will now appear in the Manage Your Applications section of the iTunes Connect website. The initial status for your new app will say "prepare for upload." This state is presumably there so that you double-check everything before going to the trouble of uploading your build. Before we can upload, we need to move things on from the prepare-for-upload state. Go back in to the Manage Your Applications page of the iTunes Connect site. Click on your app in the iOS App Recent Activity area, then click the View Details button once the app summary page shows.

Read through all of the details you have entered and double-check that everything is as you would like it to be. Once you are completely happy with it all, click on the Ready to Upload Binary button. The site may ask you a question about export compliance. The main question is, "Is your product designed to use cryptography or does it contain or incorporate cryptography?" By default, Unity does not contain or incorporate cryptography, and you can answer "no" just as long as you have not significantly modified the Xcode project source to include cryptography. Answer this question and click on the Save button to continue.

The next page on the iTunes Connect site will inform you that you are now ready to upload your binary. Click the Continue button and, on the next page, note that the status of your app should now have changed to "waiting for upload."

9.4.2 Building in Xcode and Uploading for Review

We've reached the final stage of the submission process, which means all that is left to do is build the Xcode project from Unity, compile it to an archive build in Xcode, and upload it to iTunes Connect. Xcode contains a built-in system for validating the build (where the build is checked for the correct provisioning profile and certificates prior to uploading), then we can go ahead and upload that archive build also from within Xcode.

Building the Xcode project from Unity.

- Open the Unity project.

- Open player settings (Figure 9.6) and ensure that the Bundle ID is correct and matches the app ID you used earlier for creating the distribution provisioning profile.

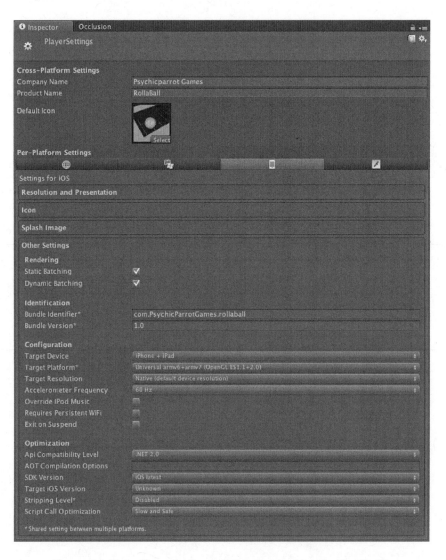

Figure 9.6. Unity Player Settings window for checking the Bundle ID.

- Hit Build and Run (File–>Build and Run) and select a file location, if prompted. Xcode should open automatically once the build process is complete. It should also try to run the game on the device (if one is plugged in), but don't worry if that fails. Hit the Stop button to cancel the process.

Compiling, validating, and uploading.

- Open the Scheme drop-down from the top left of the Xcode window. This needs to be set to the device. It should say "Unity-iPhone" on the left, which is the application name, and we want it to read "iOS Device" on the right (or the name of your device, if your device is attached via a USB cable).

- Click on the left side of the Scheme drop-down. Click Edit Scheme (Figure 9.7).

- On the left side, click on Archive. Make sure that the build configuration is set to "release" in its drop-down and that there is a check in the box for "reveal archive" in the organizer. Click OK (Figure 9.8).

- Before we can build, Xcode needs to know which provisioning profile to use. This can be found in the Code Signing section of Build Settings.

Click on the project from the Project navigator on the left of the Xcode window. (It will say something along the lines of "Unity-iPhone.")

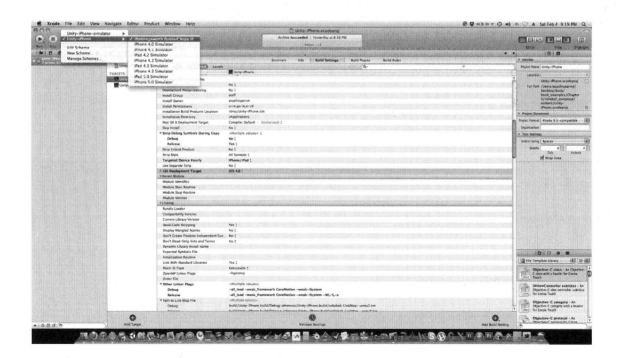

Figure 9.7. Xcode and the Scheme drop-down menu.

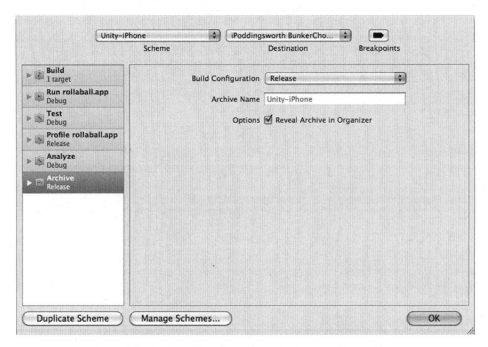

Figure 9.8. Xcode: Editing the scheme to check archive settings.

With the project selected, the right side of the window should be populated with the project summary. Click on Build Settings at the top. In the Code Signing section of the build settings, expand Code Signing Identity to show the options within it (if it is not already expanded), then click to the right of the word "release" to open the Profiles drop-down.

- Select iPhone Distribution under Automatic Profile Selector (Figure 9.9).

- Click the menu Product–>Archive to build the archive. Once Xcode has finished building, the Organizer window should pop up. If you have any problems with this build, consult Section 9.4.3.

- In the Organizer window, select your archive on the left if it is not already highlighted. On the right side, you should see your game icon, the name of your game, and a few more details. Over to the right of the window are three buttons: Validate, Share, and Submit. Click the Validate button.

- If prompted, enter your Apple ID and password.

- Once Xcode has logged you in, you will be prompted to select your application from a drop-down menu. Also on this screen, check that the Identity drop-down contains the iPhone Distribution profile, then click Next.

- If all goes well, a message will inform you that there were no issues and that the build has passed validation and may be submitted to the App Store.

Figure 9.9. Xcode: The Code Signing drop-down menu, selecting the iPhone distribution provisioning profile.

- Click Finish.

- The organizer will go back to the Archives section after validation. Click the Submit button to begin the process of sending the build to Apple for review.

- Xcode will likely ask you to enter your login details again. Enter your Apple ID and password, then click Next.

- Once Xcode has logged you in, you will be prompted to select your application again from a drop-down menu. As you did with validation, check that the Identity drop-down contains the iPhone Distribution profile, then click Next.

- A progress bar will appear. During this process, Xcode will again validate the file and upload will begin automatically. Once upload has completed, a message will inform you that your app has been submitted to the App Store for further review.

Congratulations! You just submitted your game to Apple for review. Good luck with the review process! I sincerely hope to be playing your game soon.

9.4.3 Troubleshooting Xcode Build Errors

If building the app fails in Xcode, the most likely cause is the certificates, but you can check the error message within Xcode to try and find out what has gone wrong.

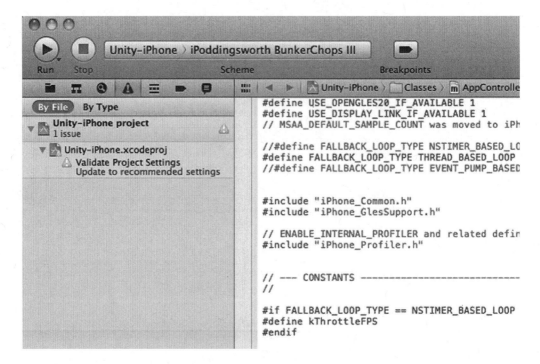

Figure 9.10. Xcode: The issue navigator.

If the "build failed" message appears, click on the Issue Navigator button (a small exclamation mark icon; Figure 9.10) on the left of Xcode, above the project navigator. The project navigator will change to show any warnings or issues made during the compilation process. If your build has failed, a small red icon (a red sign with a white exclamation mark) will highlight a message containing the issue that caused the build to fail.

Note that if the error says that the identity you are using doesn't match any identity in any profile, this is Xcode's way of telling you that you have not set up (or perhaps just not installed) the right provisioning profile for this identity. For example, if you were to select "iPhone Distribution" from the Automatic Profile Selector section of the Code Signing Identity drop-down, and the build failed with the error "Code Sign error: The identity 'iPhone Distribution' doesn't match any identity in any profile," this would suggest that no distribution provisioning profile had been installed on your machine. From there, you would log into the Developer Center, into the Provisioning Portal, and into the Provisioning section (on the left) to download or create the correct profile.

To try to build again, rather than clicking on the arrow to build and run, you may want to just build. To do this, use the menu Product–>Build.

Certificate-related errors. If the error message is related to certificates, the first place to check is the build settings. We need to make sure that the build is using the correct code signing details:

- Click on Unity-iPhone, which is located directly underneath the word "Project" and above the word "Targets."

- Look for the Code Signing section and expand if needed.

- Underneath the Code Signing heading is a Code Signing Identity property. If you click to the right of this, a drop-down should appear showing all of the profiles you have access to. Select the correct profile here. If no profile is shown or your profile is missing, you may need to download and open it from the Provisioning Portal section of the iOS Developer Center website.

Non-certificate–related errors. If the issue is unrelated to certificates and you have not modified the Xcode project, something may have gone wrong during the process of Unity creating the project file and opening it in Xcode. As long as the error is unrelated to certificates or provisioning, the best place to start is to delete the Xcode project folder, restart the machine, and start the build process again. If the error persists, you must understand that compiler errors are way beyond the scope of this book. To get help, you should begin by posting on the Unity forum (in the iOS section) or perhaps try the IRC chat or other online channels. If that fails and you are sure that the issue is not with Unity, you can try submitting a case to Apple support. I have nothing but praise for Apple's developer support; they have helped me out more than once, very quickly and very skillfully.

The iOS developer library[1] and its search function are your best friend when problems arise. If you are experiencing code signing issues or you are unsure as to how it all fits together, search the developer library for technical note TN2250: iOS Code Signing Setup, Process, and Troubleshooting.

9.5 What Happens Once Apple Approves Your Game for Sale?

There will come a day when your game is finished, approved by Apple, and ready to launch. Provided that you set your Apple Developer subscription up correctly, when that day comes, an email will drop into your inbox to let you know that your game is ready for sale. When that email arrives, it is a great feeling!

When you submit a game to Apple, you can choose to launch as soon as the app reaches this ready-for-sale state or you can choose to launch on a particular date.

9.5.1 Making Your Game Live on the iTunes Store

When you set up the new app on iTunes Connect (see Section 9.4.1), you would have set a launch date for your game. If the launch date was before your game was approved, it should automatically go live on the iTunes Store as soon as the review process is completed.

If the date you set was later than the review completion date, making your game go live on the store is as simple as logging into iTunes Connect and changing the status of the app. To do this, go in to the Manage Your Apps section, click on the application you want to launch, and change its launch date.

---

[1] https://developer.apple.com/library/ios/navigation/

9.5.2 Finding Your Game on the iTunes Store and Getting Links to Share

The easiest way to find your game and link to it is by going through the iTunes Connect interface.

- Open https://itunesconnect.apple.com and log in to the system with your Apple ID and password.

- Click on the Manage Your Applications link.

- Click on your game from the list in the iOS App Recent Activity section.

The App Information section at the top of your game's page has two headings: identifiers and links. Under links, select "view in app store." Copy this address to use as a link to send out.

9.5.3 Why Can't I Find My Game on the iTunes Store after It Went Live?

When your game first goes live in the store, it may take a while for it to propagate on all of the Apple servers. It may become available in one country several hours before another, and the keywords may not become active in the search engine for a while after.

To find the game on your own device, use the search field to find your game by exact name. Type the name you used when you set up your game in the iTunes Connect interface and it should come up in the search results.

9.5.4 Downloading Your Game to Test It Out

It goes without saying that as soon as your app goes live on the iTunes Store, you should delete any development versions from your iOS device and download your new live version. If you don't want to pay for it, of course, you will need to issue yourself a promo code—this is your choice. Personally, I like to buy all of my games at least once so that I have a record—an invoice or perhaps a receipt—of my hard work. Silly, I know, but it's just one of my little game launch rituals!

9.6 iOS Marketing

The iTunes Store is huge. Literally thousands of apps find their way in, only to silently disappear into the sea of games and utilities. It is a sad reality that a large proportion of the most popular apps are mainly where they are because of great marketing (which often means a great marketing budget). Marketing an iOS app is a difficult task that takes a lot of work, and there is no magical formula to sell millions. There are a few tips to follow to get you heading in the right direction, which will at the very least help you to present your game in a professional manner. (Of course, if you have the budget for larger scale advertising and marketing, go for it—the sky's the limit!)

This section of the book will examine some of the simplest (and cheapest) ways to get your promotion going.

9.6.1 Press Releases

Press releases are used to tell industry sites about a business announcement or product launch. They are usually distributed to a blanket of portals and relevant industry websites to be shared on their news pages or announcements sections.

Press releases tend to follow a particular format, and there are several companies that will format the release for you and distribute it across a number of different sites for a fee. The following example is an official press release from Riptide Games, announcing the release of their iOS game, *Mini Monster Smash*.

Mini Monster Smash Smashes onto the App Store

Denver, CO

Feb 04, 2011, in Games

[prMac.com] Aurora, Colorado—Riptide Games today is pleased to announce their latest game, *Mini Monster Smash 1.0* for the iPhone and iPod touch. *Mini Monster Smash* is a free game where the goal is to smash the monster as far as you can with a flyswatter. Along the way you can bounce off of trampolines, run into bombs, or float in bubbles. *Mini Monster Smash* is the most recent release from Riptide Games whose previous apps have been downloaded more than 2 million times.

Mini Monster Smash was originally developed overnight at the 360iDev Game Jam held in Austin, TX, in November 2010. The core gameplay from that initial development sprint is largely unchanged from the final product, and Riptide tried to keep true to the Game Jam sprit and kept development as minimal as possible. The final app represents only approximately 40 hours development time.

"We love the unique constraints put on by a Game Jam and are thrilled that *Mini Monster Smash* was good enough to release" said Brian Robbins, Founder of Riptide Games. "Our first release *Gravity Sling* also came from a 360iDev Game Jam and we hope that players enjoy this one just as much."

In addition to smashing the monster as far as possible, users can post their score to Facebook, Twitter, or share it via email. There are also 26 Game Center achievements to earn that provide for an extended amount of gameplay in spite of its superficially simple appearance.

Mini Monster Smash is the latest game released by Riptide Games. Previous games include the *iLookApps* series, which has well over 1 million downloads, and *Gravity Sling*, among others.

Device Requirements

* iPhone and iPod touch

* Requires iPhone OS 3.1 or later

* 17.1 MB

Pricing and Availability

Mini Monster Smash 1.0 is free and available worldwide exclusively through the App Store in the Games category.

- Riptide Games

- *Mini Monster Smash 1.0*

- http://www.riptidegames.com/2011/02/mini-monster-smash-is-now-out/

- Download from iTunes http://itunes.apple.com/app/id414176551

The press release could also include links to a splash screen, app icon, and press kit, as well as contact information. The most important part of writing a good press release is to include a suitable amount of information about the game itself, usually a quote from someone on the team (normally a CEO or equivalent), and a contact name with contact details. Keep the release official, but try to keep it lightweight to give people something interesting to read that isn't too demanding.

From there, the aim is to distribute your press release to as many websites as possible. Industry community sites such as Village Gamer[2] are ideal places to spread the word.

Press releases at this level are about indirect sales. The trick is to get the word out about your app with an aim to either getting reviewed by some industry members or, at the very least, get mentioned somewhere else that could have good public visibility. Indirectly, a few well-placed press releases can result in a big difference in sales.

9.6.2 Press Kit

As you promote your game, you will need to send out your game icon, screenshots, or perhaps your company logo to various sources. It makes no sense to have to dig those out and email them individually, so most developers now put together a *press kit*. The press kit contains everything that a website featuring your game might need, such as the icon and screenshots for a review site or a larger graphic for a portal site to show as a headline image.

9.6.3 Promo Codes

Promotional codes, or *promo codes*, are a fantastic way to get people playing and talking about your game. It works like this: you give away a promotional code that allows potential players to download and play your game for free.

A promo code takes the form of a string of letters and numbers. To redeem it, the user can either go through the iTunes application installed on a computer or via the iTunes Store on the iOS device itself. The user clicks on the Redeem link and types in the code, which unlocks the game for instant download or, if redeemed on the device, downloads the game and installs it in a single tap.

Promo codes are perfect to send to potential reviewers or give away as prizes on blog sites or social networking sites such as Twitter or Facebook. The objective is indirect sales—we want people to talk about the game, Like a Facebook page about the

---

[2] http://www.villagegamer.net

game, review it on an iOS app review site, or even just tell their friends about what a cool game they have found.

The number of promo codes you can download per game is limited to 50, but that should be plenty to get the ball rolling. I have given away codes in a number of different ways:

- *Mobile gaming forums.* I ask people on the forum to reply to my message at an exact time of the day. The first few people who reply at that exact time get a promo code. This is a fun way to get people to retain your game in their memory as they try to remember to return to the page at the time you set. It doesn't hurt to be a little lenient about the timing, either. If you give away a couple of extra codes to people who made it a minute late, it'll only make you look like a nice person!

- *Review sites.* Several iOS app review sites require two or three promo codes to be submitted along with a brief description of the game. The site may or may not actually get to review the game, but it is always worth a try since the promo codes don't actually cost anything. A good review on a high-profile app site could generate a good number of sales, so it is worth giving away a few copies for this.

- *Twitter giveaways.* You should certainly set up a Twitter account for your game or, at the very least, your company. To help generate followers, put out a few tweets about having a promo code giveaway for your followers. Ask people to retweet the message. There are also Twitter groups who cross-promote apps (you retweet links to their apps and they will retweet links to yours), so be sure to search for any app-related groups to join. We will talk about this in Section 9.7.4.

- *Email promotions.* If you have a mailing list, you could ask people to sign up to the mailing list and give away promo codes for the first x number of new subscribers.

- *Facebook.* One method to use promo codes to increase your Facebook profile would be to put the message out via another platform (such as emails, forum posts, or Twitter feed posts) that the first x number of people to Like your page from a given date or time will be awarded with a promotional code.

I am sure that there are many other wonderful ways of giving out promotional codes—perhaps printed on flyers at an event or written up on a shop window. Hopefully these are just a few to get you started and to get you thinking about how you can use promo codes to get more people talking about your game. Whenever you give away a code, be sure to ask the user kindly to review your game on the iTunes Store after he or she has played it. Reviews help instill confidence in buyers, even when they may be slightly negative; having reviews on the iTunes Store suggests that people are actively playing your game. Potential customers are far more likely to take a chance on a game that appears to have players than on one that doesn't.

9.6.4 Free App of the Day Schemes

There are a growing number of schemes that provide mobile users with regular, free games. The idea is that you pay the organizers a fee and, if they accept your game, they do a whole bunch of promotion: you offer your game for free for a day or two and ride off of some of their promotional work to raise your game's profile and position in the iTunes Store charts. By raising your position in the charts, more people become aware of the game and, in theory, more people then buy the game.

The success of these schemes varies depending on a number of factors, the biggest of which is the overall quality of your app. If your game is making zero sales, do not expect a free-app promotion scheme to solve its problems. Like any form of promotion, it is a tool to raise your profile, which may or may not increase sales. If there is no demand for your game, sadly, it will take a whole lot of promotion to generate any sales and, even then, it may or may not be possible to sell.

9.6.5 Give Away Free Copies to Reviewers

Visiting the top iOS review sites to submit your game for review often requires that you provide a promotional code so that a reviewer can download and play the game for free (unless, of course, your game is already free of charge on the iTunes Store). You should supply promo codes with your review application, and most sites demand that you include a little write up.

Sending out promo codes is the best way to allow reviewers to play your games. The alternative is to ask for device IDs and to make special Ad Hoc builds, which should be reserved for supplying builds to your testers or teammates instead.

When you are sending out promo codes, exercise some caution about whom you send them to; remember, you are limited to 50 codes within 28 days. Often, established developers will receive emails from people posing as reviewers to try and get free games. Perhaps an extra copy here and there won't hurt sales and may benefit in getting the name of your game out there, but if you do decide to send out promo codes to random people, be sure to ask them to post a review to the iTunes Store in exchange for the code.

Choose reputable, well-known sites to send review versions to. Often they will take several weeks to react and they tend to be very busy, so try to be patient and, sadly, don't expect a reply if they choose not to feature your game. Sometimes it may be that the reviewer doesn't like your game, or sometimes it may be that a bigger, higher-profile game will launch at the same time, which demands more of the reviewer's attention. Either way, don't take it personally if you don't get featured.

Make sure that your press kit is available for reviewers (include the URL to download your press kit when you submit the game for review) and that it contains, at least

- great screenshots, both low- and high-resolution versions;

- background information about you or your company;

- a game description (either the one you use in the iTunes Store or a new variation of it);

- background on the game itself, perhaps a paragraph or two about how the game came about, what it brings to the genre or market, etc.—anything that may be seen as an interesting feature or make for an interesting story;

- the game's icon, both low- and high-resolution versions; and

- a sales paragraph about your project as a whole, including quick interesting facts about the game, you, or your company.

Once you have your pack prepared, it will be much easier for you to produce professional review requests or provide information to the press quickly. While review sites are ultimately interested in good games, they are also interested in telling a story that their readers will want to hear. Provide a clean, professional-looking submission, and you will stand out from the hundreds of badly put-together and rushed applications they receive each day.

With a little luck, the site will eventually review your game. If this is the case, you may or may not receive notification of the posting of the review. You should Google search for your game regularly, just in case.

Note that bad reviews are inevitable, regardless of the game. You can't please all of the people all of the time, and there will almost certainly be bad feedback from somewhere. The trick is to focus on the productive feedback that actually helps to do things better, either through an update or in your next game. Again, this is not personal—the enjoyment of games can be a personal, individual experience that works for one but not for another.

9.7 Promotion Tips and Tricks

9.7.1 Good Icon Design

If you can afford to hire a professional designer to put together an icon for your game, you may still want to provide some guidelines as to how you need the icon to be. As this is a customer-facing representation of your game, the last thing you want to do is paint the wrong picture of the experience you are offering up.

Take a few moments to look through the iTunes Store at some of the icons heading up your competition (Figure 9.11). Find anything similar to your concept and see how representative of the product each one is—not just quality-wise (a badly put-together game may be accompanied by a great icon), but also whether or not the core game concepts actually come through the icon or whether or not the overall vibe of the game is present. The game icon should be in a similar artistic style to your game and should also attempt to represent its genre or theme.

Keep the themes simple. Try to keep in mind the word "icon"; some of the most iconic images are those that say the most with the least. For example, a monster-truck-racing game might be represented with a picture of a monster truck. Any potential customers of monster-truck–racing games will see it immediately and want to find out more about it.

Try to come up with methods to make your icon stand out as much as possible against others. If you didn't already know, there are rather a lot of games on the iTunes App Store. A potential buyer will be faced with literally hundreds of icons. If yours can stand out, even a little, from those hundreds, it may just mean that special something that piques the interest of your potential audience and leads to an increased number of sales.

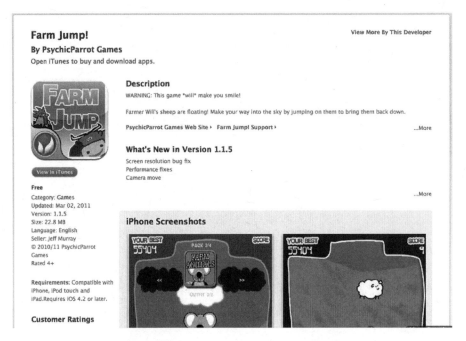

Figure 9.11. The Farm Jump page layout on the iTunes Store.

Most iOS games end up with two different versions on the iTunes Store: one full version and one lite version. The lite version usually takes the form of a scaled down or content-limited version of the game, available for free download to give potential buyers a taste of what the full game has to offer. If you do choose to release a lite version, you should follow suit and add the word "lite" to the icon. This is a convention on the store for good reason, in that people are far more likely to download free games than to blindly spend money on products they have little or no idea about.

Words on an iTunes Store icon are a bone of contention, with designers' opinions split. Depending on who you ask or which website you read, you will get a different answer on this; some say that having a single word on the icon helps to convey the game genre, and others say that a good designer could put together an icon that tells the story graphically. I have seen them both work, so I don't believe that there is a magic formula here. If your icon looks great and supports your product, it's mission accomplished!

Try laying out your icon onto a screen capture from the store to see how it will look on the page. This may sound like a silly idea at first, but if you think about it there are hardly any situations where you wouldn't want to see the full picture before designing a part of it. The iTunes Store icon should be no exception; seeing it on a page as it will appear in the store will give you a good idea of whether or not your icon works.

9.7.2 Writing Your App Description

The description of your game is unquestionably important for your iTunes Store page, and there are a few important things you need to put into it. Opinions vary as to how to do this, but there are a few things that your potential customers will almost certainly want to read.

When you get user reviews, copy some quotes from them (the good quotes, of course!) and paste them at the top of your description. If you do not yet have any reviews, mention any special features here at the top to try and interest potential customers.

Now write a small paragraph to sell your game. This is commonly referred to as an *elevator pitch*—a pitch you could tell to someone in the time it takes to reach his or her floor when travelling in an elevator. Keep it short, keep it simple, but try to make it sound exciting! Below is an example.

> Love word games? Download *Space Word* and you will have trouble putting it down! With a dictionary of over 150,000 words and an infinite number of levels, there's plenty to keep you coming back for more. Expand your mind, expand your vocabulary—into space and beyond!

Following on from your sparkling elevator pitch, you should list out what your game has. Start with the most important features, then go on to list out everything you can think of:

Features

- A 150,000 word dictionary

- An infinite number of levels

- Simple tap-and-play interface

- Automatic saving of game progress, so you can play in short bursts

- Beautiful graphics

- Exciting space-themed sound effects

- High-score table

Now that we have them interested, it is important to go into a little bit more detail about what it is they are going to be doing. We need to describe the game play itself, with a simple walkthrough description. I have left out a walkthrough description like this on two of my applications only to receive complaints from users about the fact, so I highly recommend including this.

It may be very clear to you, for example, that a word game requires the user to tap letters on the screen, but your screenshot may not be entirely clear to someone who may not be used to an iOS-based device. Better to include a brief description of the game:

> *Space Word* is a fun word game where letters appear on the screen and players tap on the letters to make words. Longer words give higher scores, but you have to be quick because time is running out!

Your description first and foremost needs to tell potential buyers what to expect from your game. It's great to write some sales material, but if your description doesn't tell buyers what kind of experience they are in for, there is much less of a chance of them making a purchase.

Put together a single paragraph that explains the game with exciting terms to make it sound interesting, then go on to list out the core features:

- Fun, cartoon-style graphics

- Sound effects by a composer who once visited the New York Philharmonic

- Four different game modes (quick play, career, time attack, and multiplayer)

- Leaderboards and over 40 achievements

Now include a paragraph to describe how to actually play the game. This should not be sales speak; this should be an actual instruction paragraph:

Tap the letters to make the longest words you can. Keep an eye on the timer because if you don't make a word within the allocated time, the words will be ejected off into space and it is game over. A bonus will be awarded for making words quickly. Look out for space aliens who will try to attack the letters—tap them to zap them! In-between levels are the bonus rounds, where you make a word before the asteroid strikes.

Once your game has been out there for a while, if you receive any positive reviews either from the iTunes Store review system or from an external source, you should return to your product description and quote them at the top. Just simple one-liners will be enough:

"Fabulous fun!" —*The Daily App Blah*

"This is the best game I've ever played!" —5 Star Reviewer

Overall, you should try not to go too crazy with the quotes and reviews (keep it to five or so), and try as much as you can to keep your description short but interesting.

Another point to remember is that you don't need to use all of the available words. Try to save some space for cross-advertising—when you have more than one game in the iTunes Store, you can use this extra space to mention and link to your other games.

9.7.3 Make a Facebook Page

Just about everyone on the planet has a Facebook page—from video games to kitchen cleaning products to little bits of plastic that cover the bolts on toilets. Modern consumers are expected to hit the Like button so that they can be kept up-to-date on all the latest developments or new product ranges. They're often led into hitting the Like button through basic promotions such as product discounts or free competition entries.

As our culture becomes more and more used to this type of advertising and promotion, the rest of us need to be sure to take advantage of it by setting up a Facebook page for our games and keeping our potential fans up to date when we release updates, sequels, or even new apps.

9.7.4 Make a Twitter Account

Twitter is a fantastic place to actively connect and engage with your customers, promote your games, promote your brand, and network with fellow game developers.

Twitter allows users to send and receive messages containing no more than 140 characters. This limitation means that the messages, or *tweets* as its users call them, need to be focused and direct. Many users have literally thousands of followers, meaning that whenever they tweet a message, it will appear to all of their followers to read.

You should use Twitter to post updates, to link to screenshots of the game in development, or to post links to your page on the iTunes App store after release. Game developers love to see what other game developers are working on and, if you build up a rapport, often they will retweet your message to their own followers. The idea here is, of course, that your post gets passed from just your followers to their followers, then to their followers, and so on.

By signing up to groups such as the #IDRTG (Indie Developers Retweet Group),[3] you can both promote your own games and promote other developers' games by retweeting their messages. The #IDRTG has a points system whereby its members can rack up a score for how much they retweet and how well they adhere to the #IDRTG guidelines for Twitter posting.

Note that everything you post on Twitter is public: avoid telling people about your hangover, your shopping list, or anything that may paint an unprofessional picture of your company. What you post on Twitter will decide what kinds of people follow you and may show up in search results in the future. Be aware of everything that you post and never give out personal information or log-in information such as usernames or passwords.

Sign up for a free Twitter account[4] and start building your followers. My Twitter handle is @psychicparrot and I would love to see you in my follower list!

---

[3] http://www.innovatty.com/twitter/IDRTG
[4] http://www.twitter.com

///

CHAPTER 10

Thinking Outside the Box

As you know by now, Unity is an amazing and powerful tool to have in your game-making toolbox. Now that you have the knowledge to build iOS games and to publish them yourself to the Apple iTunes Store, where to next? There is a whole world out there!

This chapter looks at things you can do outside of Unity to improve your Unity games or add functionality to Unity that doesn't come standard. We'll be looking at some simple tweaks you can do to the Xcode project to squeeze a little extra performance out, some of the plug-ins available for iOS Unity development, tips for porting to other mobile devices, and, finally, we will look at how you can use something called TestFlight App to deliver builds more easily to testers.

This section is the experimental chapter, where we get a little crazy, bend the rules a little bit, and step outside the box.

10.1 The Democratization of Game Development: Anyone Can Make Games!

If your budget is low and you don't have enough confidence in your own artistic talents, the great thing about developing with Unity is that there are plenty of options for purchasing or finding free downloads of assets for your games. Developers should never feel as though assets stand in the way of them making their dream game anymore. Anyone can make a game, and by using a few stock or free items here and there, anyone can actually make a good-looking game without paying megabucks for the privilege.

To access the Unity Asset Store, either click the link from the welcome popup that appears when you first start Unity, or click on the menu Window–>Asset Store (Figure 10.1).

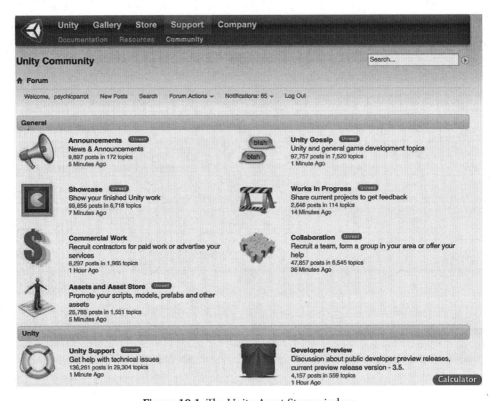

Figure 10.1. The Unity Asset Store window.

10.1.1 Get Assets

The Unity Asset Store, built right into the Unity editor, is a great place to start when you are looking to put together a project. It has everything, from small scripts to entire game source code. You can purchase starter kits to get a head start with coding games in a particular genre, or purchase models, animations, sounds, and special effects. Prices vary, ranging from just a few dollars all the way up to hundreds of dollars for full game source code. If you are looking for game art, browse through the Asset Store to see if there is much there that could help you bring your project to life. Use the resources you have and make the game you always wanted to make—don't let artistic difficulties stand in your way!

10.1.2 Premium Assets

Alongside the Unity Asset Store, there are a number of other online stores selling prefabs and assets. They usually take the form of either full project files that can be opened easily by Unity, or sold as .unitypackage files, which are compressed files that are extracted by Unity into an existing project file for easy integration.

Stock items are usually sold under a particular license, which may or may not limit how you may be allowed to use them. Be very careful to read any license or terms and conditions before downloading. The last thing you need after putting in all the hard work in bringing your game to market is some kind of legal problem preventing you from selling it, so please do be sure that you take the extra time to read the boring legal guff.

- *ActiveDen*[1] is a large library of stock files (not just for Unity). It offers Flash, Flex, and Unity developers a range of assets, from individual packs (such as vehicles, models, or scripts) to art packs and even full game starter kits.

- *Unity Magic*[2] offers a small library of high-quality stock items, such as visualizers, A* path-finding, and shader code. It is also home to the UnityCar Vehicle Simulation Package, a high-end car simulation pack.

- *GamePrefabs.com*[3] has a myriad of prefabricated content, from top-down shooter kits to camera scripts.

- *Psionic 3D Game Resources*[4] provides some amazing models from my good friend Psionic, who kindly gave permission for me to use some of his 3D models in the kart racing game example included with this book.

- *TurboSquid*[5] is a well known site for purchasing stock 3D models.

10.2 Tweaks to the Compiled Project Code in Xcode

Changing the code in the Xcode project that Unity builds is not exactly for the faint of heart. Unless you understand Objective-C, the source Unity builds might as well be the works of a broken word processor. But there are a few things that you can play around with to squeeze a tiny bit of extra performance out of your game, or perhaps add the slightest bit of extra polish. There are a few values we can tweak, such as the frequency of accelerometer updates or the target frame rate, which can make a real difference to the final product. In this section, we take a look at those options, what they mean, and how you can change them. No knowledge of Objective-C is required!

10.2.1 Getting A Little Extra Performance From Unity

Unity is an amazingly flexible engine, giving its users the power to build any kind of game for a number of different platforms. More specific engines, tailored to a particular genre or game type, may be optimized and built to perform well under the intended conditions but would perform badly when taken out of their original genre and asked to do something different. Unity does everything very well, regardless of genre or game type, but may have some of its default settings not exactly optimized to your type of game.

For example a UI-based game, which relies on a lot of user input, requires more checks to the iOS touch system than, say, an accelerometer-driven driving game. When

---

[1] http://www.activeden.net
[2] http://www.unitymagic.com/shop/en/assets.html
[3] http://www.gameprefabs.com
[4] http://www.psionic3d.co.uk
[5] http://www.turbosquid.com

Unity builds your game, the number of times that the accelerometer is checked and the frequency at which the touch system is checked will be set to values somewhere in the middle so that everyone, regardless of genre or game type, will have a decently functioning product. We can, however, change these values to suit the type of project we are working on and, in doing so, squeeze out a tiny bit more performance from our iOS project.

10.2.2 Changing Accelerometer Input Updates

The default number of *updates*, or times that Unity talks to the accelerometer, is perfect for games that use this feature. If your game doesn't use the accelerometer, there's absolutely no reason to waste processor cycles checking it, and we can easily go ahead and stop this from happening. It won't make the largest performance difference, but it will be one less thing for the processor to do as your game is running. Even if you don't disable it completely, it may be worth experimenting a little to see if you can bring down the number of updates to an acceptable level without affecting your accelerometer controls.

First, open up your game in Unity. Open the player settings (Edit–>Project Settings –>Player) and select your accelerometer frequency from the drop-down. The value here determines the processing frequency for the accelerometer. When this is high, it takes more CPU power to process, and when it is low, of course, it takes less. If your game is not reliant on fast updates from the accelerometer (say, for example, that your game is touch-driven only), you can go ahead and lower this, or even disable it. When the kAccelerometerFrequency is disabled, the game will completely ignore the accelerometer.

In versions of Unity prior to 3.5, this setting is in the Xcode project that Unity creates. Open Xcode, load up your project, and on the left (in the project navigator), expand the "classes" folder. Within that folder is a file called "AppController.mm." Click on that to open it for editing. Scroll down to find the line

```
#define kAccelerometerFrequency        60.0
```

Change the number as you see fit for your application.

10.2.3 Changing the Desired Frame Rate

iOS devices have their frame rates locked to either 20, 40, or 60 frames per second. This means that if your game is not fast enough to run smoothly at 60 frames per second, it will be downgraded to run at 40. Within the Unity Xcode project is a value that attempts to force the frame rate to a default of 40 frames per second. This value is normally completely acceptable and the best target frame rate for most games to aim for, but there is nothing stopping you from upping this to 60 frames per second if your game has some extra processor cycles to spare.

If your game is pushing it and you are already at the limits of what can be rendered or played on the iOS device, setting this up to 60 frames per second could result in laggy performance (or make no difference if the iOS device chooses to stick to 40). The best way to deal with it is to try it and see.

Setting the frame rate is as simple as adding a single line of code to one of your scripts. You should place it somewhere that will be executed early on, preferably before game play begins, such as the `Awake` function of a main menu script or similar. All you do is set `Application.targetFrameRate`:

```
Application.targetFrameRate = 60;
```

This would set the frame rate to 60 frames per second.

In versions prior to Unity 3.5, you will need to edit the Xcode project that Unity creates. First, open up your Unity project in Xcode. Open the "appController.mm" file and scroll down to find `#define kFPS 30`. This is the target frame rate. By lowering this, your game will use less battery power with the payoff of rendering less frames per second. If your game performs extremely well on the device, you may want to increase this value to provide a smoother game play experience. Keep in mind that you should still try to support older devices, which may run slower, so if you have any doubt that an older iPhone will run at 60 fps, you should consider leaving it at 30.

10.3 In-App Purchases

Unity does not, at the time of writing, provide a method to connect to Apple's *StoreKit* and deal with the payment side of things. To accomplish In-App purchases, some work will need to be put into building an Objective-C plug-in, which is way beyond the scope of this book. Plug-ins are available to take care of the StoreKit side of things for you, thanks to companies like Prime_31.

Once you have a solution in place to talk to Apple's StoreKit, some method for unlocking the content in your game will be required.

10.3.1 Unlockable Purchasable Media

This method has all of the purchasable content included within the main game files, but it's locked until the purchase is made. Your game will check with the StoreKit system to see which (if any) purchases have been paid for and unlock them for the players. There should also be some code to check with the StoreKit to find out what has been purchased and whether or not it needs downloading, just in case the player loses saved data, reinstalls the OS, or is playing on a new iOS device.

10.3.2 Downloadable Purchasable Media

This method downloads new content upon purchase, rather than having it already within the game files. Both of these methods require code to check with the StoreKit to find out what has been purchased and whether or not it needs downloading.

The Unity documentation contains full instructions on dealing with the downloadable media system, including source code. For the best method to deal with downloading media, you should consult the Unity documentation under the In-App Purchases section.

10.4 Other Uses for Unity iOS and Available Plug-Ins to Expand Its Functionality

iOS devices provide a lot of functionality, and features such as piracy detection or iPod music playback, sadly, are not currently included as part of the Unity iOS engine.

Thankfully, Unity is open to the possibility of extending the engine with Objective-C code. If your Objective-C programming skills are up to it, there is nothing to stop you from adding any or all of the native iOS functionality to the Unity engine via its plug-ins interface.

If you don't feel like building the plug-ins on your own, or you are new to Objective-C programming, a paid solution is available! Prime_31[6] are the leaders in the field of Unity iOS plug-ins that provide the quickest, easiest way to incorporate iPhone and iPad native features into your games and applications. They provide the largest range of extra functionality for Unity, such as iAd support, the ability to record and play back sound from the iOS device microphone, StoreKit integration, and a lot more.

The best thing about Prime_31 plug-ins is how easy they are to use. Usually, it is as simple as importing a .unitypackage file and calling commands from your own scripts. Full documentation is included, and their support is second to none.

10.5 Tips and Questions to Ask for Porting to Other Platforms

Try to design a GUI that can be scaled easily to suit different screen resolutions. Android in particular is available across a range of devices with many different sizes of screens. This means we have to be intelligent about UI design and try to build either systems that scale dynamically and work regardless of aspect ratio, or systems that stay the same size and work on everything from tablets to 3.5-inch mobiles.

Make sure that your controls will work well across your targeted devices. A game designed for a touch interface may not work as intuitively when the gestures are carried over to a mouse input system and vice versa. Consider the platform and any special input devices it has, and prototype first to get the best results!

Is your game suited to tablets, desktop machines, consoles, or phones? Without trying, of course, this may sometimes be a difficult question to answer. The best most of us can do is try to consider each device and score it based on the suitability of its components, such as inputs, screen sizes, delivery mechanisms (download, disk, etc.), and audience.

If you intend to use plug-ins, are they available for your target platforms? Plug-ins such as in-app purchasing or device-specific functions such as gyroscopic controls or camera inputs will most likely not transfer across platforms and you may find extra work in building out other versions of your code to work with the different plug-ins.

Owlchemy Labs[7] provides what they call a Multiplatform Toolkit to help Unity developers produce cross-platform builds from the same Unity projects. It allows for per-platform configuration and can automate the process of changing button sizes, swapping out textures, or solving the resolution-independent conundrum across multiple targets. You can find their system on the Unity Asset Store. Be sure to check it out if you plan to go cross platform with your game(s) in the near future.

10.6 Using TestFlight to Get Builds to Your Testers

Installing an unreleased iOS app onto multiple devices for testing can be a frustrating and long-winded process. As well as keeping your profiles updated on the Apple

---

[6] http://www.prime31.com
[7] http://owlchemylabs.com

Developer Portal with the UUIDs of any new devices, you will also have to redownload profiles each time a new tester joins and package the profile up with each new build. The time spent talking users through the process of installing builds via iTunes or through an .ipa file (not to mention staying on top of keeping all of your testers informed about new builds via email) could be put to better use.

TestFlight is a free online solution providing over-the-air installation—that is, it's a solution that means that your testers don't need their devices to be tethered via USB cable to a computer for installation. In essence, TestFlight provides one-click installation straight from your tester's iOS devices, adding a friendly front end to an installation procedure that may have otherwise been an intimidating process for novice users. It also offers user management for your testers, meaning that you can organize your testers into groups and distribute either group-specific builds or builds for everyone.

As well as the distribution and management of your test builds, TestFlight can aid the debugging process further with its software development kit (SDK). The SDK includes such functionality as remote logging, crash reports, checkpoints, tester feedback via in-app questions, and more.

Implementing the functionality of the SDK and setting up Unity to build projects suitable for TestFlight can be daunting, but there is an alternative solution. The Unity Asset Store sells a low-cost system named Autopilot (for TestFlight SDK),[8] which automates the entire TestFlight build and uploading processes. I highly recommend it if you intend to use TestFlight, since it not only simplifies the process to a single click but also provides access to the Autopilot SDK, meaning that you can easily get crashlogs, user feedback, checkpoints, and session data from your users in real time. During testing, the extra functionality it provides could easily save you from a lot of extra work diagnosing bugs or providing support to your users.

10.7 Mantis

One of the most common tracking systems is Mantis. Mantis is a PHP-based free, web-based bug-tracking system working with MySQL, MS SQL, PostgreSQL databases, and a web server. If all that means nothing to you, don't panic. Most low-cost hosting packages will have these features, and some hosts may even have the ability to automate the installation in a single click. If you are in any doubt, of course, consult your hosting provider.

The full installation instructions for Mantis are beyond the scope of this book. Mantis does have extensive installation instructions in its documentation if you feel competent enough to take that on yourself, but I would recommend http://www.simplescripts.com as a great web-based utility for automating the Mantis installation to your server.

10.8 The Unity Online Community

One of the best things about Unity is the amazing community of experts and artists that use it. On my Unity journey, I have met some incredible people and made friends with people from all around the world via Twitter, the Unity forums, IRC, and conferences. One trait you tend to notice is that most Unity users are more than simply users of the

---

[8] http://u3d.as/content/cratesmith/auto-pilot-for-test-flight-sdk/2cU

software, but people passionate about their tool of choice and, perhaps even in some cases, a little defensive about it. Unity, for many, provides a voice that we didn't have before and a playground for our imaginations to run wild in. The freedom and power that this software gives to the independent or hobby coder is something unrivaled by anything else.

If you find yourself with a problem you can't solve, or perhaps you have an idea and you are looking for the best way to make it happen in Unity, there are a number of places to get help from within the community. There is a vibrant and exciting independent game developer community out there, too, which means awesome support and places to pick up useful free code snippets.

10.8.1 The Unity Site Forum

The forum provided on the Unity website[9] is a well-established resource and hangout for Unity users. Here, you will find product announcements, a showcase, news about the Asset Store and items on it, gossip, and forums for both collaboration and commercial work. Unity support is also provided here.

Be sure to do a quick search before posting up support questions, as your problem may have already come up before and an answer may well already have been posted. Generally, people are extremely friendly within the Unity community, though not always rich with time, so you should never expect an instant answer. Sometimes it can take a while to get a response, but I can't think of a time when any of my posts have ever gone unanswered.

10.8.2 Unity Answers

To quote the Unity Answers site, "Unity Answers is the best place to ask and answer questions about development with Unity."[10] I couldn't have put it better myself. It works by users and Unity staff providing answers to questions posted by other users. The voting system also makes it easy to find the best answers quickly.

The community is quite spectacular and Unity Answers is a great resource for problem solving. At the time of writing this book, more than 29,457 questions have been answered with more than 40,278 answers!

10.8.3 IRC Chat

The Unity3D IRC Channel is not an official Unity creation, but you will often find Unity staff using it and ready to help out. The discussion is mostly Unity-related, but don't be surprised to find the occasional conspiracy theory discussion or trout-slapping session. Grab an IRC client and point it to irc.freenode.net.

Join the #unity3d room to chat in real time with other users. Remember to be polite and courteous at all times—these are real people, after all!

10.8.4 The Unify Wiki

The Unify Wiki[11] is part of what is know as the Unify Community,[12] which is made up of a wiki, free tutorials, a gallery of Unity-based games (called the "Unicade"), and the

---

[9] http://forum.unity3d.com
[10] http://answers.unity3d.com
[11] http://unifycommunity.com/wiki
[12] http://unifycommunity.com

Unitree project. Everything here is free and available for download, although you should note that the Unify Community relies on contributions from its users or money generated through the sale of merchandise available on the website. Grab yourself a Unity mousepad and t-shirt and, if you can afford it, please make a donation to keep this valuable resource online.

The wiki is the place for Unity users to find and share their knowledge. It contains a wealth of goodies from shader code to wizards, game code (in-game elements like radars or car physics, character controllers, utility scripts, camera code, GUIs, and more), particle systems, tips and tricks, articles, tutorials, and more. I have to emphasize this as much as I can, though—if you take, please try to give back either through donation or through contributing your own useful scripts. Not only is it a great way to help out your fellow Unity users, it's a great way to get your name out there as a code guru and earn some respect and reduce bad karma!

10.8.5 Twitter

Twitter[13] is rife with Unity and game developers, as well as a vibrant and exciting indie game community. If you are new to Twitter and looking to build up your follow list, here are some Unity-related accounts you should add right away (including my own, of course!):

- @PsychicParrot
- @Unity3D
- @TornadoTwins
- @DavidHelgason

For more general game development chat, news, and information, you should consider following:

- @Dubane
- @VillageGamer
- @Envato
- @CartoonsByRic
- @RichPantsOn
- @GeorgeBray
- @GamaSutra
- @OwlchemyLabs
- @SpiltMilkStudio
- @BugbearGames

---

[13] http://www.twitter.com

Glossary

A

(Apple) Developer Center: Available to subscribers to the Apple Developer Programs, this is where certificates are issued, development software is downloaded, and development devices are registered with Apple.

ARM: ARM is a 32-bit RISC (reduced instruction set computer). The ARM architecture is used in the design of processors for low-power applications. Originally introduced by Acorn Computers in 1987, the architecture is used today in the design of the processors in most mobile devices, including those produced by Apple such as the iPhones, iPods, and iPads.

ArrayList: An ArrayList is an array, a dynamic data structure suitable for the storage, retrieval, and manipulation of data.

artificial intelligence (AI): In this book, we use a simple path following system for our AI players.

assets: In the games industry, almost all parts of a game project that are not hardware or software are referred to as assets, such as graphics, audio, or animations.

audio listener: Unity requires at least one audio listener to be present in every scene of a project. The audio listener acts as an ear to the 3D world. Whatever audio would be heard at that point in the 3D space will be played out through the computer's audio system.

AudioSource component: The AudioSource component is used in Unity to emit sound within a game environment. It is a component that is applied to a GameObject.

B

batching: The combining of objects in Unity.

Boolean: Refers to a system of thought developed by mathematician and computer pioneer, George Boole. In this book, we use variables declared as Boolean that may be one of two states, either true or false.

breakpoints: During debugging, it is useful to be able to pause script execution at a chosen point. This may help to diagnose issues by looking at variable values at a particular time or perhaps seeing what is being rendered on screen at the point of pausing. To facilitate this, developers place breakpoints into scripts to tell the engine where to pause execution of a debug build (breakpoints will only stop execution in a debug build).

bundle identifier: Think of a bundle identifier as an application's ID, used to identify it during certification. An application's bundle identifier ties it to a provisioning profile during development or ties it to a distribution profile when it comes time to distribute or upload to Apple.

C

cache: A collection of data, normally a temporary store.

cells: Culling necessitates the environment to be broken up into smaller areas. Each small, square area, known as a cell, contains information used to calculate visibility of the objects in the scene.

certificate signing request (CSR): A small file generated by an OSX application called Keychain, from a Mac, used to describe the developers system to the Developer Center when generating Development Certificates.

checkbox: A simple user interface element that can be set either on or off by clicking or tapping on it.

collider: A collider is a Unity component that provides collision detection to your GameObjects via the PhysX engine.

color depth: The number of bits used in image data to indicate the color of a single pixel. The higher the number, the more colors but with the disadvantage of using more memory to store the image.

cube mapping: The most common method for simulating reflection, such as the surface of mirrors or chrome. It uses six textures (or, in some cases, a texture split into six areas) to represent up, down, left, right, forward, and back views.

D

dependencies: When one task relies on the completion of another before it may be completed, we often refer to those other tasks as the main task's dependencies.

development provisioning profiles: Development profiles contain information on which devices your application is allowed to run on during development. Without the correct provisioning profiles, your app will not run on any iOS device.

draw call: This term normally refers to function calls within or between scripts.

draw call batching: Combining draw calls to reduce the amount of information sent to the graphics cards and therefore reducing the overhead in the transport and processing of graphics data.

drop-down menu: A drop-down menu is a menu that appears upon clicking on a button or icon. The menu "drops down" from an area close to or within the button or icon.

E

elevator pitch: An elevator pitch is the summary of a concept that may be delivered within the time it takes for an elevator to reach its floor. The idea is that elevator pitches summarize something quickly and in the most exciting way possible, usually in order to achieve a sale or authorization to go ahead with building a larger project.

Euler angles: Three angles introduced by Leonhard Euler to describe the orientation of a rigid-body. In Unity, these angles are defined as 3D vectors such as `Vector3(1,2,3)`.

F

first-person-shooter (FPS): The game is played out through a first-person perspective, usually as though you are looking out at the game world through the eyes of the main character.

flat velocity: In the context of this book and the code within it, the flat velocity is the velocity of a rigidbody physics object in a 3D space without taking into account its vertical (y) axis. For example, we use this in Chapter 6 to calculate the speed of our kart so that we can stop it from going too fast. If we were to take into account its y-axis, the calculated speed would be incorrect on slopes.

flythrough: This term refers to the flying action of some form of floating, disembodied camera. It may be controlled by a user or automatically moved by the computer.

G

game design document (GDD): A document outlining some or all of the elements and concepts within a video game.

GameObject: A GameObject is an element within a scene in a Unity project. This is discussed in detail in Section 4.1.2.

Gantt chart: An informational diagram. See Section 1.9.

garbage collection: In programming, we create objects and references to objects throughout our scripts. These objects and references use up an amount of RAM and must, at some point, be cleaned up and the memory freed up for other purposes. This process is known as garbage collection.

graphical user interface (GUI): See user interface (UI).

H

homepage: A main page of a website, usually the page that appears by default when a website is visited for the first time.

hot keys: Keyboard shortcuts.

I

instancing: An instance may be thought of as an occurrence of an object, although it is usually used in the context of being a reference copy of an object (not an actual object), which reduces overhead in either memory or processing or both.

instantiate: In programming terms, instantiation is the process of forming a copy of an existing object that is independent of its template object. Unity instantiates objects into game scenes on demand, such as player objects, character rigs, or effects. We look at this in more detail in Section 6.2.7.

iOS: The name of the operating system used by Apple Inc. mobile devices such as the iPhone or iPad.

iPad (1, 2, or 3): The iPad is Apple's tablet computer system. To date of writing, there are three generations of iPad.

iPhone: A brand of smartphone made by Apple Inc.

iPod: Apple Inc.'s mobile MP3 player.

iPod Touch: A mobile MP3 player with added functionality to run apps and games the same way as the iPhone produced by Apple Inc. Essentially, iPod Touch are iPhones without the phone.

iTunes Store: Commonly known as the App Store, this is the place for iOS users to download and purchase applications and games for iOS devices.

J

JavaScript: The JavaScript programming language. See Section 4.1.6.

L

layers: The Unity interface provides access to a layering system, used to help easily identify game elements.

lightmapping: A lightmap is a data structure containing information on the brightness of surfaces. Unity uses the Beast lightmapping system to create the effect of a computationally expensive lighting system (offering shadow projection) by applying lightmaps to its surfaces.

M

(Mac) OS or OS X: The operating system that Apple Macintosh computers use. An operating system is a vital part of any computer system, as it provides a suite of programs managing hardware resources and providing services for other software such as games or applications.

massive multiplayer online game (MMO): A video game where a large number of players can interact with each other.

massive multiplayer online roll-playing game (MMORPG): We won't be building any of these, but we do touch on just how much work it takes to build one!

memory footprint: The peak amount of space in memory that a software application takes up as it is running.

mind mapping: A form or diagram suitable for studying and organizing information such as ideas or story elements.

mipmapping: A system of filtering intended to reduce aliasing artifacts and increase rendering speed. Mipmapping should be used sparingly on limited memory devices, as it uses several precalculated, optimized images that require extra memory to store.

modeling: The act of building 3D models with modeling software.

MonoDevelop IDE: A script editor and debugger bundled with all versions of Unity.

N

.NET libraries: A library of classes, interfaces, and value types designed to be the foundation on which .NET Framework applications are built. In Unity, .NET support is provided by the MONO platform, which is an open source, cross-platform framework. Unity uses MONO to support C#, which uses the .NET framework.

null reference exception: This is an error that occurs when code tries to access an object that has a value of null. Normally, these types of exceptions will be caught by the engine and reported to you before compilation is possible; however, there are always exceptions to the rule and it is always possible that objects are initialized in a different order on different platforms, which may lead to null referencing on a device that is not immediately apparent in the editor. A simple null value check before accessing objects is usually all it takes to stop the exception occurring. See Section 6.2 for more information.

O

occlusion culling: A line-of-sight–based system that means the renderer will only draw when it needs to, freeing up precious CPU cycles and helping to keep up the frame rate.

P

PHP: A scripting language generally used for web development.

pickups: Virtual objects in a game world that may be picked up by the player.

powerups: Virtual objects that change the behavior of the player, environment, or other objects.

prefabs: Precomposed objects in a Unity project. See Section 4.1.10.

press kit: A collection of product information put together (usually in one download location) to make it easier for members of the press, such as a reviewer or PR agent, to be able to include screenshots during a review or write-up of a product.

promo (promotional) codes: To provide users with free copies of normally-paid-for iTunes Store published games, developers can distribute promotional codes generated through the iTunes Connect portal. Promotional codes (also known as promo codes) usually take the form of a string of letters and/or numbers. A user may redeem codes by typing them into the iTunes Store, which will reward them with a copy of the app being associated to their account and available for download and installation. Promo codes have a limited lifespan and will expire, which means that once they are generated, they should be distributed immediately.

Provisioning Portal: The section of the Apple Developer website dedicated to the management of provisioning certificates. See Section 2.7.4.

Q

quality assurance (QA): The Quality Assurance team normally provides support to the technical and creative teams in finding and diagnosing issues. This may include providing feedback on issues such as functional problems (bugs), game-play issues, or asset problems such as audio or graphics problems. A QA team may also be responsible for designing and building additional tools or environments to support teams in providing robust products, such as automated testing systems, logging software, or specific hardware set-ups.

R

rect: Short for rectangle, the rect object provides a method to define a 2D rectangle in code (part of the Unity library and applying to all languages supported by the engine).

renderer: The renderer is a component applied to a game object in the Unity engine that adds functionality to render 3D geometry.

replayability: Generally a term for the likelihood of players returning to a game to play again.

reproduction (repro) steps: During testing, it may sometimes be difficult to define an issue with just words. Most commercial QA/testers will provide steps to reproduce the issue so that the team can see the problem for themselves.

RGB (red, green, blue): A color scheme used in additive color modeling.

rigidbody: A physics object. See Section 4.5.

S

shader: A small program used to calculate rendering effects on graphics hardware. Unity ships with many different shaders. See Section 4.1.3 for more information.

shoot 'em up: A type of game focused on the firing of some kind of weapon and the destruction it causes.

sidescroll (or sidescroller): A term used to describe a game that has a moving background, normally (but not limited to) a jump-and-run platform game.

spaghetti code: A common term for a messy scripting style whereby scripts that could normally operate independently are intermingled and mixed up with references to functions within other scripts, creating a reliance on each other. Complex relationships created between several scripts can make it especially difficult for a third party to unravel or to debug.

splash screen: An image (which may include text) displayed on-screen for a period of time, most likely a company logo or a logo from some third-party middleware. In the case of this book, the splash screen refers to the compulsory image shown at the start of loading applications created with any of the free versions of Unity.

split screen: Where the screen is split into more than one area to allow more than one viewpoint or more than one player to participate.

Standard Assets (mobile): The assets bundled free of charge with Unity for use on mobile platforms.

StoreKit: The API provided by Apple Inc. for interacting with the App Store.

structured query language (SQL): SQL is a type of database most commonly found on web servers.

T

Tag Manager: The interface within the Unity editor for managing tags.

textures: Images that are displayed in a 3D environment or wrapped onto 3D meshes.

time stamp: A record of the current time.

transform: A transform is used by Unity to store and manipulate the position, rotation, and scale of an object.

tweets: Messages posted to the Twitter network. Tweets are required to be less than 150 characters in a single message.

U

Unity: A game engine that may be used to build games for iOS, Android, PC, Mac, Xbox360, Nintendo Wii, PS3, and other platforms through the Union program.

universally unique identifier (UUID): It is a 128-bit number used to identify a system. In the case of this book, iOS-capable devices are assigned a UUID and we use this to describe the device as Development Certificates are made in the Developer Center. Unless a devices UUID is registered for development, it will not be available for testing.

updates: The Unity engine updates the physics and rendering engines at separate times during execution. Three functions are provided, called automatically by the engine at particular times, to facilitate time-critical scripting. See Section 5.3 for more information.

user interface (UI): Also known as GUI, UI is a graphical system allowing users to interact with a computer system. In computer games, menus and buttons are generally thought of as UI whereas the in-game display is referred to as heads-up display (HUD).

V

Vector3: A description of a 3D vector.

W

WorldWide Developer Relations (WWDR): The WWDR certificate links your development certificates to Apple, making you a "trusted" source.

X

Xcode: A development environment provided by Apple Inc. for iOS and OSX developers. Unity builds Xcode projects that are opened in Xcode and compiled to an iOS device or in a file format suitable for submission to the iTunes Store.

Index